40 $1

✓ **W9-AEA-085**

The Rush Hour of the Gods

H. NEILL McFARLAND

THE
RUSH HOUR
OF THE
GODS

A STUDY OF NEW RELIGIOUS

MOVEMENTS IN JAPAN

THE MACMILLAN COMPANY, *NEW YORK*

COLLIER-MACMILLAN LTD., *LONDON*

Library of Congress Catalog Card Number: 67-10576

FIRST PRINTING

The Macmillan Company, New York
Collier-Macmillan Canada Ltd., Toronto, Ontario
Printed in the United States of America

For permission to reprint from copyrighted material acknowledgment is made to:

Random House, Inc., New York, and Secker & Warburg, Ltd., London, for *Japanese Inn* by Oliver Statler, Copyright © 1961 by Oliver Statler

Alfred A. Knopf, Inc., New York, and Secker & Warburg, Ltd., London, for *Homecoming* by Jiro Osaragi

Alfred A. Knopf, Inc., New York, for *The Religions of the Oppressed* (Mentor edition) by Vittorio Lanternari and *Japan Past and Present* (3rd edition revised, 1964) by Edwin O. Reischauer

Asahi Shimbun-sha, Tokyo, and Mrs. Tsuya Masamune for "Thoughts on the New Religions" by Masamune Hakucho, which originally appeared in the *Japan Quarterly*, Vol. 4 (1957)

The International Institute for the Study of Religions, Tokyo, for their pamphlet "Rissho Kosei Kai: A New Buddhist Laymen's Movement in Japan"

Iwanami Shoten, Publishers, Tokyo, for *The Manyoshu: One Thousand Poems Selected and Translated from the Japanese*, translated by the Japanese Classics Translation Committee

Charles E. Tuttle Co., Inc., Tokyo, for *History of Japanese Religion* by Masaharu Anesaki and *Japanese Popular Culture* edited by Hidetoshi Kato

Twayne Publishers, Inc., New York, for *Modern Japanese Religions* by Clark B. Offner and Henry van Straelen

D. Van Nostrand Company, Inc., Princeton, N.J., for *Modern Japan, A Brief History* by Arthur Tiedemann, Copyright 1955, D. Van Nostrand Company, Inc., Princeton, N.J.

1. Japan — Religion — 20th century

To The Japanese People,

who—being immoderately blamed and immoderately praised, in neither case without cause—are one of the world's greatest enigmas and one of its greatest treasures

Contents

Preface

In September, 1956, when I had been in Japan only about two weeks, I went with several American and Canadian friends to Tenri City, near Nara, to visit the headquarters of *Tenri-kyō*, one of Japan's so-called New Religions. Though I had some previous knowledge of these flourishing sects and of this one in particular, what little I knew had not led me to anticipate fully what we actually saw and experienced there that day. The scope and grandeur of this headquarters precinct and the orderliness and vigor of the life that centers there were simply astonishing.

Having been very cordially received and patiently briefed by sect officials, we were assigned knowledgeable and personable guides for a tour of the various installations. They took us first to the heart of the compound to see the sect's two massive sanctuaries, one dedicated to the worship of the deity, Tenri-O-no-Mikoto, and the other maintained as the abode of the living spirit of the foundress, Nakayama Miki. Built of wood in a classical Japanese architectural style, these impressive structures stand at what is presumed to be the very center of the universe.

From there we were led through the many other varied facilities—some traditional and some modern in design—that have been erected in the surrounding area. There we saw the quarters for a complete school system (kindergarten to university), a publishing house, dormitories and dining halls to accommodate thousands, a hospital and sanatorium, an orphanage, an Olympic-style swimming pool, and numerous office buildings, residences, and training facilities. Among these, the two principal showplaces are the university library and an ethnological museum, institutions that fully justify the pride of their sponsors. The library, which now must hold more than seven hundred thousand volumes, is a special project of the patriarch of Tenri-kyo. A bibliophile, he buys books avidly during his rather numerous trips abroad and has acquired a number of quite rare and valuable items. The ethnological museum, housed in a modern ferroconcrete building, includes a large, well-classified collection of artifacts, many of remarkably fine quality, gathered especially from east and southeast Asia.

Wherever we went on our tour, we encountered eager, cheerful, devoted people for whom this place is the center of creation, the locus of their faith and hope, and the symbol of their identity and purpose. They had come as pilgrims from all parts of Japan. Many wore the distinctive costume of their sect, a short black *happi* coat bearing the name of the sect in white characters on the back and that of a local church on the lapel. They were occupied in a variety of ways—worship, training, sightseeing— but perhaps the majority were engaged in "consecrated labor" (*hinokishin*), their voluntary contribution to the construction, maintenance, or improvement of the headquarters properties. Buildings, people, activities—all combined to give an impression of intense vitality.

My amazement at what I had seen and experienced at Tenri was enhanced later that same day, when, on our return journey, we stopped briefly at Horyuji, said to be the oldest extant Buddhist temple in Japan. Lovely, quiet, hoary, this temple is seldom now the goal of earnest pilgrimages. Maintained in part and protected by the government as a "national treasure," it seems to be more a museum than a religious center. The visitors are largely sightseers, schoolchildren on excursions, photographers, and picnickers. The priests are ticket sellers and ticket takers, vendors of pictures, postcards, and religious articles, and guardians of the artistic treasures.

To me, encountering directly for the first time these two aspects of Japanese religion, the contrast between Tenri and Horyuji was somewhat startling. Are Japan's New Religions displacing the old ones? Is Buddhism in Japan as passé as Horyuji? Actually, as I was to discover very soon, neither Tenri-kyo nor Horyuji is completely typical of the branch of Japanese religion that it represents. Tenri-kyo, founded in 1838 and numbering upwards of two million adherents, is the oldest (some regard it as the forerunner) and one of the largest and most influential of all the New Religions. Horyuji, on the other hand, is one of three nominal "head" temples of the almost defunct *Hosso* sect, which passed the zenith of its religious vitality more than a thousand years ago. Not all the new sects are flourishing, and not all the old sects are decadent. Nevertheless, in character, if not in intensity, this experience proved to be an accurate orientation in one important aspect of the religious life of present-day Japan. The old traditional religions, largely failing to demonstrate their relevance to current needs, are indeed losing much of their vitality. The New Religions, accepting as their special mission the assuagement of those needs, are mushrooming in number, in size, and in apparent effectiveness.

During the remaining ten months of my initial stay in Japan, as I sought to immerse myself as thoroughly as possible in various dimensions of the religious life of that country, I had fairly numerous contacts with still other New Religions and began to collect data concerning them. This involvement made it quite clear, I thought, that the New Religions of Japan constitute a socioreligious phenomenon which should be of considerable interest and importance to students of the history of religions and which also must be taken into account in any comprehensive effort to understand modern Japan, particularly in the postwar period.

Soon after my return to the United States, I drafted and published a rather impressionistic report of my observations;[*] and, thereafter, for the next six years, I attempted at long range to keep in touch with the continuing developments in this field. Then, for the academic year 1963–1964, aided by a grant from the American Association of Theological Schools, I went back to Japan for the more intensive field research that has issued in the preparation of this book.

[*] "The New Religions of Japan," *The Perkins School of Theology Journal*, Vol. XII, No. 1 (Fall, 1958), pp. 3–21; reprinted in serial form in *Contemporary Religions in Japan*, Vol. I, Nos. 2, 3, and 4 (June, September, and December, 1960).

At the time that this project was conceived, there was no book in English on this subject. I hoped, of course, that mine would be the first. However, just prior to my return to Japan, *two* such books were published: *Modern Japanese Religions* by Clark B. Offner and Henry van Straelen (Tokyo: Rupert Enderle, 1963) and *The New Religions of Japan* by Harry Thomsen (Tokyo: Charles E. Tuttle Company, 1963). Thus, I lost the "scoop." Nevertheless, I do not feel any necessity to apologize for bringing out yet another book on this subject. This field is broad and complicated, and its exploration really has only just been begun. Offner and Van Straelen concentrated particularly on the examination of doctrines and methods of healing. Thomsen sought to let the various sects speak for themselves, so far as possible, concerning their own beliefs and doctrines. Certainly, what they have done acceptably well I could find no reason for doing again; but it happens also that my own interest and approach seem to differ considerably from theirs, so that from the outset my inclination has been to explore certain dimensions of this subject that have received very little, if any, treatment in the English language. Specifically, I am chiefly concerned with tracing the historical and cultural roots and with discerning the actual or potential social functions of these movements. There is room for this book, and there is room for still others as well.

Even so, I must acknowledge a sense of misgiving of another sort. It derives from the futility and inadequacy that one always must feel in attempting to interpret the phenomena of a culture other than his own, and it is compounded in this instance by an awareness that the subject is dynamic and constantly changing. In such a circumstance, one is reluctant to turn his work loose; for he knows that as soon as he has done so, he will want to recall it in order to record some new insight or datum that had not been accessible before. But while it is frustrating to have to acknowledge that one cannot write a definitive book on a living subject, there is some satisfaction in the thought that one may render a useful service by calling attention to something potentially presageful and thus involve others also in pondering its significance.

My ambition in this regard is rather pretentious, though I hope

not presumptuous. As a historian of religions, I aspire to serve
my colleagues by helping to open this realm of study to their
fuller view. As an educator, I desire to contribute to the edifica-
tion of the student or general reader who is curious to know
what is going on in his world. As one who has been a guest in
another land and has been permitted to see things that others
hold to be sacred, I want to be faithful to my trusting hosts and
fair in the portrayal of that to which they have given me access.
Perhaps it is wholly unrealistic to essay all three of these purposes; for, in a sense, the fulfillment of any one of them militates
against the fulfillment of the other two. Thus, it may be inevitable that some specialists will regard my account as too journalistic and uncritical, that some general readers will find it to be
too technical, and that some of my Japanese informants will consider it to be too unsympathetic. My real hope is not that all of
these will find my work wholly satisfactory, but that any one of
them occasionally will find herein some rewarding moments.

No matter the outcome of this hope, I cherish the opportunity
now to record an expression of gratitude to the many people who
have given me aid and encouragement. I am indebted first of all
to Dr. Merrimon Cuninggim and Dr. Joseph D. Quillian, Jr., my
former and present deans, respectively; to Mrs. J. J. Perkins of
Wichita Falls, Texas; to the American Association of Theological
Schools; and to Kwansei Gakuin University for their help in making possible my two sojourns in Japan.

Among the Japanese, I had so many benefactors in the data-
gathering stage of my project that I must forgo trying to list
them all. Anyone who has been a recipient of Japanese hospitality
can imagine something of the extent of my debt; others could
not be expected to believe the account. However, there are five
persons whom I must acknowledge by name. More than to any
other, I am beholden to Professor Kobayashi Sakae, who in 1955
was my first graduate student in the United States but who in
1963–1964 was my mentor in Japan. I also owe special thanks to
Mrs. Teshima Sachiko, to the Reverend Fujimoto Haruyoshi, to
Miss Miyazaki Chieko, and to the Reverend Kuwahara Ryozo
for invaluable research assistance.

Some of the most substantial help has come from those who

have read portions of my manuscript. My principal indebtedness for this service is to Professor Hori Ichiro, of Tohoku University and Tokyo University, who read the first nine chapters. Parts of the manuscript also were read by Professor Joseph M. Kitagawa of the University of Chicago; Dr. William P. Woodard, Director of the International Institute for the Study of Religions in Tokyo; the Reverend Miyake Toshio, Chief Minister of the Konko-kyo Church of Izuo in Osaka; and officials at the Konko-kyo headquarters. In acknowledging my gratitude to these persons for their helpful suggestions, I want also to absolve them of all responsibility for any errors that may remain.

Finally, I should like to thank Mrs. Anne Norris for typing my manuscript and to acknowledge the patience—sometimes heroically maintained—of my long-suffering family.

Throughout this book, Japanese personal names are rendered in the traditional Japanese order, surname first. In both personal names and place names, the long vowels are not marked. Names of sects are printed in italics with the long vowels marked in the initial occurrence of each term and in any other instance when such details seem crucial. Otherwise they are treated as anglicized words, according to the practice of English-language news media.

A set of color slides with notes is being prepared for use with this volume. Inquiries concerning these materials may be addressed to the author.

H. NEILL McFARLAND

Southern Methodist University
Dallas, Texas
January 10, 1966

The Rush Hour of the Gods

❀ I ❀

Introduction

AN OUTSIDER ATTEMPTING to understand Japan is confronted again and again by the realization that in effect there are two Japans, distinguishable variously as the *old* and the *new*, the *historical* and the *contemporary*, and the *traditional* and the *modern*. This is a tantalizing circumstance, for wherever he turns, he may encounter this juxtaposition of seemingly antithetical elements.

Is there no vantage point from which the *real* Japan may be seen as an entity? There is, but if the inquirer is in the least incautious or impatient, he is quite likely to miss it and, instead, to identify *one* of the two Japans as the *real* Japan. For example, he may find the historical dimension in Japanese life to be overwhelmingly impressive. If so, he may insist that no contemporary aspect of that life is either explicable or demonstrably authentic apart from a detailed century-by-century reconstruction of its antecedents. Or he may be so thoroughly enthralled by the surviving monuments to the aesthetic refinement of old Japan that he finds it difficult to concede that the term "Japanese," which for him identifies these traditional works, may with equal propriety be given to innovations. For such a one, the *real* Japan is *traditional* Japan and what may be called *modern* Japan is essentially a regrettable superimposition of alien and corrupting elements.

On the other hand, if the observer is impressed most profoundly by the remarkably rapid rate at which Japan has modernized and industrialized, he may take the position that history really began for Japan in 1854 or 1868 or even in 1945, the dates, respectively, of the opening of Japan for trade with the West, the Meiji Restoration, and the end of World War II. According to this perspective, the *real* Japan is *modern* Japan and what may be called *traditional* Japan is the vestige of an outmoded and discredited feudalism and sentimentality.

That the outsider who seeks to know Japan may gravitate toward one of these two positions is natural enough. He takes with him to Japan his own predispositions and preconceptions, and while there, he collects his own set of unique experiences. Even among the Japanese whom he meets, there will be individuals who are oriented to one Japan or the other, but not to both. No one who essays to interpret Japan to the rest of the world can do so reliably if he focuses on one of the two Japans to the exclusion of the other, if he insists on choosing between such options as the temple and the pinball parlor, the thatched-roof farmhouse and the apartment building, and handicraft arts and modern technology to serve as symbols of Japan in the mid-twentieth century. Rather, he must acknowledge that if present-day Japan is to be described, it must be as a dynamic process, not as a static entity.

The present, said Nishida Kitaro, Japan's greatest modern philosopher, is "the point where future and past, negating each other, are one. . . . Past and future are confronting each other as the dialectical unity of the present."[1] The *old* and the *new*, the *historical* and the *contemporary*, the *traditional* and the *modern*—Japan is the dialectical unity of their negation of each other. This does not mean that Japan essentially is unknowable and indescribable, as some suppose it to be; but it does suggest that Japan is unknowable to anyone who has no awareness of this dialectical ferment and that it cannot be described in categorical terms.

This perspective is nowhere more crucial than in the effort to comprehend the religious life of Japan. In matters of religion, Japan now is an enigma both to the Japanese themselves and to the outside world. In only a few other countries has religion been more conspicuous historically than in Japan. The numerous temples and shrines, together with their art treasures and colorful festivals, continue foremost among the attractions of that land. Yet, paradoxically, among contemporary nations, Japan is also notable for its lack of religious identity.

Is Religion a Viable Factor in Japan?

Two religions, Shinto and Buddhism, historically and traditionally have been major determinants of Japanese culture and character, and they still are prominent features in the Japanese scene; however, the extent to which either of them is now an important influence is a moot question. The impression is strong and widespread that they have lost much of their former vitality. Outside observers often report that most of the Japanese whom they meet through professional, business, governmental, and other similar contacts seem to be almost totally indifferent to all religion. Though they may acknowledge some nominal, usually Buddhist, religious affiliation, they frequently are explicit in disclaiming any real interest in religion. Their interests and goals are avowedly secular, pragmatic, and materialistic. But is this impression an accurate index? Is the mood that it records really dominant, extending beyond the rather sophisticated contacts just cited? Even the testimony of many Japanese commentators suggests that it is—that indifference to religion is one of the most conspicuous characteristics of present-day Japan.

However—as one of my Japanese associates[2] consistently has cautioned me—on the basis of such evidence as this, it is quite easy, in attempting to gauge Japanese indifference toward religion, to generalize too extravagantly. There are indeed many concrete indications that attitudes toward religion are changing significantly in Japan, but in considering these, it is important to bear in mind that casualness toward religious involvements is not in itself an innovation in that land. Hence, a given instance of apparent indifference may be only a contemporary manifestation of traditional casualness, or indeed it may be the result of a fundamental reorientation that does leave traditional religion almost completely out of account. This ambiguity is of sufficient consequence that we shall examine it more fully at a later point in this study.

Here it is more important to our purpose to state that over against this impression of religious indifference—an impression widely shared by both Japanese and non-Japanese—there is another order of evidence that suggests that the incidence of religious interest and participation in Japan is, in fact, remarkably high. This evidence comes from the so-called New Religions, a host of popular religious movements, of indeterminate number, that have emerged sporadically, but especially in times of intensified crisis, during approximately the past century and a half and have flourished particularly since the end of World War II. Appealing initially to peasants, but now expanding more rapidly among urban dwellers, these movements have gathered followings that may include twenty percent of the total populace of Japan. So rapid and spectacular has been the burgeoning of these religious groups since the war that this period has been dubbed facetiously the "rush hour of the gods" (*kamigami no rasshu awā*).[3]

The Rush Hour of the Gods

Prior to 1945, the Japanese people suffered through a long period of totalitarianism, during which religious bodies usually were either suppressed or regimented as thought-control agencies. Hence, at the end of the war, when complete freedom of religion was guaranteed as one of the cardinal principles in Japan's new day,[4] the way was open for innumerable captive and incipient religious movements to become independent sects and for new "prophets" to let their voices be heard. The characterization of this period as the "rush hour of the gods" captures rather effectively the almost frenetic quality of the response to this first laissez-faire religious policy in the history of Japan. The

levity of this label, however, betrays the prejudice of many Japanese observers who still are reluctant to take the New Religions
seriously. They look upon them generally as false religions or
quasi-religions and tend to regard their founders as charlatans.
It is perhaps largely for this reason that in assessing the importance of religion in present-day Japan, many Japanese dismiss
the New Religions from their consideration. Now, however, two
decades after the end of the war, there are reasons for asking
whether the "rush hour of the gods" may not prove to be a period
of considerable long-range significance in the religious and social
history of Japan.

Several of the most prominent of these movements have
acquired such large followings and have developed such efficient
organizations and effective means of financing that the dissolution
of any one of them within the foreseeable future is an unlikely
prospect. The five groups that will receive our principal attention
in this study (*Konkō-kyō*, *PL Kyōdan*, *Seichō no Ie*, *Risshō
Kōsei-kai*, and *Sōka Gakkai*) report membership enrollments
totaling more than fifteen million people. *Sōka Gakkai* alone—
whose militant tactics and rapid growth have been described
several times in popular news media in the West[5]—claims to have
enrolled more than five million families, or well over ten million
persons.

While admittedly the membership figures released by all such
groups probably are inflated, it is evident that the popular following involved is significantly large. Furthermore, this fact is
manifested not only statistically but also—less ambiguously and
more dramatically—in some of the actual activities and projects
of these movements. This is particularly notable in three areas
of endeavor: large-scale mass gatherings, numerous and costly
construction projects, and extensive use of the media of mass
communications. Sometimes on their own property, sometimes
in public halls and stadia, these groups sponsor mass meetings
that often involve ten thousand to fifty thousand devotees. Occasionally the number of participants will go even as high as one
hundred thousand. The building programs customarily are long-
range undertakings intended to create distinctive headquarters
and training facilities. As proselyting agencies, these movements

continually seek ways to disseminate their messages as widely as possible. Hence, they make fairly frequent use of radio and television and various novel advertising devices; and they are particularly committed to the use of printed materials—books, tracts, newspapers, and magazines—which they produce in immense quantities.

Thus, the existence and evident vitality of these religious movements clearly indicate that the religious situation in present-day Japan is much more complex and portentous than many observers have supposed. The story cannot be told simply in terms of the deterioration of traditional faiths in the face of secularism and modernity. But just what is this story, and how is it to be told? To an inquisitive student of Japanese life, the prominence of these New Religions is an invitation to attempt to understand their nature and significance and to explain them to the outside world. This is not easily to be done, for in accepting this enticement, he finds himself almost immediately in the "two-Japans" dilemma with which we began this discourse. What is called *new* may in fact be *old*. What is presumed to be *historical* may be of *contemporary* origin. What is vaunted as *modern* may be controlled subliminally by what is *traditional*. Thus, the effort to understand is impeded by the problem of recognition and labeling —by the very difficulty of demarcating a field of study among phenomena which at first glance seem to constitute a generic entity but which on further examination tend to melt into the dialectical ferment that is present-day Japan. Hence, an indispensable prelude to this study is a discriminate definition of terminology and perspective.

Demarcation of the Field

The term for these groups used by most non-Japanese observers—"New Religions" in English and its equivalent in other European languages—is derived from Japanese nomenclature that even *in situ* has proved to be troublesome and imprecise. In Japanese, these movements most frequently are called *shinkō shūkyō* (literally, "newly arisen religions"), a term that seems to have gained currency early in this century through journalistic usage.[6] However, because it was used in news media to denote certain groups that also were being described therein as nonscientific, magical, and deceitful, it very quickly acquired a pejorative connotation, and in common speech it has continued to be used oftentimes as a term of opprobrium. As we shall see, certain Japanese scholars do attempt to use the term *shinkō shūkyō*, qualifiedly and arbitrarily, to achieve some scientific preciseness; but since their practices in this regard are not uniform, they actually have done very little to redeem this particular term.

The use of another term, *shin shūkyō*, which literally simply means "new religions," has been urged by the Union of New Religious Organizations (Shinshūren),[7] a body representing more than one hundred of the movements in question. This, however, is primarily an effort to counteract the harmful effects of the common appellation, and the alternative offered only compounds the problem of scholarship.

When the student—be he Japanese or non-Japanese—observes the religious life of present-day Japan and attempts to apply either of these terms to the phenomena that they seem loosely and inconsistently to designate, he needs to know, historically, how *new* is "new" and, substantively, how *novel* is "new." Not all the religions that sometimes are called "new" really are very new. For example, *Tenri-kyō*, which seems to have been the movement specifically denoted in the first use of the term *shinkō shūkyō* but which by some scholars no longer is so classified, was launched in 1838. *Konkō-kyō* and *Ōmoto* also were begun in the nineteenth century, and several other movements already had been in existence, at least in an incipient form, for several decades prior to the end of World War II. If, then, one has only a category called "New Religions" and is confronted by religious movements that vary in age from a few months to well over a hundred years, in what ways and for what reasons ought chronology to govern the choice of what is to be so classified?

Moreover, the designation of certain groups as "New Religions," especially with pejorative overtones, seems to imply that they are distinct from the traditional religions. However, several of these movements either claim, acknowledge, or actively maintain a relationship with Shinto or with one or another of the Buddhist sects; and all of them unmistakably have been "made in Japan." How, then, is one to determine whether to classify a given movement as a "New Religion" rather than as a sect or subsect of Buddhism or Shinto?

While these numerous religious movements are acknowledged to be generically related, there is no single way by which they can be neatly packaged. Here, then, in the terms of the "two-Japans" dilemma, one must proceed under the imperative of seeking the dialectical rather than the categorical identity of this field of study. In my own effort to respond to this imperative, I have sought a means by which to denote both a range of data that actually characterize a discernible field of inquiry and a perspective that seems relevant to the examination of that field. Thus, while I shall continue the use of the term "New Religions" throughout this book, I shall employ it primarily as simply a convenient and economical stand-in for another preferred, though less wieldy, designation. The field I wish to explore comprises *contemporary popular religious movements*. Each of the words in this description has been chosen carefully for a quite specific purpose.

To speak of these movements as "contemporary" is literally and simply to acknowledge that they are an aspect of the life of our time. However, as the word is here employed, two additional nuances of meaning also are intended: a suggestion of *newness* and a suggestion of *historical sequence*. These developments are contemporary in the dual sense that they are in part products of this time and in part current manifestations of a tradition whose sources are in the past.

The word "popular" is used in this instance in its primary meaning, "of or pertaining to the common people," which characterizes both the present movements and their historical antecedents. While admittedly the designation of the "common people" in any complex society is always a relative matter, in the case of Japan I mean to include in this general category such persons as farmers, laborers, housewives, clerks, and proprietors of small businesses, who usually rank no higher than lower-middle class on the socioeconomic scale. The adherents of the New

Religions are for the most part just such persons, and the use of the term "popular" is intended to indicate that fact. In addition, however, this term also specifies the generic identity of these movements with the ongoing tradition of Japanese popular religion. That they have among them certain new features, some of which are the results of non-Japanese influences, is clearly evident, but the movements themselves belong essentially to the "folk faith" (*minkan shinkō*) of the Japanese tradition.

Finally, I choose to speak here of "religious movements" rather than of religions in order to avoid needless involvement in the semantic problems concerning the definition of religion and religious associations; this term is sufficiently broad to include a wide variety of groups without the necessity of making quibbling distinctions. Others have classified these groups in different ways and for different reasons. For example, some observers prefer to speak of one or another of these groups as a *sect* or a *subsect* or a *quasi-religion,* while a devotee of one or another of them may insist that he is part of a *lay organization* or a *publishing agency* or an *interfaith association.* In any of these instances, one may argue quite cogently that the term "religion" is a misnomer; however, actually to engage in such argument serves generally to obscure rather than to further real understanding of the matters in question. In such a situation, the term "religious movements" appears to be at least descriptively applicable to all the groups commonly called "New Religions" and also to have some promise of being acceptable both to observers and to devotees.

Thus conceived, the field of study to be essayed here is fairly inclusive, yet it has its own consistency. Numerous elements are present in some form in almost all these movements. It is precisely for this reason that the movements have been lumped together in the otherwise rather undiscriminating attention generally accorded them by the Japanese populace. For my part, I want to affirm still more emphatically that the character of these likenesses—which I shall identify and discuss in Chapter IV —compels us to recognize the New Religions as phenomena that must be treated as a phenomenon, as movements that are a movement. This is to say that collectively the New Religions con-

stitute a definable socioreligious movement—one of considerable
size and potential significance.

At the same time, the diversity of the separate groups is also
impressive. Each of the movements has certain claims to distinctiveness. Indeed, the very intention to achieve uniqueness and
novelty is in itself an important, though little noted, characteristic
of the New Religions. Much of this diversity, especially that
which results from novelty for novelty's sake, is quite superficial.
Beyond this, however, some very significant differences may be
discerned at more profound levels. In their basic attitudes and
teleologies, whether these are explicit or implicit, conscious or
unconscious, certain of these movements seem to be playing
distinctive, complex, and perhaps portentous roles in the emerging society of Japan.

As a movement, then, the New Religions, as here defined, are
characterized by simultaneous similarity and diversity—a circumstance that leads me to assert immediately that therefore the
effort to comprehend their nature and significance also requires
both a long-range historical perspective and a special sensitivity
to the moods and trends of recent and present-day Japan. On the
one hand, a long-range historical perspective is necessary if one
is to be able to identify and examine the long-term influences
and traditions that have contributed to the development of the
New Religions and have imparted to them their corporate character. On the other hand, sensitivity to recent and current moods
and trends is needed if one is to perceive both the precipitating
function of recent critical events in relation to the rise and growth
of the New Religions and the social and religious roles that these
movements themselves have played, are playing, and may yet
play.

Perspective: Historical and Sociocultural

Because the most rapid mushrooming of the New Religions
occurred in the immediate post-World War II period, it is tempt-
ing to concentrate too narrowly on this one era and the dramatic
effects of the defeat of Japan. However, to take so short a view

in attempting to analyze the New Religions is a serious mistake, for their emergence must also be seen in association with a long-range pattern in the history of Japan.

In retrospect, we can see that by about the middle of the eighteenth century, the feudalism of the Tokugawa period (1603–1868) had begun to decay and the development of a new social structure was being heralded by the rise of a merchant class. From at least that time until now, social crisis, afflicting the common people in particular, has been endemic in Japan. By what must have seemed a relentless and often demonic process, familiar ways of life were being disrupted. There were also rather frequent realignments of political power and major changes in governmental policies that resulted, in almost every instance, in additional and more oppressive burdens for the people. Beginning with the forcible opening of Japan to foreign trade in 1854, the seriousness of this sustained social crisis was intensified from time to time by various other similarly cataclysmic events that rapidly increased Japan's susceptibility and responsiveness to outside influences. Thenceforth, the transition of Japan tended to assume rather definite patterns: from feudalism toward democracy, from isolationism toward internationalism, and from medievalism toward modernity. Thus, altogether, for approximately the last two hundred years, in response to either internal or external influences, Japan has been undergoing a process of radical restructuring that never has been fully consummated.

From the standpoint of the common people, it is important to observe that throughout most of this extended period of transition, they usually have been the victims, almost never the architects, of social change and national policy and that only recently have they begun to derive many benefits from either. Their situation has been one of subjection to political, economic, and social forces that often have seemed far more threatening than supporting. Required to work hard and sacrificially, with the principal inducement being some vague prospect of future victory, they could neither realize nor anticipate many really satisfying achievements.

Though seemingly powerless to exercise any significant control over their environment and generally incapable of comprehending either the causes or the long-range implications of the social changes and governmental policies to which they have been subject, the masses of Japan have not been unresourceful. Within themselves and among their own traditions, they have sought some means of defense against both the political establishment and natural exigencies. Their stolidity of character and their inurement to hardship perhaps have provided their basic staying power, but from our standpoint, it is their recourse to religion that is most noteworthy. As they have sought aid and security in the resources closest to them, their most accessible resource has been their religious tradition. As a discerning sociologist has noted, "different groups have different kinds of anxieties and different preparation, by experience and culture, for various proposed solutions."[8] Among the Japanese masses, the anxieties of those who have accepted the solutions proffered by the New Religions have stemmed from poverty, illness, powerlessness, and confusion of values, especially those governing personal and familial relations; their preparation has occurred within a residual feudalistic pattern and folk faith.

In its diversity and flexibility, Japanese popular religion is at least a hospitable refuge in time of crisis. It is a rather loose compound of Shinto, Buddhist, Confucian, and Taoist influences, together with innumerable, often quite rudimentary, folk elements that have no clear affinity to any institutionalized religion. There are instances of what the philosopher Nishida Kitaro has called "dazzling obscurity,"[9] moments in which life seems to impart to man something of profound yet ineffable meaning. There may also be found examples of the crassest kind of manipulation to effect man's own material purposes. Many other apparently contradictory elements find equal hospitality here, with the result that the reconciliation of opposites has become one of the hallmarks of the Japanese popular religious heritage. For the most part, it is from this popular religion that the New Religions have emerged to provide a refuge, and in some instances also a means of social protest, for the harassed masses. Why this is so can be seen only by means of a long-range historical perspective.

As we have already noted, it is also necessary to see the New Religions in relation to recent trends and moods. Though initially they functioned as crisis religions, it must not be assumed that they will continue to play only this role. Japan no longer is a crisis-ridden land. To be sure, there still are social conditions that serve to keep a large number of people responsive to the original ministry of the New Religions, but after two decades of religious freedom and continuing improvement in the over-all economy of the nation, some of the New Religions are performing a greater variety of functions through involvement in the arts, education, politics, social action, and international outreach. It is perhaps a little ironic that while the New Religions arose primarily to shelter the masses from the impact of a threatening world, some of them are turning out to be a means of admission to that larger world—a world that increasingly is seen to be less threatening than promising.

In summation, despite widespread indifference toward all religion in present-day Japan, the New Religions, as herein defined, constitute a very significant socioreligious movement in that country. My understanding of what has been and is transpiring is well expressed by J. Milton Yinger in the following statement:

Religion is part of a complex interacting system. On some particular issue and from the perspective of a given point in time, religious developments may best be understood as responses to fundamental changes in their social environment. The new religious forces then "feed back into" the system from which they came, influencing the course of its development. On another issue, viewed again from a given point in time, religious change may be the dynamic factor. The influences thus set in motion become, in turn, conditioning and constraining forces that affect the religion which released them.[10]

The principal purpose of this book, therefore, is to describe the New Religions as a development within the religious and social history of Japan and to explore the dynamic relations between these religious movements and the emergent society. An effort is made in the chapters that follow to characterize the Japanese religious heritage, to sketch the record of social crisis in Japan since the early seventeenth century, to identify the chief characteristics and functions of the New Religions, and to describe some of the more representative and prominent of them.

Analogues in Other Cultures

This study also has a place in the general history of religions. The New Religions of Japan, while certainly distinctive, are unique only in particulars, not in their essential character. Their analogues can be found throughout much of the world. For example, the New Religions of Japan invite comparison with the "messianic" or "millenary" cults of primitive societies, such as the Ghost-Dance Religion of the American Indians and the Cargo Cults of Melanesia.[11] From various anthropological reports and analyses, it appears that such cults exhibit remarkably similar patterns of development in which at least five factors recur: (1) social crisis intensified by an intrusive culture, (2) a charismatic leader, (3) apocalyptic signs, (4) ecstatic behavior, and (5) syncretic doctrine. The milieu from which they arise is a "ferment of half-abandoned old and half-understood new."[12]

These cults are also to be understood as the reactions of in-groups to certain overt threats to their traditional existence at times when radical transition has already begun. In such a situation, the integrity of a group thus threatened is doomed if the choice is to retreat into the old or to dash into the new. Its only defense seems to lie in a commitment to reaffirm the old and at the same time to reform it, to repudiate the new and simultaneously to adopt it. Such a paradox cannot be converted directly into polity, but it may be resolved in a religious experience and may thus become the means of reaffirming in-group solidarity and the motivation for developing new patterns of group behavior.

The New Religions of Japan also have their counterparts in other societies in which "higher" religions predominate. Such groups as pentecostal sects, storefront churches, and the Black Muslims in the United States, Cao Dai in Vietnam, and Iglesia ni Cristo in the Philippines may be so considered. Some of the factors that characterize the primitive cults are also prominent in these movements. They too are crisis religions, attracting especially those people who live in conditions of social disprivilege and for whom the usual channels of protest and hopeful endeavor are blocked by their powerlessness and the complexity of the modern world. In each such group, there is usually a strong leader who purports to have received a new revelation, who formulates a new myth, who claims a new power, and who creates a new community. Frequently, the doctrinal expressions are syncretistic.

The existence of these movements in complex societies serves in part to highlight the occurrence of new forms of the transcendence-immanence dichotomy. Among presumably more sophisticated people, concepts of the Ultimate characteristically are quite hazy. Even among those who are nominally religious, there is a tendency to regard the Ultimate as being so far transcendent as in effect to be almost nonexistent, and there is an inclination toward universalism and relativism that minimizes any expectation that religion really will prove to be relevant to concrete situations. Throughout much of the world, this attitude is increasingly becoming characteristic of the older major religions, which have lost much of their appeal except in those areas where they can be identified with dramatic and worldly matters, such as nationalism, peace of mind, and accepted patterns of success. In contrast to this outlook, some very vivid notions of immanent power may be found in certain new religious movements. These notions thrive among those who feel the great pressure of life in the modern world but who have too little discernment to be fully aware of the real complexity of current issues. To such persons, the prospect of finding immediate solutions to persistent problems seems not only attractive but quite feasible. The causes of crisis, they suppose, must be knowable and susceptible to some kind of direct counteraction. This is the general outlook of most new religions. Their grasp of issues often may seem naïve or superficial, but in faith they approach them hopefully and expectantly.

Japan's Religious Heritage

DESPITE THE NOVELTY and modernity that they so frequently manifest, the New Religions of Japan unmistakably are *Japanese* religious movements. Though not typically traditional in character (they would not be called "new" if they were), they are nevertheless preeminently products of the Japanese tradition and experience, and they cannot be understood except in relation to the religious culture that supplies most of their basic motifs. The purpose of this chapter, therefore, is to sketch the background against which these movements must be considered and to communicate something of the flavor of the Japanese religious consciousness and commitment that permeates them.[1]

Sources of Japanese Religion

The religious heritage of present-day Japan, like the total culture of that nation, is the product of many diverse influences. From as yet unidentified areas of the Asian mainland and the Pacific islands, some of the components of this heritage were brought by the early immigrants to the islands of Japan. Other elements have developed indigenously and reflect a close connection with topography and climate, local legends and history, and the emergence of the Japanese nation.

Still other influences have been introduced more formally through the entrance into Japan of major institutionalized religions. The first of these was Buddhism, which arrived from China via Korea in the sixth century A.D. In a sense, Buddhism came to Japan as part of a "package deal." Infatuated by the remarkably rich culture of China, the Japanese in effect placed themselves under her tutelage. In the resulting process of acculturation, Buddhism was established in Japan as one of that country's most pervasive influences. One of the effects of this development was to make the Japanese more self-conscious concerning their own indigenous religious life. Since previously Japan had known very little of institutionalized religion, the presence of so sophisticated a religion as Buddhism exposed the generally primitive, amorphous character of the native traditions; but in so doing, it also evoked a considerable defensiveness on their behalf. Thus, presumably for the first time, a name was given to the old traditions in order to differentiate them from the new. They were called *Shintō*, etymologically a Sino-Japanese term, which means "the way of the spirits."[2] Thenceforth much of the history of religion in Japan could be written in terms of the various patterns of relationship between Shinto and Buddhism.

In addition to Buddhism, three other important religious influences—Confucianism, Taoism, and Christianity—entered Japan from abroad. The first two of these came from China in the same "package" with Buddhism. While neither has functioned prominently as a "religion," both have exerted important effects upon religious life—Confucianism through its ethical and political influence, Taoism in the realm of magic and divination.[3] The other foreign import, Christianity, first entered Japan in the sixteenth century, much too late to participate in shaping the basic patterns of Japanese culture. Its chief opportunities for growth and creative influence have come within the past century, as Japan once again—as in her earlier relations with China—has sought to remake herself, utilizing another, seemingly more advanced culture as a source for new borrowings. In this instance,

however, the technology rather than the religion of the bene-
factor culture has been the chief interest.

Difficulties of Categorical Analysis

In identifying these principal sources from which the components of Japanese religion have come and in ascertaining that
Shinto and Buddhism are Japan's major institutional religions,
the outsider has no particular difficulty. He has only to consult
the historical record. It is when he attempts to follow the leads
that he expects these basic facts to supply that his problems
begin. Particularly if his aim is a categorical and statistical
analysis of the sort frequently essayed in the West, he discovers
very quickly that these obvious facts do not necessarily imply
what his Western orientation prompts him to expect.

For instance, in a Western nation it is taken for granted that
the total membership of all religious bodies will be less than the
total population of the country. Characteristically, one person
adopts one religion or he adopts none, and this clear-cut choice
is presupposed in the compilation and interpretation of religious
statistics. In Japan, however, no such assumption can be made.
According to statistics compiled and published by the Ministry
of Education of the Japanese government, in 1963 there were
66,415,817 Shintoists and 53,558,613 Buddhists.[4] This would indicate that the total membership of just these two principal com-
munions exceeded the population of the country—at that time
around ninety-six million persons—by approximately twenty-four
million.

Because of plural religious affiliations, such a quirk as this has
been characteristic of Japan's religious statistics for a long while,
and it continues to provide an important clue to understanding
the nature of religious commitment in that land. However, one
must wonder whether these particular statistics have much real
interpretive value. Some of the figures from which the totals were
derived seem to be entirely arbitrary estimates; other surveys indicate that if all the Japanese people were asked to declare their
religious affiliations, the results would be significantly different.

These statistics released by the Ministry of Education indicate that about 55 percent of the Japanese are Buddhists and about 68 percent are Shintoists. However, a recent survey[5] conducted among 614 households in a large commuter housing area between Osaka and Kyoto revealed that 52.4 percent of the households were Buddhist and only 1.3 percent were Shintoist. Furthermore, 32.9 percent of the respondents claimed to have no religion, and an additional 10.1 percent simply ignored this question; thus, in the case of 43 percent of the households, there was either an unwillingness or an inability to designate a religious affiliation. Since this survey was conducted principally among young and middle-aged city-oriented people, the results are not necessarily typical of Japan as a whole; nevertheless, they may reflect fairly accurately the situation that prevails throughout the country within this one very large and influential segment of society.

In a more cross-sectional survey, which I personally supervised among 250 persons in Kobe, Osaka, Kyoto, Wakayama, and the surrounding area, 67.6 percent identified themselves as Buddhists (55.2 percent listed Buddhism as their sole affiliation; an additional 12.4 percent described plural affiliations, including Buddhism), and 8.8 percent identified themselves as Shintoists (only 2.0 percent claimed Shinto as their sole affiliation, and 6.8 percent acknowledged plural affiliations, including Shinto). Those claiming to have no religious affiliation amounted to 13.6 percent, and only 1.2 percent failed to respond to this question.

The results of these two surveys at least suggest that in the matter of religious affiliation, the Japanese people see themselves somewhat differently than does the Ministry of Education. While these data do tend to confirm the latter's figures on Buddhism, they disagree markedly with its figures on Shinto. To be sure, these surveys represent far too limited a population sample to support any general conclusions; still, even if their base could be expanded many times, I should not be surprised to find approximately the same results accruing—more than fifty percent of the people identifying themselves with Buddhism, a very small percentage identifying themselves with Shinto, and a fairly large number acknowledging no religious affiliation at all.

One of the principal purposes of this discussion of statistics is to make the point that this kind of statistical analysis actually tells us very little (at least in terms of Western expectations) about the religious constituency of Japan. Except in relatively few instances, the religious institutions of Japan do not even attempt to keep accurate membership records that would enable any agency to compile a reliable statistical report on the religious population of the country. Most of these institutions do not require or even provide for the kind of profession of faith or commitment to membership that is the *sine qua non* of meaningful religious statistics in the West. Thus, even if one turns to the people themselves and asks them to identify themselves religiously, he will find that many of them cannot do so with any certainty. My experience in this regard has been that Japanese people generally feel considerable discomfiture in being obliged to file themselves in one or more religious categories. They may do so, but often it is with misgiving.

Therefore, even if it could be demonstrated that, given the opportunity, slightly more than fifty percent of the people of Japan would identify themselves as Buddhists, there still would remain a question concerning what this statistic would mean. From one point of view, it could be argued that the percentage is much higher than that. Because Buddhism is so pervasive an influence in the culture of Japan and is so closely identified with family life, the individual who has absolutely no association with Buddhism is a rarity. From still another perspective, however, this percentage should be reduced drastically. Although many millions of Japanese nominally or formally are affiliated with Buddhism, the number of those who really are committed to this religion in understanding and faith is comparatively small.

Similarly, in the case of Shinto, even if it could be shown that somewhat less than ten percent of the population consider themselves to be Shintoists, this statistic also would have to be put into perspective. There is a significant sense in which virtually every Japanese, no matter his personal profession, may be said to be a Shintoist. This link, in most cases, is cultural, not confessional or institutional. It may show itself in an individual's closeness to nature or in his pride in things Japanese or in innumerable other habits of mind and conduct that result from his having been reared in Japanese society. Because of the peculiar character of Shinto, this tenuous relation, even though it may be almost entirely unconscious and informal, still merits Shinto sanction.

Clearly, the Japanese religious heritage is in part institutional. This is to say that there are religions with names, chiefly Shinto and Buddhism; and there also are people who will accept or who may be assigned religious labels. However, it may obscure certain dimensions of the subject to begin with the institutionalized religions and attempt to use their names for the purpose of categorizing people and phenomena. Rather, it seems preferable to identify the typical Japanese perspectives in religion and, in the light of these, to consider all other religious phenomena, including the institutionalized religions. It appears that the religious life of Japan is governed largely by such perspectives, to which the religions have contributed significantly but which they do not control. There are contexts in which, with proper qualification, it is appropriate to speak of Japan either as a Shinto nation or as a Buddhist nation or perhaps even as both; but if one's purpose is to characterize Japan religiously, it seems preferable to attempt to do so in less categorical terms. This, of course, is the point of real testing for the analyst.

In my opinion, there are two mutually implicative perspectives that in effect do govern the religious life of Japan.[6] To attempt to state them is in part to distort them, for by their very nature they have consistently eluded codification. They are attitudes of mind, subliminal propensities, not credal statements or affirmations of faith. Yet to the extent that they are explicable, they should be set forth for the purposes of this study. The first of these is the *centrality of experience*; the second is the *reconcilability of opposites*. In both instances, we are confronted by outlooks significantly different from those with which we are most familiar in the West.

The Centrality of Experience

If there is a single aphorism that typifies the cast of the serious mind in the West, it is possibly Socrates' dictum: "The un-examined life is not worth living."[7] Much of the purpose and dedication of Western man seems to be summed up in these words. They focus quite aptly one of his most conspicuous concerns, namely, to utilize his rational powers both efficiently and responsibly. They reflect as well a value orientation that in varying degrees pervades many areas of Western life, even among persons whose outlook characteristically is philosophically informal but who nevertheless have a standard of rationality. Thus, even though it expresses an ideal that may be honored more in the breach than in the practice, Socrates' watchword may be said to be virtually axiomatic in the attitude of the West.

In Japan, on the other hand, there is generally far less confidence in the reliability of rational processes. "The Japanese attitude is phenomenological, and as such is indefinite. Phenomena are accepted as wholes, without analysis or definition."[8] The Japanese bent is "to receive a phenomenon as it appears and not to codify it."[9] This cast of mind contrasts so sharply with that intimated for the West that perhaps it can be characterized best by means of a conversion of Socrates' epigram: "The unlived life is not worth examining." If such an utterance has something of the flavor of a Zen *koan*, it is all the more appropriate, for it suggests the priority that the Japanese tend to assign to living rather than to thinking. They are inclined to see affective implicitness as more adequate than rational explicitness for understanding reality. That is, in general they emphasize the *centrality of experience*, letting life deliver its messages directly.

The Reconcilability of Opposites

In the West, there is a tendency to see reality as dichotomous or dualistic. We think that we are sensitive to contradictions, and as we identify the more salient ones, we are inclined to classify them in terms of polar opposition. This habit is especially characteristic of our general religious orientation. As evidence of this, consider the pairing of the following as mutually contradictory elements: truth-falsehood, good-bad, God-man, divine-human, sacred-secular, religion-superstition, monotheism-polytheism, devotion-diversion. In each of these instances, the two factors commonly are regarded as essentially fixed poles that stand in a relationship of mutual negation. To be sure, there is also the general recognition that between the two poles there is a field within which the actual phenomena of the workaday world are to be found. Some of these will lie closer to one pole than to the other, but most will be permeated to some degree by the influences of both. Thus, for example, we acknowledge that in the matter of moral choice, we may not always be able to choose between the *good* and the *bad* but often must be content rather with the "lesser of two evils." Nevertheless, the fact remains that among those of a religious persuasion in the West, there is a strong tendency to see the two poles as absolute opposites. Confusion and compromise between them may be inevitable, but ultimately only one is meritorious or ideally desirable—only one is deserving of triumph.

In Japan, a very different orientation to reality prevails, one in which apparent opposites are seen as complements or factors of each other. Polar opposition is conceivable but usually not as a relationship between fixed positions; rather, it is only one in an infinite number of possible relationships. It is as if the poles were represented by two beads threaded on a large ring. They may be set opposite each other, but they may also be moved toward each other or may even be joined at any point on the ring. Reality, then, is not so much a contest between opposites as it is interaction between them. The discovery of the real does not result from the elimination of contradictions; it comes instead from an awareness of the unity of opposites. This is not, as one might suspect, a complete distortion of logic (as in Orwell's "doublethink") that enables one to believe that black is white. Logical negation is recognized, but it tends to be seen as in itself a means by which reality is apprehended. A prominent Japanese philosopher has stated it this way: "At the base of the world, there are neither the many nor the one; it is a world of absolute unity of opposites, where the many and the one deny each other."[10] Most Japanese, of course, are not so articulate as this, but the general mood and orientation to life that this statement reflects are deeply embedded in their minds. The *reconcilability of opposites* seems to be assumed.

The Concept of Kami

Though there are many phenomena (some subsequently to be noted) that illustrate or exemplify these two closely related perspectives, it is appropriate at this point to cite the one aspect that seems to be most typical of the Japanese religious consciousness, namely, the concept of *kami*. The word *kami* is an honorific term used to designate the objects of worship in Shinto. Usually it is translated as "deity" or "spirit," but while the etymology is as yet unclear, the essential meaning of the term seems to be rendered more adequately by such words as "superior" or "sacred" or "miraculous."[11] For an observer from the West especially, it is most important to realize that the term *kami* does not designate a unique order of being or a self-contained category of phenomena. Rather, the *kami* (in this instance a plural noun) theoretically are the "spiritualizations of all things in the Universe."[12]

Among the phenomena that at one time or another have been designated *kami*, and thus have been singled out for worship at various Shinto shrines, are the following: (1) fundamental life principles, such as fertility, growth, and productivity; (2) celestial bodies, preeminently the sun and the moon; (3) natural forces, such as wind and thunder; (4) prominent topographical features, such as mountains and rivers; (5) many natural objects, especially trees and rocks; (6) certain animals, notably the horse and the fox; and (7) spirits of the dead. This last-named category is especially copious. It features most prominently the spirits of the imperial ancestors, but, in effect, all other ancestral spirits are also included in it. In addition, it includes the spirits of innumerable persons who lived or died distinctively—persons of inventive or creative genius or artistic skill, the doers of great deeds, the possessors of great virtues, and all those who have given their lives for the nation or the community. Finally, as if to contradict all the rest, even the spirits of the *pitiable* dead may be regarded as *kami*.[13] These include quite conspicuously the so-called *goryō* or *goryō-shin*, the spirits of those who suffer an untimely death. Being justifiably resentful, such spirits might also be vengeful; thus, they occasion particular solicitude on the part of the living.[14]

In traditional Japanese usage, a customary reference to this vast assemblage of phenomena is the phrase *yao-yorozu no kami*, which literally means "eight millions of *kami*" but which, in fact, never was intended to convey any precise numerical image. To the extent that this term is used with a conscious purpose, its intention is to emphasize that the number of the *kami* actually is infinite, constantly increasing, and, in itself, ultimately unimportant. Much more significantly, this term reflects rather the distinctive Japanese religious consciousness, an expectation that in one's experiences anywhere within the whole vast range of life's phenomena, something salutary can be apprehended intuitively. In this there is reflected an orientation which permits participation in rather than observation of reality—which sees the divine and the human in a relationship of interpenetration rather than of confrontation. According to this most typical Japanese outlook, "gods, spirits, men, and any natural objects or phenomena pass easily . . . from one realm to the other."[15]

In this *kami* notion, therefore, we can perceive the *centrality of experience* and the *reconcilability of opposites*, the two closely related perspectives that seem largely to govern the religious life of Japan. "The Japanese people themselves," a contemporary spokesman for Shinto admits, "do not have a clear idea regarding the kami." Immediately, however, he goes on to say: "They are aware of the kami intuitively at the depth of their consciousness and communicate with the kami directly without having formed the kami-idea conceptually or theologically."[16] Here is the centrality of experience. In an earlier generation, another Shinto interpreter, employing phraseology derived from the West, described the religious outlook of Japan as a "theanthropic religious consciousness," according to which "it is a matter of course that man ascends to God, and God descends to man."[17] Here is the reconciliation of opposites. Confronted by these perspectives, the observer from the West must acknowledge that many of his own preconceptions and analytical categories simply do not fit this situation. Hence, to a considerable degree, he must concur in the conclusion of one of his tutors: "Therefore, it is impossible to make explicit and clear that which fundamentally by its very nature is vague."[18] And according to a logic other than the one that begot the phrase, he must be able to say, "*Quod erat demon-*

strandum." Hopefully, then, he is ready to examine in more detail the religions and religious phenomena of Japan.

Shinto

Shinto is the custodian of many of the most ancient and primitive traditions of the Japanese people. To attend the rites and festivals of some of the shrines, especially those in rather remote sections of the country where commercialization is still minimal, is in effect to be transported hundreds of years back into the past of Japan. Particularly if the setting is a mountainous or wooded area, as it often is, one has a sense of witnessing something that still retains the flavor of the primordial. Here, in a measure, is the numinous experience, as yet still unrationalized and unmoralized.

On the other hand, Shinto also is the chaplain of much of the industrial and technological enterprise of modern Japan. Before the construction of a new building is begun, a Shinto rite of purification customarily is performed at the site. Small shrines frequently are to be seen on the roofs of department stores and office buildings and in out-of-the-way corners of large industrial compounds. Ribbon-cutting ceremonies for the opening of a new highway, subway, vehicular tunnel, or some other major public facility usually include a Shinto rite.

As just these two roles suggest, the range and diversity of phenomena included within Shinto are extensive, and they point also to what probably is the most distinctive characteristic of this religion, namely, the intention to be identified through ritual with the whole range of Japanese history, tradition, and aspiration. Doctrinally and ethically amorphous, jealous of no absolutes, Shinto acknowledges no necessary contradiction between primitive animism and modern scientism. Its time always is the present, defined as *naka-ima* (literally, "middle-now"), the time between past and future.[19] Shinto is "that which continues to live in the most valid form in conformity with the age."[20] Preeminently it seeks *from* the Japanese only their acknowledgment, through their attendance and support, that its rites are a continually relevant symbol of their identity as a people. It seeks *for* them mainly the perpetuation of their sense of peoplehood.

In view of these circumstances, it is not surprising that some Shinto leaders object to the classification of Shinto as a religion. They insist that it should be identified as the way of life of the Japanese people. As such, and in fostering and maintaining a national or social faith, it is said to be a special agency that does not compete with religions that have messages of personal salvation, such as Buddhism and Christianity. Neither an option among religions nor an alternative to religion, Shinto claims its own reason for being.

The record of Shinto's involvement in Japanese history provides precedents for not considering Shinto as a religion, but the question remains unresolved. As we have already observed, what was first called Shinto was just an unstructured assortment of native Japanese traditions that had to be distinguished from cultural and religious acquisitions from China. Throughout many centuries thereafter, Shinto generally was subordinate to Buddhism. The *kami* were identified as incarnations of Buddhist deities and often had as their chief function the task of guarding Buddhist temples. Buddhist priests frequently were authorized to be the ministrants of Shinto rites. In the nineteenth century, however, there was a revival of powerful support for Shinto, leading first to an abortive effort to establish it as the state religion and subsequently to its designation as the "national faith," with a special nonreligious status. It was in this latter role that Shinto became the accomplice of the militarists who led Japan into World War II. Following the defeat of Japan, Shinto was disestablished, but since the adoption of constitutional guarantees of freedom of religion and the separation of church and state, it has attempted to maintain itself as an independent religion. However, among avowed Shintoists, such a status is considered to be both arbitrary and artificial, hence inappropriate for Shinto. They would like to see the restoration of at least limited official recognition and support.

For the most part, it seems that the Japanese people have little interest in this problem; yet if a steady increase in the number of shrine visitors is an accurate index, the people still are interested in Shinto. Perhaps few think of themselves as Shintoists, but during the three-day New Year's season and on the occasion of other major festivals, immense crowds of people go to the

shrines. "Is this devotion or diversion?" an observer might ask.
But within the Japanese religious context, this is not really an
appropriate question. In Japan, the two are not necessarily antithetical.[21]

Buddhism

As we have noted, Buddhism came to Japan by way of Korea.
The date traditionally given for its arrival is A.D. 552. Though
initially there was widespread suspicion of "the god of a foreign
country" (*ikoku no kami*), the new religion quickly gained favor
at the court level and thereafter, through official patronage, had
every opportunity to establish itself. Since the regency of Prince
Shotoku (593–622), one of Buddhism's most effective champions
in Japan, Buddhism and Japanese culture have been inseparable.

The forms of Buddhism that have flourished in Japan belong to
the Mahayana branch, the religion of the Great Vehicle, which
by its very nature is permissive of expansion and modification.
Because of this fact, coupled with Japan's penchant for remolding
its cultural acquisitions, Buddhism has been assimilated into
Japanese life as much by adaptation as by adoption. Thus, in the
process of putting its indelible mark upon Japan, Buddhism itself
has also undergone fundamental changes. Japanese Buddhism
has emerged as a very special kind of Buddhism.

Under the tutelage of Chinese masters, promising young Japanese scholars were prepared from time to time to introduce to
their countrymen the teachings of the major sects of Mahayana
Buddhism. Some of these men were exceptionally gifted and
attractive personalities and used the founding of Japanese
branches of the sects as occasions for popularizing Buddhism
among the masses. Such efforts, however, resulted not only in the
rapid extension of Buddhist influence but also in the obscuration,
through policies of accommodation, of some specifically Buddhist
emphases.

As it has been widely accepted among the common people of
Japan, Buddhism represents an otherworldly concern and the
hope of salvation by faith and invocation. This is evident in the

three most popular and thoroughly Japanized forms of this religion: the Pure Land, or *Nembutsu*, tradition, devoted to the adoration of Amida (Amitabha) Buddha; the *Hokke* faith, or *Lotus Sūtra* tradition; and *Shugendō*, the way of the mountain ascetics (*yamabushi*). The particular objects of the people's devotion are a number of compassionate Buddhas and bodhisattvas, whose special purpose is the rescue of the weak and the helpless, who after death will be admitted to Paradise. Within a religious orientation such as this, there is little place for the monastic discipline that characterized original Buddhism and still is emphasized within the Hinayana branch in southern Asia. Instead of celibate monks, the Buddhist clergy in Japan consists mainly of married temple priests, whose ministry centers in mortuary and memorial rites.

Some of the schools or sects of Buddhism in Japan have been identified mainly with certain abstruse metaphysical problems that are of interest only to a very limited number of scholars. Much of Japanese Buddhist scholarship is very meticulous and highly specialized and often is pursued without any regard to its possible relevance to everyday life. The gulf between scholarly Buddhism and temple or popular Buddhism is very wide, and there appears to be little interest on either side in attempting to bridge it.

The type of Japanese Buddhism that has attracted the most attention abroad is Zen (Meditation) Buddhism. Defined as being essentially indefinable, Zen has intrigued a wide range of Westerners, from beatniks to psychoanalysts, because of its "existentialist" distrust of rationalism and formalism in favor of individual experience and intuition. Significantly, news of this Zen boom in the West surprises the Japanese very greatly, for most of them have not thought of Buddhism, in any of its forms, as one of Japan's exportable commodities. Though there still are some Zen monasteries that shelter or produce a few real devotees of Zen, most of their "graduates" simply become temple priests who perform essentially the same functions as all other Buddhist priests in Japan. Historically, however, Zen has played a quite distinctive role. For example, it contributed significantly to the molding of *Bushidō*, the famous "way of the warrior"—the so-called

code of chivalry. While relatively few Japanese are conscious of
it any more, its influence is still discernible in many of the most
characteristic and admirable aspects of Japanese culture, such as
brush painting, landscape gardening, flower arranging, the tea
ceremony, and even some of the martial arts (archery and judo,
for example).

Almost every discussion of contemporary Buddhism in Japan
seems to go downhill. Historically and culturally, to be sure,
Japan belongs within the Buddhist orbit. Obviously, the importa-
tion of Buddhism has been of inestimable importance to the
development of Japan. In Asian diplomacy, it still is customary
to cite Japan's participation in the Buddhist heritage as a basis
for affirming the commonalty of nations. Within Japan, millions
of people continue to follow a traditional pattern of life that
involves formal Buddhist observances. The question is, to what
extent is their Buddhist heritage available to the Japanese people
as a real resource for living in the modern world? At the moment,
the answer seems to be that, for the most part, they see it as
almost entirely irrelevant to the preparation of a modern man
and to the task of decision making in the modern world. Efforts
are being made within Buddhism to alter this trend. It remains
to be seen whether or not they will succeed.[22]

Confucianism

Whether or not Confucianism should be classified as a religion
is one of the questions perennially debated among Sinologists;
but no matter the verdict on that issue, it has not been as a religion
that Confucianism (*Jukyō*) has functioned in Japan. From
A.D. 604, when Prince Shotoku promulgated his Seventeen-Article
Constitution—the "really first example we have of Confucian
ethical and political principles being understood and utilized in
Japan"[23]— until the period of World War II, when the militarists
sought to undergird their cause by appealing to Confucian principles,[24] the impact of Confucianism was basically political, social,
and ethical in character. Nevertheless, by contributing substantially to the definition of normative social relationships, duties,

and values, Confucianism also pervaded the religious life of Japan.

Of special importance to the Japanese have been the Five Great Relationships: sovereign and subject, father and son, husband and wife, elder brother and younger brother, and friend and friend. Each of these relationships will conduce to over-all social harmony if it is governed by propriety or decorum and motivated by filial piety or loyalty. This teaching was the basis of feudal ethics and, along with Zen Buddhism, was a contributor to the shaping of *Bushidō*. In modern times, it has been made to support the ethics of patriotism, centering in devotion to the Emperor. Generally, the virtue of loyalty has been supreme in Japanese Confucianism, whereas in China, filial piety has ranked highest.

Since the end of World War II, the study of Confucian literature and teachings has been continued mainly by a few specialized scholars. Among the Japanese populace generally, most of those who had progressed as far as high school by 1945 are still conscious of their Confucian heritage, but because of the context within which they received it, they may not treasure it or think of it as viable. Younger people have little, if any, specific awareness of Confucianism; still, without their knowing it, some of their most deeply ingrained habits are traceable to this source. For a while at least, residual Confucian influences will remain an important, though vague, part of the Japanese cultural heritage; but at this juncture, it is impossible to tell whether they will ever again be purposefully renewed.

Christianity

It is conceivable that some Nestorian Christian influence reached Japan by the ninth century in association with the many other cultural commodities then being acquired from China, but this is almost entirely conjectural. The documentable history of Christianity in Japan begins in 1549 with the arrival in Kagoshima of the far-ranging Jesuit missionary Francis Xavier, a Spaniard commissioned for foreign service by the king of Portugal.[25]

Originally mistaken for a variant sect of Buddhism but accurately identified as an agency whose presence would favor the development of good trading relations with the Portuguese, Christianity for a time was tolerated, sometimes even encouraged and abetted, by certain Japanese feudal lords. Also, the new faith proved to have a considerable attraction for the hard-pressed peasantry, the particular victims of the political instability of the times. Thus, after only slightly more than a half century of evangelism, the number of Christians in Japan stood at an estimated five hundred thousand, approximately two percent of the total population, a much higher percentage than has ever been achieved in modern times. However, the tide turned abruptly. Suspected of being an advance agent of European imperialism and feared because of its demonstrated ability to subvert feudal loyalties, Christianity was banned, first in 1587 by the powerful military leader Toyotomi Hideyoshi (1536–1598) and then, more effectively, in 1614 by Tokugawa Ieyasu (1542–1616), founder of the Tokugawa shogunate, whose policy for the next two and a half centuries was to seclude Japan from the outside world.

How deep was this initial Christian penetration of Japan? Obviously the appeal of this foreign religion was much more than a passing fancy for many thousands of its adopters. Persistent ruthlessness, including the massacre of more than thirty thousand people at Shimabara in 1637, was deemed necessary by the Japanese authorities in order to control this intrusive movement. One effect of their effort was simply to drive the movement underground. More than two centuries later, in 1865, it was discovered that in western Japan, possibly as many as fifty thousand people were practicing a religion that was still identifiably Christian. These were the so-called *Kakure Kirishitan*, "hidden Christians" or "crypto-Christians."

The surprising persistence of Christian influence even in limited areas of Japan suggests that the presence of Christian ingredients in the folk-religious matrix may account for certain distinctive, seemingly non-Japanese features in particular New Religions. There are scholars who think that some such influence underlies Konko-kyo and Tenri-kyo, both of which originated in areas geographically proximate to regions inhabited by the *Kakure Kirishitan*. Undoubtedly, Christianity contributed some-

thing to Japanese folk religion, but its influence is so diffuse that
it cannot be traced to any points of definitive impact. Certain
aspects of the New Religions might be explicable on this basis;
none seems to require the presence of *Kirishitan* influence as its
sine qua non.

When Japan was reopened to the outside world in the middle
of the nineteenth century, Christianity was still a *religio illicita.*
Though missionaries began to enter the country in 1859, for
fourteen years thereafter they were denied almost all contact
with the Japanese people, and edicts against the religion were
posted throughout the land. It was not until 1873, when the
Japanese government realized that its discrimination against
Christianity was a barrier to the negotiation of favorable treaties
with Western nations, that Christians were given the right to
propagate their faith. Immediately thereafter, partly because of
the close association between Christianity and the then ardently
coveted Western civilization, many converts were made among
the upper and middle classes.

Over the long range, however, Christian successes in modern
Japan, at least in terms of membership statistics, are modest.
The total membership of all Christian groups has never exceeded
about two-thirds of one percent of the population. Converts have
come chiefly from among urban-dwelling and somewhat Western-
oriented people. Rural areas and the laboring classes have been
penetrated very little. Nevertheless, it is justifiable to claim—as
Christian leaders do—that the extent of Christian influence in
Japanese society is disproportionate to the unimpressive size of
the Christian community. Through such media as schools, Bible
classes, and social-service agencies, the Christian church has influ-
enced untold thousands of persons whom it has been unable to
win as converts. Seeds sown in Japan by Christian evangelists
often germinate and bear fruit in fields other than those tended
by Christians.

Aspects of Japanese Folk Faith

In every complex society, there are many interesting and important ways in which the religious life of the folk both includes

and remains separable from the official or institutional or otherwise systematically presented religion or religions of the whole
body politic. Though more or less exposed to and affected by
sophisticated forms and interpretations of religion, folk-religious
life is never completely informed by what is "handed down
through channels." There seems always to be an element of
residual autonomy in folk life—a jealous defense of something
that the masses *know* to be real in the face of all sophisticated
formulations. Such a defense, to be sure, in some degree is fed
by ignorance and is offered in behalf of what many are wont to
call superstition; but it may also be an effort of the folk to ensure
their continued access to certain wellsprings that their more
sophisticated fellows, no longer supplied therefrom, are likely to
choke by their very heedlessness. It is not always easy to say who
has the edge in the search for the "real"—the sophisticates or the
folk. There are moments that favor the folk.

As we have intimated, the domain of Japanese folk religion is
especially commodious and encompasses much of the data upon
which this present study is based. Throughout this treatise, we
shall be alluding to and describing various features of this folk-
religious tradition, such as the syncretistic *shinbutsu* faith, veneration of ancestors, shamanism, divination, magic, and the expectation of concrete results.[26] Our purpose at this point is more
general, namely, to sample a bit further the noninstitutional character of much of the Japanese religious heritage.

For this undertaking, Fanny Hagin Mayer offers a useful point
of departure in an article on Japanese folk tales. She concludes
her essay with the following observation: "Closeness to nature,
humor, and compassion seem to be characteristic of religious
elements as revealed in the folk tales and, surely, something of
these outlooks has remained with the Japanese even in the more
complicated present."[27] Something of these does indeed remain,
and I think it worthwhile to follow up the clues here provided.

CLOSENESS TO NATURE

It is difficult to ignore or be indifferent to nature in Japan.
Usually it is alluring in its beauty, variety, and temperateness;

occasionally it is terrifying and devastating. No matter where one goes, he is almost always within sight of a mountain and never very far from the sea. Each section of Japan and each season of the year feature natural phenomena that are a delight to the observant. Perhaps in no other nation are the people so knowledgeable concerning the topography of their homeland or so eager to visit its scenic places. Perhaps nowhere else do people find such enjoyment in moon viewing or flower viewing. According to ancient Shinto mythology, the islands of Japan are themselves divine, having been born of the union of two deities. While such a story no longer receives much credence and while the Japanese more and more are crowding into mammoth cities, one of the most widespread qualities among these people is a kind of reverent attachment to the natural beauty of their land. At the same time, they have learned also to be wary of nature. Frequent earthquakes, typhoons, tidal waves, and fires have taught the Japanese (more effectively perhaps than have the Buddhist sutras) lessons concerning the fragility and transience of men and things, but disasters have also taught them resiliency. In their closeness to nature, the Japanese acquire directly an essentially religious perspective, although it may never be articulated as such.

HUMOR

In their attitude toward and involvement in religious activities, many Japanese exhibit a casualness or playfulness that to the outsider often must seem sacrilegious. Perhaps in some instances it is, but in general this attitude simply reflects another aspect of the Japanese religious orientation. Remember that devotion and diversion are not necessarily antithetical in Japan.

This outlook is reflected in many of the Zen stories and riddles (*koan*) that currently delight so many readers in the West. It is one function of these seemingly nonsensical utterances to demonstrate that frequently the most direct route to enlightenment lies through the ridiculous. Still another, more earthy facet of this mood is suggested by a historian's observation that in premodern Japan, "a pilgrimage was an excuse for a journey and a journey was an excuse for a spree."[28] This is still true in modern Japan.

One of the most engaging examples of this humorous vein is the Japanese treatment of Daruma (Bodhidharma), the semi-legendary first patriarch of Zen in China. In painting and sculpture, he is represented in the most grotesque ways. He is even fashioned as a legless, roly-poly doll that, having been kicked over, immediately rights itself again. Yet, while playful, this treatment accorded Daruma is not necessarily disrespectful. It may even acquire a certain dignity when seen in association with a popular proverb, "Seven falls and eight rises" (*nana-korobi ya-oki*), which is meant to strengthen one's determination to get up one more time than one goes down.[29]

If nothing else, the presence of humor indicates that while the Japanese religious outlook is seldom profound, it is relatively free of rigidity.

COMPASSION

The quality of compassion in Japanese life is principally the product of Buddhism; however, as in other Buddhist lands, it remains rather vaguely and inconsistently focused. To an outsider, the Japanese generally appear to be a kindhearted, sentimental people; yet it is sometimes difficult to predict their responses in various situations. Some of their expressions of compassion seem maudlin; at other times, their apparent apathy and callousness in the face of a specific need are shocking. For example, on the one hand, a recent newspaper story from Japan told of a Buddhist priest's wife who personally cares for about fifty dogs that have been dumped at the temple. So demanding in time and energy is this task that she has had to abandon almost all other activities, including the religious instruction of the neighborhood children.[30] On the other hand, Japanese editorial writers often criticize their fellow citizens for their alleged reluctance to assist persons who have been injured or are being assaulted in public places.

Thus, like so much else in Japan, the true nature of compassion is not easily to be assessed; but to live for a while among the

Japanese is to receive many assurances that compassion still is an important, if sometimes rather ambiguous, ingredient of their character.

Summary

Anesaki Masaharu, the first great Japanese historian of religion, once wrote that throughout the history of Japan, "the fundamental character of the people seems to have remained fairly unchanged, highly responsive but hardly penetrating, active and seldom pensive."[31] His words are an apt summation of much that I have intended to say.

There has been a strong tendency in Japan for genuinely profound or penetrating religious insights (both original and borrowed) to follow a course of sophistication that spirals upward to abstruseness and final repose in the archives. Along the way, they have at times exerted some influence upon the manners of the aristocracy or imparted some further refinement to aesthetic temperament and its tangible products, but they have seldom been accorded a definitive motivational status in Japanese society. Hence, the life of the masses rarely has been permeated by profound religion but usually has been characterized by credulity and its colorful but frequently nonsalutary accompaniments. Among the elite, through whose domains profound religious insights have filtered, a general contempt for the abominations of popular religion has often prevented them from recognizing the real worth of that which has passed through.

At the present time, much of the religious heritage of Japan, while it is intriguing and in many ways instructive, seems far too vague and naïve to be a very effective resource for life in the modern world. It continues to satisfy many among the uncritical masses, but among the better-educated Japanese, great numbers already have rendered their judgment that the religious heritage of their nation is passé. Even so, it is not uncommon, among these same persons, to find evidence of a real nostalgia for their former security in faith. Therefore it is important to ask not only how the New Religions reflect the religious heritage of Japan but also how they may in turn affect that heritage. Ultimately, will they be an aid or a hindrance to "spiritual" recovery, which most Japanese at all levels seem to acknowledge as one of their nation's most urgent needs?

Social Crisis and the Rise
of New Religions

ONE PREREQUISITE for the study of the New Religions of
Japan is a long-range historical perspective. It is true, of course,
that these sects are particularly a characteristic of the post-
World War II period and that the conditions most propitious for
their rise and development were created by the cataclysmic
events of the mid-1940's. Nevertheless, considered altogether,
these movements must be viewed not simply as features of this
one critical epoch but rather as variously dated products of the
history of a people for whom crisis has been endemic for centuries. It is fundamentally important to understand why this is
so if one is to comprehend the essential nature and function of
the New Religions—hence the necessity of historical perspective.

Yet, in attempting to comply with this prerequisite, no matter
how far back one goes, there is always something more to be
considered; for it is a truism that all historical antecedents in
turn have their own historical antecedents, and so on *ad originem.*
Eventually, then, one must decide somewhat arbitrarily at what
juncture in Japanese history the story of the New Religions
really begins. Not everyone can be expected to agree on this

point. For reasons that I hope to make clear, I see the story beginning with the founding of the Tokugawa shogunate at the start of the seventeenth century.

What follows in this chapter, therefore, is first of all an effort to filter more than three and a half centuries of Japanese history in order to discern the social conditions that seem to have contributed most significantly to the rise and persistence of the New Religions. Thereafter, the beginnings of specific religious movements will be noted in their relation to these conditions and to particular periods of intensified crisis. Finally, the usefulness of certain typologies in classifying and analyzing the various sects will be considered. The over-all time period to be covered includes the four eras customarily employed as frames of reference in the chronicling of modern Japanese history: the Tokugawa period (1603–1868) and the succeeding three imperial reigns, known respectively as the Meiji period (1868–1912), the Taisho period (1912–1926), and the Showa period (1926 to the present).

History of the Japanese Nation Since 1600

After two and a half centuries of political turbulence, marked by intermittent civil war, Japan entered the seventeenth century under a leader who was determined above all else to achieve an enduring political stability.[1] In the year 1600, Tokugawa Ieyasu (1542–1616) defeated his principal rivals for power and went on to establish his authority over all the formerly almost autonomous feudal domains. In 1603, he assumed the title of *shōgun* (generalissimo), which implied that his authority to rule had been delegated by the Emperor; whereas, in fact, the Emperor was completely bereft of political power, except for the latent charisma of his office, and was kept in seclusion in the old city of Kyoto, which remained the nominal capital. The actual capital was established many miles to the east in Edo (later Tokyo), from which lines of rigid control went out to all parts of the nation. Thus, in peace and political stability, and by effective design almost completely isolated from the rest of the world, Japan lived for more than two and a half centuries under the rule (at times actual and at other times nominal) of successive scions of the Tokugawa family. But if respite from warfare and the maintenance of political stability were boons to the nation, they were dearly bought "by ruthless suppression of many of the most creative tendencies in the Japan of that day, and by a return to many of the outmoded forms of feudalism—in short, by resorting to what was essentially a reactionary policy even in the early decades of the seventeenth century."[2]

During the latter half of the Tokugawa era, certain Shinto scholars[3] began to question the authenticity of a regime which denied the Emperor his inherent right to rule. Though their ideas apparently found many receptive hearers and contributed to a growing dissatisfaction with Tokugawa rule, the opportunity to effect a change in government was a long time in coming. The event that opened the way to this eventual development also proved to be the pivotal event in modern Japanese history— Commodore Matthew C. Perry's negotiations opening Japan to trade and diplomatic relations with the United States in 1854.

Though initially the foreigners used only a show of force, no actual violence, to secure compliance with their demands, the Japanese authorities knew that they had no choice but to accede. Their capitulation, however, was generally objectionable to the Japanese people, many of whom, rallying to the slogan, "Honor the Emperor—expel the barbarians," attempted to take matters into their own hands. After a few ill-considered efforts, they soon learned the futility of attempting to "expel the barbarians," but to "honor the Emperor" remained an option. In the autumn of 1867, under persistent pressure, the unnerved and clearly anachronistic government of the shogun abdicated to clear the way for the restoration of imperial rule. The one into whose hands the ruling power ostensibly was to be transferred was a recently enthroned fifteen-year-old boy named Mutsuhito, later known to history as the Emperor Meiji. Imperial rule was resumed officially on January 3, 1868.

During the Meiji era, the actual power to govern was vested in an oligarchy, which at first ruled in the name of the Emperor but later included him as an able participant. These were young visionaries, former samurai, who became the architects of a crash program designed to bring Japan abreast of the modern world. What followed must be recognized as one of the most remarkable periods of development in all of human history. The feudal structure of society was abolished (officially in 1871), and in effect the whole world was engaged to be tutors to Japan in all endeavors deemed essential to modernization. Finding its models in various Western nations, Japan set out to achieve nothing less than advanced status in education, technology, industry, economics, and, particularly, military strength. Yet behind this deliberate exposure to foreign influences and this bold commitment to modernization lay a deep concern for the preservation in all things of the essential spirit and character of Japan. From this there emerged a nationalism which proclaimed the Emperor to be the embodiment of national identity and which recognized loyalty to him as every citizen's highest virtue and duty. This nationalism provided much of the motivation that enabled Japan to achieve the seemingly impossible, but it also issued in the distorted perspective that prompted, step by step, the Japanese commitment to totalitarianism and imperialism. Thus, the Constitution of 1889 was the "gift" of the Emperor to his subjects; Shinto, revived as the original faith of Japan, received a favored status and then was utilized to some extent as an instrument of thought control; success in foreign wars (the Sino-Japanese War of 1894–1895 and the Russo-Japanese War of 1904–1905) fed the notion of a manifest destiny to rule vast areas.

By the end of World War I, Japan had progressed in all her endeavors to the point where she was ranked as one of the Big Five among international powers. For a decade or so thereafter, liberal democratic influences were able to thwart the tendency toward a complete commitment to militarism; but by the early 1930's, immoderate forces prevailed. With the so-called Manchurian Incident in 1931 and the outbreak of war with China in 1937, Japan embarked upon the conquest of east and southeast Asia; and in 1941 she attacked the United States, thus opening the Pacific phase of World War II.

In 1945, a nation in shambles, Japan surrendered unconditionally and was occupied by the Allied forces under the command of General Douglas MacArthur. Immediately, in accordance with directives issued by the victors, major changes were made in the structures of Japanese political, social, economic, and religious life. Less than two years later, in 1947, a new "democratic" constitution was adopted as the chart for a new course for the nation.

In Japan's darkest days following surrender, the most poignant and perhaps also the noblest figure was Emperor Hirohito. For many years, he had been kept in mystic seclusion as "manifest deity" (*akitsu mikami*) and had been named as the authority for the totalitarian programs devised by others; but when the nation lay devastated, he could at last reveal himself. A gentle, sensitive man, he emerged in that moment as one who perhaps really did symbolize that which is enduring in Japan. On January 1, 1946, he issued a New Year's message to his people.[4] The outside world and perhaps most of the Japanese heard it only as his denial of the divinity that had been ascribed to him, but it was also much more. It was a reaffirmation of traditional virtues that had been tragically perverted. It was an appeal to his countrymen to find in Japanese tradition a basis and an initiative for effecting reforms that others would require of them. It was a word of deep sympathy and encouragement for a distraught people.

Within that same month, the Emperor also released a poem that he had composed for the nation:

> Be like pine trees,
> Which do not change color
> Although they bear the weight
> Of continuously falling snow.[5]

While we cannot gauge the effectiveness of the Emperor's words, it is clear that his confidence in the resourcefulness and resiliency of the Japanese people was not misplaced. In his poem for the following year, 1947, he wrote:

> The day dawns hopefully
> Upon the town of Mito;
> The sound of the hammer
> Is heard clearly.[6]

Japan was at work, shaping another miracle—a miracle of physical restoration perhaps even more impressive than the earlier miracle of modernization.

Once again, however, as in the Meiji era, the question had to be asked: "Who are we as Japanese?" The answer, quite confidently given in the former instance, had resulted in the near ruination of the country and therefore had largely been rescinded. Thus far, in response to the second asking, no clear new answer has been forthcoming.

Endemic Crisis Among the Common People

Up to this point, we have sketched the recent history of Japan in such a way as to leave out of the account any very specific references to the life of the common people. How did they fare during the period just surveyed? Since this is the question that is most pertinent to our purpose, we shall go back now and attempt to answer it.

Apart from the exempt status of the imperial household, the feudal society of Tokugawa Japan, patterned on an accommodated Confucianism, was divided into two main categories: the warrior-aristocrats (samurai), who were the administrators, and the commoners. The commoners in turn were classified according to three castes: farmers, artisans, and merchants. Under Tokugawa rule, perhaps the life and property of the commoners were more secure than they had been previously,[7] for at least the peasants were no longer exposed to attacks from predatory warlords. Since rice was still the basis of the economy, agriculture was encouraged, and the farmers flatteringly were called the foundation of the nation. Because there was a continuing demand for the products of the artisans, they were able to develop during this time some of the distinctive arts and crafts for which Japan has become famous. Only the merchants, regarded as unproductive people, were officially despised. But, as shall be explained momentarily, it is the greatest irony of this period that real power was not always confined to its official doctrinaire categories.

Despite the relative security of the commoners, such freedoms as they were given were permissible only within narrowly circumscribed limits. They were not allowed to have surnames or to wear a family crest or to bear arms. Peasants were discouraged from wasting their time on recreational pursuits. Townsmen were permitted their own amusements but could not indulge in those belonging to the higher orders. In all their enterprises, they lived in fear, for they were under the surveillance of an extensive and effective secret police force.

"From the political and historical point of view this was a period of peace and calm, but from the social and cultural standpoints it was a period of revolutionary change"[8]—a fact which the samurai never explicitly acknowledged but which they were obliged to accept implicitly. The positions of real power actually were reversed during this period. With the shift from a rice to a money economy, the merchants, though still ranked last, became the most powerful segment of society. The samurai, still toprated, were becoming anachronisms in a society where martial skills no longer were required, and often they were heavily in debt to wealthy merchants. Moreover, it was due to mercantile enterprises that cities began to grow and flourish, until at length they became a dominant factor in Tokugawa life; and it was the merchants themselves who, more than any others, contributed to the shaping of the culture that centered in those cities. Their values, their arts and literature, their amusements were supreme.

Many of the stories from this period contain a Horatio Algerlike advocacy of frugality, industry, and resourcefulness as the means by which a lowly man might make a fortune.[9] At the same time, though including many wealthy and influential men, the merchant class remained vulnerable to political whim. A single precipitate action by the shogun, such as the declaration of a moratorium on debts, could be ruinous. It is quite significant, however, that the typical response of the merchants to the transience of their fortunes was not otherworldliness, though they were ready enough to attempt to guarantee the success of their ventures by the invocation of supernatural powers. Rather, they turned to a kind of hedonism, a determination to enjoy what they had while they had it.[10]

The lot of the peasants differed markedly from that of the merchants. Though honored in word as the foundation of the land, the peasants lived terribly deprived lives throughout the Tokugawa period. Obliged for much of each year to work inhumanly hard and long and exposed to many natural exigencies, they also had to bear a heavy burden of taxes, often capriciously levied. They also faced a persistent shortage of all economic necessities and were denied almost all pleasures. Some measure of their desperation is provided in the fact that during the Tokugawa period, more than one thousand peasant uprisings were recorded, and for the last one hundred and fifteen years of that time, they occurred at an average rate of about six per year.[11] These protests, however, were sporadic in nature, and while they did occasionally lead to a redress of grievances locally, they apparently had little over-all effect on social conditions.

When the Tokugawa period ended, the farmers and the lower classes of the cities, together with many of the lesser samurai, were frightfully impoverished; but perhaps even more tragic and ominous than this was the transformation that had been wrought in the people themselves. E. O. Reischauer has summarized the effect of Tokugawa rule in this way:

> The bellicose, adventurous Japanese of the sixteenth century became by the nineteenth century a docile people looking meekly to their rulers for all leadership and following without question all orders from above. They grew accustomed to firmly established patterns of conduct. A thousand rules of etiquette, supplementing instructions from their rulers, governed all their actions.[12]

Since, as one might surmise, the Japanese masses were not very politically conscious, they probably cared little whether their ruler was the shogun or the Emperor; however, the Meiji Restoration of 1868 did renew their hope for social reform. After 1871, when the feudal structure was dissolved, all commoners were freed from many of the restrictions of their former caste status, but unfortunately most of their gains were more theoretical than actual. "The hardships of the lower classes in the feudal period were replaced with new hardships."[13] The new conditions that had the greatest effect upon them were a widening of the gap between the wealthy and the poor and a thoroughgoing revolution imposed from above. The first was a socioeconomic condition that meant perennial disability for the masses; the second was a program that brought crisis after crisis and increased their distress. We shall need to remember the former while we focus upon some of the details of the latter.

A Japanese social analyst stresses the point that "modernization was begun not because of popular demand but because the government willed that it should be so."[14] Reischauer has observed still further that "the ruling group was interested in developing a powerful nation rather than a prosperous people."[15] In view of the general docility and impoverishment of the Japanese masses, and in light of the comments just quoted, we can see how four projects of the forced revolution inaugurated in the Meiji period precipitated particularly severe crises, many of which, in some form or influence, persist even in the present. The four undertakings were: (1) universal education, (2) military conscription, (3) industrialization, and (4) control of religion.

UNIVERSAL EDUCATION

In 1872, the Meiji government decreed that education be made available to everyone. Though the new program "was founded on such lofty ideals as equality for men and women, compulsory education for all subjects, and respect for individual freedom,"[16] its forcible imposition upon the people at that juncture was both economically and culturally premature. With little money to appropriate for the building of schools, the government demanded that each designated district supply its own. This requirement produced a serious drain on village finances and in some cases resulted in so much discontent that riots ensued. Furthermore, for a long while both farmers and merchants resisted sending their children to school, because the new education had no apparent relation to the latter's preparation for their lifework. In the long run, of course, Japan's commitment to universal education produced many significant results, including the first literate populace in Asia and sustained exposure to many elements of Western culture. At the same time, it must not be forgotten that from the early Meiji period until the end of World War II, education in Japan was "essentially a tool of government, training obedient and reliable subjects who could serve as technically efficient cogs in the complicated machinery of the modern state."[17]

MILITARY CONSCRIPTION

In feudal Japan, military service had been solely the province of the warrior class; in modern Japan, after 1872, it was proclaimed to be the duty of every able-bodied male citizen. Initially, however, there were so many loopholes by which exemptions could be secured that the new citizens' army was composed mostly of boys drafted from the farms and from among indigent city dwellers. Deeply resentful of the conscription law, the common people devised all sorts of ruses—among them the worship of "gods who were supposedly able to keep them out of the army"[18]—to evade being drafted.

In 1882, the rules governing conscription were revised to eliminate the original terms of exemption and to place military service more nearly on an egalitarian basis. Thereafter, army training gradually became accepted as a normal part of a young man's maturation. Over a long period, military service, like universal education, contributed significantly to the modernization of Japan. Innumerable rustics from remote provinces and small islands were first exposed to modern life in the army. Many were much better fed and clothed in the army than they had ever been in civilian life. But, here again, the great tragedy was the almost complete impersonality of the whole enterprise. Subject to an iron discipline and exposed to the often sadistic treatment of their superiors, soldiers generally were deprived of all initiative and were taught to rely on obedience in its stead.[19] The individual had only instrumental value. Sometimes, it is alleged, a soldier was told, "You are cheaper than a horse. Another man can be bought for the price of a postcard."

Yet, particularly during the 1920's and 1930's, as the militarist tradition matured and the imperialist design took form, there were many who found a sacred vocation in military life, especially among those enlisted from the peasantry—remarkably changed from the "draft dodgers" of the 1870's. Fired by nationalism and devotion to the Emperor, these men found in the army their entrée to prestigious involvement. "As peasants they were insignificant members of a poor and downtrodden class. As soldiers they were honored members of a mystic elite corps, participating directly in all the glories of Japan as a world power."[20] Never having known a better bargain, they sold their birthright to totalitarianism.

INDUSTRIALIZATION

In dismantling the old feudal system, which bound a person to a social class and hence usually to specific duties or means of livelihood, the Meiji government recognized in principle the right of a citizen to choose his own occupation and to seek employment wherever he wished. In reality, the shadow of feudalistic paternalism and indentured labor never disappeared completely from the Japanese scene, but certainly the general character of Japanese life was altered radically and quickly by modern industrialization.

Encouraged and abetted by the government, new industries were introduced rapidly, thus opening up a wide range of new types of work for people of all classes. Especially crucial to this development was the creation of a large labor force, which was recruited mainly from rural areas and which included a high percentage of young women, the daughters of financially desperate farmers.

The evils attendant upon the industrialization of Japan were essentially the same as those that characterized the Industrial Revolution in the West: long hours, low wages, boring work, unhealthful and unsafe working and living conditions, and use of child labor. Again, from this dimension of Japan's program of modernization, many benefits accrued to the nation, but as in the other enterprises already considered, these gains resulted from the dehumanization of large numbers of people. Japan's ability to compete for world markets depended upon the production of a large quantity of goods with low-cost labor; therefore, demands for shorter hours and higher wages were severely suppressed. Not until after World War I could organized labor function legally, and it was largely ineffectual until after World War II.

One of the earliest and most consequential by-products of industrialization in Japan (as in other modern countries also) was urbanization. With the establishment of new industries, workers recruited from rural areas moved into the industrial centers, and this trend was further enhanced by a sudden and dramatic increase in the rate of population growth. Throughout much of

the Tokugawa period, the population total apparently had remained fairly constant at approximately thirty million,[21] but a
marked increase began after the seclusion policy was ended in
1854. After the Russo-Japanese War (1904–1905), the rate of
population growth and the tendency toward urban concentration
became particularly pronounced. By 1912, the end of the Meiji
period, the population stood at fifty million; in 1937, it was
seventy million; and in 1945, at the conclusion of World War II,
it was seventy-two million, with an additional six million still
living abroad. Due to repatriation and a greatly accelerated birth-
rate during the immediate postwar period, the population grew
to eighty-three million by 1950. Now, in the mid-1960's, with a
more moderate rate of growth, the total is approaching one hundred million.

At the end of the Tokugawa period, considerably less than
10 percent of the total populace lived in cities. By 1912, the
urban population still amounted to no more than 17.5 percent;
by 1935, it was about 30 percent; and by 1941, at the outbreak
of the Pacific war, it had increased to about 40 percent. In 1960,
approximately 64 percent of the Japanese lived in urban areas,
and since that time the percentage has continued to swell due
to the annual exodus of more than a half million people from
farms and villages.[22]

CONTROL OF RELIGION

Along with everything else, the Tokugawa government attempted to regulate religion. Confucianism was adopted, with
some rather startling accommodations, as the official philosophy.
Christianity, feared as an advance agent of European imperialism,
was sternly suppressed. Buddhism, officially favored, was organized into parishes whose temples were used by the government
as observation posts. Shinto was regarded as subservient to
Buddhism.

The Meiji government, also committed to controlling religion,
quickly adopted some quite disruptive policies. Concomitant with
the restoration of imperial rule, the new government sought to
destroy the privileged status of Buddhism and to "recover" a more

authentically Japanese condition known as *saisei itchi*, "the unity
(or congruence) of rites and government." The historical referent
thus invoked was a primitive stage in Japanese society during
which the rulers also had been priests.[23] This period was recalled
idyllically as a time when the Japanese had constituted a kind
of liturgical community, and it was this that the Meiji government
sought to reestablish.[24] To accomplish this purpose, it was
deemed essential to end the centuries-old syncretism of Buddhism
and Shinto. The desirable condition of bygone days antedated
Buddhism in Japan and was associated with Shinto. In the blending of Buddhism and Shinto, the latter generally had been subordinate; therefore, it seemed necessary to free Shinto from this
demeaning relationship and to revive it as the national faith.
Hence, one of the early acts of the new Meiji government was
to adopt a policy known as *shinbutsu bunri*, "the separation of
Shinto from Buddhism."

There followed a complicated succession of measures reflecting
the government's determination to control religion and to identify
the rites of Shinto with the functions of government. The immediate result was general confusion in the religious life of the
nation. Because of two factors in particular, the government
eventually was obliged to modify its approach. On the one hand,
Buddhism and the syncretic *shinbutsu* faith were too intrinsic a
part of the life of the masses to be much affected by a governmental decree. On the other hand, the government discovered to
its surprise that its failure to grant religious freedom (and especially its persecution of Christians) was a barrier to developing
good diplomatic and commercial relations with the leading
nations of the world.[25]

The long-range policy that finally emerged was based upon an
arbitrary distinction between "religion" and "national faith."
Buddhism, Christianity, and thirteen popular religious movements
designated collectively as *Shūha Shintō* or *Kyōha Shintō* (Religious Shinto or Sectarian Shinto) were recognized officially as
"religions." The Constitution of 1889 included, as Article 28, a
carefully qualified guarantee of religious freedom: "Japanese
subjects shall, within limits not prejudicial to peace and order,
and not antagonistic to their duties as subjects, enjoy freedom

of religious belief." In contradistinction to the "religions," traditional shrine Shinto was declared to be the "national faith," the further development of which entailed an unrelenting emphasis on the sacredness of the Emperor, the recasting of Japanese history in the light of ancient myths, and the take-over of Shinto shrines and priests as governmental agencies and agents.

There is no reason to doubt that during the Meiji period and thereafter, many Japanese were fully sincere in their conviction that Shinto need not be considered a religion. Such is the character of Shinto and such has been its relation to Japanese life that its entitlement to a special status in that culture may be argued quite cogently. Yet from the eighteenth century onward, there was in Shinto revivalism, along with a thoroughly valid quest for national identity, a fundamental irrationalism that tended toward arrogance and fanaticism. The Meiji and later the militaristic use of Shinto was in large measure a subterfuge, insofar as it was a response to the issue of religious freedom. There was no real freedom of religion for the Japanese people so long as each subject had to give evidence that his ultimate loyalty and devotion were directed to the Emperor, hence to the state. Furthermore, the manner in which Shinto was offered as a nonreligious national faith was a prostitution of the sensibilities of the people. They were deliberately beguiled. It is not too much to say that "Japan's great modern tragedy was that the genuine affection of the people for their emperor was . . . misused by politicians."[26]

The centuries-old record of endemic crisis among the masses and the long succession of events that periodically intensified the critical character of their existence reached a climax in 1945 in the defeat of Japan at the end of World War II. Physically, economically, and politically, the nation was a shambles. Many people were homeless; many more were undernourished, sick, or maimed; all were bewildered and dispirited.

Time has proved that the material damage, though enormous, was by far the least consequential affliction incurred by Japan during the war. The ingrained industriousness and discipline of the Japanese people survived sufficiently intact to support them in the task of rebuilding. Now few of the visible scars of war remain, and materially the general standard of living is higher than ever before.

The more serious and lasting damage was inflicted at a deeper level. The nation's commitment to warfare had been to "do or die." *Everything* had been ventured on the premise that a divine emperor was leading a divine people inhabiting a divine land to the achievement of their manifest destiny as leaders of the world. Thus, for many of the Japanese, their surrender signified not only defeat in war but also the total failure of their way of life. Had their whole endeavor been based on fantasy? Had they been exposed in the clear light of truth as an inferior people? Had their culture been so completely discredited that it would have to be discarded? Though the passage of time has produced a drifting away from unequivocally affirmative answers to these questions, the effects of deep-running disillusionment are still evident, especially among those of middle age or above. Furthermore, it was inevitable that from the national government down to the family, both the philosophy and the structure of Japanese social institutions would undergo significant change. In this process, apparently the most effective influences have been the numerous and variable factors of two major postwar developments plus their common catalytic agent. One is the weakening of traditional authority; the other, correlative to the first, is the increase of individual freedom. The catalyst is universal education.

Particularly the young people in postwar Japan are the beneficiaries, yet in some ways also the unintended victims, of social change and reforms. The repressive character of social relationships and obligations has been significantly moderated, and educational reforms have been instituted to provide more favorable opportunities for individual development. At the same time, the new freedom has also brought new problems. A comment in the UNESCO study of youth in Japan is descriptive of the entire postwar period thus far: "Probably never before in the sociological history of Japan have the cultural options been so numerous or so contradictory."[27] In Japan, as elsewhere, the problems occasioned by the granting of personal freedom center in the problem of choice. Many a Japanese, largely because of the ambiguities of his own personal values, finds the alternatives before him to be almost disabling. He has available to him no authoritative perspective and no real ethic to inform his freedom. The incidence of personal and social tragedy stemming from the misappropriation of freedom continues to be very high. What is the solution? Says one Japanese: "A rigid discipline formerly applied from outside must now be applied from within."[28] But what or who is to minister to the interior life?

The Rise of New Religions

The New Religions of Japan are variously dated products of or responses to the endemic, recurrently intensified social crisis that has been the burden of the Japanese people for approximately the last three and a half centuries. The first of these movements began in the feudal society of the Tokugawa period. These flourished and others arose after the Meiji Restoration and in association with a succession of traumata occasioned by rapid social change, involvement in foreign wars, and subjection to totalitarian rule. Their great boom came when climactic crisis and unprecedented freedom were conjoined at the end of World War II. In what follows here, we shall identify some of the most prominent and pivotal New Religions and attempt to indicate something of the relationship between their rise or growth and coincident social conditions. It appears that five periods were especially conducive to the development of the New Religions:[29] (1) the declining years of the Tokugawa shogunate in the mid-nineteenth century; (2) the middle years of the Meiji period, about 1880–1900; (3) the end of the Meiji period and the Taisho period, from the Russo-Japanese War (1904–1905) to about 1925; (4) the early Showa period, about 1930–1935; and (5) the post-World War II period, since 1945.

THE DECLINING YEARS OF THE TOKUGAWA

During approximately the last hundred years of the Tokugawa period, there was an increasing restlessness among the commoners in reaction to the oppressive policies under which they lived. As we have seen, local peasant uprisings were numerous during this time, but the hard fact was that the common people had no possibility of instigating any direct action that might force a change in the existing political structure. Overtly they had no choice other than to submit to the dictates of the ruling power; however, to some extent it was possible, through their more intimate and trustful associations with one another, to attempt "to solve political problems in religious terms."[30] As a result, there were numerous popular religious developments during this period, some of which seem to have been directly tributary to the earliest of the New Religions. We shall consider three of these here: (1) the dissemination of popular ethicoreligious teachings, (2) community-sponsored pilgrimages to distant shrines and temples, and (3) frenzied dances intended to effect social reforms.

1. *Popular ethicoreligious teachings.* Among the most interesting phenomena of the late Tokugawa period are two popular "schools" of teaching that disseminated religion-oriented moral instruction among commoners. One of these, the *Shingaku* ("heart learning" or "mind learning") movement, was primarily directed to the merchant class in the towns and cities; the other, called the *Hōtoku* ("repayment of blessings") movement, was intended for the peasants. Both were "humanitarian in principle and popular in method."[31] Without challenging the existing power structure, they stressed sincerity, genuineness, and naturalness in such ways as to help safeguard the merchant from his greatest enemy, temptation to moral corruption, and the farmer from sloth and self-pity. Thus, within their circumscribed lives, many commoners found a wholeness and dignity that enabled them to achieve both a measure of personal satisfaction and an improved standard of living.

The older of the two movements was *Shingaku*, begun in 1729 by Ishida Baigan (1685–1744),[32] who, though born a peasant and apprenticed as a boy to a merchant family, educated himself in Confucian literature, Zen meditation, and Shinto. Lecturing regularly, chairing question-and-answer meetings, and encouraging the practice of meditation, he urged people on to the attainment of a workable ethic. Under the leadership of other capable teachers, the movement continued to flourish for more than a hundred years.

The *Hōtoku* movement issued from the activities of the eminently attractive Ninomiya Sontoku (1787–1856).[33] Though deservedly called the "peasant sage," he was not so much a teacher in any formal sense as he was an exemplar of and a counselor on attitudes and techniques that proved to be workable in rural Japan. The particular forte that first won him recognition was the restoration of neglected farmland and villages, but his underlying purpose was "to help the poor and to aid them to unite in helping one another."[34] He advocated and practiced the virtues of love, diligence, and self-help and placed his confidence in the simple principle that "Nature rewardeth abundantly them that obey her laws."[35]

The relationship between these two movements and the subsequent New Religions has not been carefully studied, but it seems fully evident that, though lacking the element of social protest, they belong in any consideration of the background of these sects. Like the New Religions, they were eclectic or syncretistic, drawing together the resources of Confucianism, Buddhism, and Shinto and disseminating their essence in the form of simple doctrines. Like them also, they joined together faith and an expectation of concrete results. It has been said that from the *Hōtoku* teachings, "one gets the impression that salvation in the religious sense and economic recovery seem to be conceptually fused. There is indeed an almost millennial expectation. . . ."[36] One may get much the same impression from *Shingaku*, and this conjunction of factors is without question one of the most conspicuous characteristics of the New Religions.

2. *Sponsored pilgrimages.* Though their occasional riots secured none of the freedom they sought, the masses discovered that through various other kinds of group action, it was possible to express their bitter protest—if only surreptitiously—and, at the same time, to keep alive their hope. One such artifice, described as a method "of passive resistance without precedent in Japanese history,"[37] was the *okage mairi* (sponsored pilgrimage), a community undertaking. The inhabitants of a particular rural area would pool such money as they could spare and send certain ones

of their number on a pilgrimage to a distant temple or shrine. Increasingly, such journeys were made to the Ise Shrine, which, as the abode of the sun-goddess, Amaterasu, ancestress of the imperial line, later became one of the chief symbols of nationalism. However, no such significance attached to the *okage mairi*; rather, it embodied, somewhat ironically perhaps, "an embryonic theory of social reform."[38] For no other purpose than a pilgrimage could a peasant leave his own area, but as a pilgrim he could go great distances. Hence, the *okage mairi* became, if only in the eyes of the masses, a kind of demonstration in support of their demand for personal freedom.

3. *Frenzied dances.* As social unrest reached its peak in the final years of the Tokugawa regime, some people in Nagoya, claiming to have seen amulets falling from the sky, began to perform frenzied dances, which came to be called *ee ja naika*, from the magic formula chanted by the dancers.[39] These dances quickly spread to other communities where apocalyptic signs were also supposed to have been seen. Wherever they broke out, they may be understood as translations into spontaneous group action of the feverish desire for social reform that burned in the hearts of the Japanese masses. Because they were Dionysian in character, the dances sometimes were preludes to riots. In retrospect, they are most impressive as dramatic evidence of the popularity of the assumption that religious faith and action are directly related to the alleviation of social and economic distress. This notion, then, awaited codification and formalization in the New Religions.

"The social atmosphere in the first half of the nineteenth century," wrote Anesaki, "was redolent with something verging on the Messianic conception of the Jews in the first century before Christ."[40] In the face of severe crises, sustained and repeated, the masses were powerless to alter their circumstances by direct political action. Their only compensatory alternative was religion or, more specifically, "folk faith" (*minkan shinkō*). Perhaps it is still better to speak of "folk resources," for the religious dimension in the life of the Japanese masses was a broad one, including a combination of industriousness and ingenuity, a closeness to nature, and an intimate involvement in the family and local community. These plus the usual gimmickry of unsophisticated religion helped to maintain a working balance between hope and hopelessness. But, as Anesaki's statement implies, all this really was not enough. To the longing of the people for deliverance was added the expectation that deliverance was imminent and that it would involve the changing of the world itself.

During the declining years of the Tokugawa shogunate, there appeared a number of religious movements promising the fulfillment of that expectation. Among these there were two, Tenri-kyo and Konko-kyo, that I regard as the earliest of the New Religions. More adequately than the others, these two caught up into themselves both the traditions of the masses and their growing restiveness. They imparted to the people a hope that did not destroy itself in futile sorties against their oppressors. Though deeply rooted in the past, they were the harbingers of a new order and, especially in the case of Tenri-kyo, became the prototypes for many of the religious organizations that developed subsequently. These two alone, of all their original contemporaries, have survived in strength to the present and have suffered or flourished in more recent periods for the same reasons and at the same times as the New Religions of later origin.

Of these two precursors, perhaps Tenri-kyo has had the greater influence upon the over-all movement we are surveying. However, since Tenri-kyo is much the better known of the two outside Japan, I have elected in this volume to devote a greater amount of attention to Konko-kyo (see Chapter V). At this point, it will suffice to inject only a few pertinent facts and observations concerning the rise of both movements.

Tenri-kyo was begun in 1838 by a country woman named Nakayama Miki (1798–1887), who lived in the Yamato area near Nara. Like many other women in the history of religion in Japan, she was thought to be possessed by a deity and became a medium of divine instruction and healing; but there was something in Miki and her work that marked the real convergence of the past and the future. Anesaki has noted two features: "One is the idea of a transformed world in which a vague consciousness of the falling regime is combined with an ideal aspiration for a better world, a human world saturated with divine spirit. The other point is the strong tendency to discard all doctrinal subtleties and to establish a religion of the simple pure heart."[41] In Tenri-kyo, the fury and abandon of the *ee ja naika* dances were sublimated in a dance of creation "which provided religious inspiration in addition to the promise of practical relief."[42] Though Miki was arrested and the movement was otherwise harassed by the government, by the early years of Meiji the devotees of Tenri-kyo constituted colonies of refuge and hope in many Yamato villages.

Konko-kyo was founded in 1859, also by a peasant, Kawate Bunjiro (1814–1883), a resident of what is now Okayama Prefecture. The original characteristics of Konko-kyo did not differ greatly from those of Tenri-kyo; though of the two features specifically noted above, perhaps Konko-kyo placed more stress upon the "simple pure heart" than upon the "idea of a transformed world," thus reversing the order of priority that seemed to obtain in Tenri-kyo. In both religions, there was a tendency toward a more strongly theocentric orientation than was usual in Japan. However, although both began among farmers, Konko-kyo rather quickly gained followers also among the merchant class and subsequently achieved its greatest growth in towns and cities.

THE MIDDLE YEARS OF MEIJI

The second period in which conditions were especially contributive to the rise and development of New Religions was the middle years of Meiji (about 1880–1900), when the anxiety-producing effects of rapid modernization were reaching their first peak and the relentless advance of political absolutism had made social reform impossible.[43] This was also the time when Shinto was being established as the official cult of the nation.

In this connection, it is worth noting that even from the very early times reflected in Japanese mythology, an uneasy compromise has existed between two opposing kinds of Shinto—the official Apollonian cult of the sun-goddess, on the one hand, and a vast range of mysterious, occult practices on the other. Anesaki has pointed out that throughout the history of religion in Japan, whenever official Shinto, with its tendency toward formalism and the neglect of the mysteries of religious life, has been in the ascendancy, the people have been inclined to resort more conspicuously to such occult practices as magic, divination, and exorcism[44]—elements often found also in the New Religions.

During this period, presumably for all the reasons just intimated, both Tenri-kyo and Konko-kyo expanded rapidly and developed stable organizations. It was at this time, too, that *Ōmoto-kyō* (now known simply as *Ōmoto*) had its beginning. Though this movement no longer is very large or effective, its earlier successes and its contributions to the development of still other sects were so considerable that some scholars regard it as the first of the New Religions.[45]

Omoto traces its origin to the revelatory experience in 1892 of an illiterate peasant woman, Deguchi Nao (1836–1918), who lived in Ayabe in Kyoto Prefecture. She was at that time and for several years thereafter an adherent of Konko-kyo. Though her behavior was so strange and unpredictable that many thought her to be demented, she also showed signs of possessing remarkable powers. Untrained in writing, she is said to have written thousands of oracles under divine inspiration, using the *hiragana* phonetic syllabary. Consistently, during the early years, she pointed beyond herself to a savior who was still to come. In 1898, the expected one appeared, a young man named Ueda Kisaburo (1871–1948), who in the following year married Nao's daughter and was adopted into the family. Known thereafter as Deguchi Onisaburo and recognized as the cofounder of Omoto, he became the real organizer and developer of the religion; but his activity belongs principally to the following phases of our survey.

THE LATE MEIJI AND TAISHO PERIODS

The third period favoring the development of New Religions extended from the end of the Russo-Japanese War to about 1925. At the outset, national pride and confidence, reinforced by the outcome of the recent war, were counterbalanced by individual restlessness and by increased social tensions resulting from industrial expansion and urbanization. Later, in the World War I era, the industrial and commercial successes of Japan produced unprecedented wealth for persons at the top but, in so doing, further widened the gulf between them and the disprivileged masses. The latter sought almost any means by which to register their discontent; the former, fearful of every challenge to their privileged estate, resorted to reactionary methods of repression. The period ended in the gloom of the severe financial depression of 1921 and the devastating and demoralizing Kanto earthquake of 1923.

Religiously this period was a time of ferment. During the first decade of the twentieth century, individual interest in religious issues probably was more widespread than at any other time in Japanese history. Yet, coupled with the aftermath of the war with Russia, the very earnestness of this pursuit contributed significantly to the growth of a general distrust of the major institutionalized religions—Shinto, Buddhism, and Christianity—all of which seemed to be too much identified with formalism or special interest and too little aware of people's needs and longings. From a long-range point of view, one of the most important developments resulting from this agitation was the revival of interest in Nichiren (1222–1282), a Japanese Buddhist prophet whose nationalism, apocalypticism, messianism, literary skills, and outspoken criticism of formalistic religions seemed to commend him as an apt hero for the new times. We shall pursue the significance of this development in our discussion of the early Showa and post-World War II periods and see its culmination in *Risshō Kōsei-kai* and *Sōka Gakkai.*

For the New Religions that had originated in the nineteenth century, the early 1900's was a time of dramatic growth, preeminently so for Omoto. Under the acutely skillful leadership of Master Onisaburo, this religion enlisted a vast popular following, acquired extensive property holdings, and used mass media effectively to communicate its message to the general public. However, such was the character and style of Onisaburo that eventually he incurred opposition from the government. Apparently he was very sensitive to social injustice and was firmly opposed to most of the national policies; perhaps also he was a bit incautious in expressing his feelings. He rode an almost white horse when the privilege of riding a white horse was reserved for the Emperor. Was this a transparently disguised challenge to governmental authority? No matter the intention, the government found in this and other related behavior, combined with the Omoto prophecy concerning a new world, the excuse it needed to take action against the sect. In 1921, in what is known as the First Omoto Incident, Omoto was accused of lese majesty, and its leaders subsequently were brought to trial in three sessions over a protracted period of time. However, because of a declaration of amnesty following the death of the Emperor Taisho in 1926, the case was dismissed without judgment. Still, a new pattern had been set. Henceforth, the charge of lese majesty repeatedly would be brought against various New Religions and their leaders; and, as we shall see in the next section, Omoto would not again be so fortunate.

During this period, numerous other sects were begun. We shall mention only two—one from the beginning and the other from the end of the Taisho period—*Tokumitsu-kyō* and *Reiyū-kai*, founded in 1912 and 1925, respectively. Subsequently we shall discuss Tokumitsu-kyo as the predecessor of more successful movements; here we shall let it stand as the symbol of one important aspect of the period of its origin, namely, a shift of the principal support of the New Religions from rural areas to the towns and cities. Tenri-kyo, Konko-kyo, and Omoto all were founded by peasants and prospered initially among farming people before making any inroads into urban settings. Tokumitsu-kyo was born in Osaka, the most commercial of all Japanese cities. The founder was Kanada Tokumitsu (1863–1919), the son of a merchant and himself the owner of a prosperous cutlery business, who was also a mystic and a mountain ascetic. His merchant-oriented religious philosophy, compounded from various Buddhist and Shinto sources and his own experiences, so impressed some of his fellow businessmen that they undertook to sponsor him as their leader in a religious fellowship. The new movement was launched as Tokumitsu-kyo in 1912 and flourished quickly during the subsequent business boom of the World War I era, when it became especially renowned for its stock-market tips and advice to mine operators.[46]

The year 1925 seems to have been a fruitful one for the New Religions. Of the several sects launched in that year, the most

noteworthy was Reiyu-kai, Spirit-Friends Association, which appeared in Tokyo. Though several persons contributed to the
creation of the movement, two are generally regarded as having
been the founders, Kubo Kakutaro (1892–1944), a carpenter's
apprentice who was adopted into a devout Nichiren Buddhist
family, and Kotani Kimi (1901–   ), Kakutaro's sister-in-law, a
high-strung, energetic woman of low birth and varied, sometimes
questionable experience.[47] The principal emphasis of Reiyu-kai
was the possibility of salvation in this world through the faithful
veneration of ancestral spirits. The movement was also linked
with the newly-reviving Nichiren Buddhist tradition, which features, above all else, reliance upon the *Lotus Sūtra*.[48] In its
ascendancy, Reiyu-kai was to become the precursor of a host of
Lotus Sūtra sects, several of which resulted from schisms in
Reiyu-kai itself—but this story comes later.

THE EARLY SHOWA PERIOD

The inexorable advance of fascism was the hallmark of the
1930's in Japan. Though social conditions were right for spawning
more New Religions, only those that cooperated with the state
could hope to prosper, and—as one group discovered—even the
way of accommodation could be ruinous.

This was a time of stern antireligious measures and propaganda, when people were encouraged to think of the New
Religions as bogus religions and the term *shinkō shūkyō* gained
its greatest currency as a pejorative label.[49] It was then, too, that
a showdown occurred between the government and Omoto in
the so-called Second Omoto Incident. In 1935, charging that
Omoto had the appearance of a religion but that the real purpose
of its leaders was to usurp the place of the imperial family and
that Onisaburo himself hoped to become the ruler of Japan, the
government ordered the dissolution of Omoto. Its buildings in
Ayabe and Kameoka were razed, and its landholdings were ceded
to these two townships. The leaders were arrested, brought to
trial, found guilty, and sentenced to prison terms varying from
two to fifteen years—except for Onisaburo, who was sentenced to
imprisonment for life. When the case later was appealed, all were

adjudged to be not guilty; nevertheless, the movement was kept helpless by sustained persecution until the end of World War II.[50] Thereafter, Omoto was reorganized, but it has not fully recovered its former power. However, it should not pass unnoticed at this point that the influence of Omoto on other sects, some of which continue to thrive, has been substantial. As we shall note again in due course, some of the principal mediators of that influence were individuals who, having been schooled in Omoto, left that religion under persecution and later founded their own sects.

Though the arrest of religious leaders on charges of lese majesty was a common occurrence in the 1930's, during that period a few New Religions, by supporting the ruling power, were able to flourish—at least temporarily. These were, notably, *Hito no Michi*, *Seichō no Ie*, and *Reiyū-kai*.

Hito no Michi, an outgrowth of the previously mentioned Tokumitsu-kyo, will be presented more fully in Chapter VI. Here it is sufficient to observe that in order to avoid the fate of Omoto, the leaders of Hito no Michi recognized Amaterasu, the sungoddess, as the supreme deity, subscribed to the "orthodox" interpretations of the ancient myths, taught the morality of the Imperial Rescript on Education (*Kyōiku-chokugo*),[51] and in other ways sought to go with the tide of official ideology. For a time, the movement flourished, but the government, fearing the rise of mass power, eventually found it unbearable that its line should be supported so closely by such "suspicious" people.[52] Therefore, in 1936, having decided that the sect's teaching concerning Amaterasu was disrespectful and that its interpretation of the Imperial Rescript was vulgar,[53] the government initiated a series of charges and arrests that destroyed the effectiveness of Hito no Michi for the remainder of the militarist regime.

Other than to name Seicho no Ie as one of the sects that arose and flourished in this period and to identify its founder, Taniguchi Masaharu, as one of the aforementioned defectors from Omoto, we shall not discuss it further at this point, since it is the subject of Chapter VII.

Just prior to the Pacific war, Reiyu-kai was the most successful of all the New Religions, and it continued in that role throughout the war and for several years thereafter. Although in its early years Reiyu-kai was a small group, from about 1934 it expanded quite rapidly. The easy harmonization of its teachings with the official line extolling the virtues of the family and the imperial system was one asset. Still more fortuitous was aristocratic patronage, including a relative of the imperial family, who was listed as honorary president. Because of such support in high places, Reiyu-kai was never hindered by the government.[54] Nevertheless, while free from all external harassment, the sect was continually troubled by internal dissension. Throughout its history, Reiyu-kai has been schism-prone. From the standpoint of our narrative, the most notable early split occurred in 1938, when a new branch was formed which, though little regarded at the time, was to become, as Rissho Kosei-kai, one of the most prominent New Religions in the postwar period.

THE POST-WORLD WAR II PERIOD

With the collapse of the old authoritarianism and the granting of unprecedented religious freedom at the end of World War II, "the New Religions rose like mushrooms after a rainfall."[55] Initially most of them were either prewar religions or their offshoots, whose leaders, coming out of hiding or camouflage or jail, quickly took advantage of their opportunities to restore their enterprises and to begin a new advance. The fortunes of some of the most prominent of these will claim much of our attention hereafter, but at this point we must not overlook the addition of a steadily increasing host of new sects—most of them small, many of them bizarre, and some of them corrupt. It has been determined that by 1952, at the end of the Occupation, there were almost six hundred New Religions in Japan.[56] This was indeed the "rush hour of the gods."

In the generally confused condition of society at that time, many diverse and some dubious enterprises were linked with the cause of religion. One electrical appliance dealer founded a sect called *Denshin-kyō* (Religion of the Electricity God), dedicated to the worship of its eponymous deity and Thomas Alva Edison.[57] Another sect, called *Kōdōji-kyō*, was organized specifically for the purpose of tax evasion. The founder, a man knowledgeable in the law, saw an opportunity under the then existing legislation to register any business enterprise as a religious juridical person and thus gain exemption from the payment of income taxes. For instance, the owner of a restaurant could call his business a church and could say that its purpose was to propagate the teaching that "life is religion." His customers would be devotees. The satisfaction of hunger would be salvation. Money received would be offerings made by the faithful in gratitude for salvation. Ergo, the restaurateur really would receive no income, hence he need not pay income taxes. This idea proved so attractive to business proprietors that for about two years (1947–1948), the founder was the head of a thriving organization that licensed as churches a wide range of enterprises, including restaurants, dress shops, art shops, beauty salons, and even brothels. Needless to say, the law was amended to close these loopholes.[58]

Two other sects that received a great deal of publicity just after the war were *Jiu-kyō* and *Tenshō Kōtai Jingu-kyō*, each founded by a very unusual woman. The foundress of Jiu-kyo was a former Omoto devotee, Nagaoka Yoshiko, known as *Jikōson*, who, claiming to be an incarnation of the sun-goddess, declared that since the Emperor had renounced his divinity, she would become the divine ruler in his stead. Toward this end, she formed a "cabinet," which included a champion *sumo* wrestler and a champion *go* (Japanese chess) player.[59] For a time, she had a considerable group of fanatical followers and received from them a large amount of money. However, due to adverse publicity, the movement soon dwindled, being so severely ridiculed that it was almost laughed out of existence.[60] The movement has survived as a minor group in the suburbs of Yokohama.[61]

Tensho Kotai Jingu-kyo, popularly known as the Dancing Religion (*Odoru Shūkyō*) because of an "ecstasy dance" performed by the devotees, is still a flourishing movement. The foundress is Kitamura Sayo, a farm woman who stirred up widespread interest, amusement, and resentment by her bold claims to be the spokesman of a deity and by her sharp diatribes directed at those she considered to be in error. Short and stocky, dressed in a man's-style suit, completely self-assured, she was an unforgettable figure as she preached on trains and street corners and wherever else she found people. The recalcitrant and heedless she called "maggot beggars." All others she invited to accept the riches of faith and to join together to build a new Japan and establish peace throughout the world. Two decades after the war, she remains a compelling presence.

Because there were many aspects of the New Religions that seemed base and unsavory, the press and the general public had an unsympathetic attitude toward them. To be sure, there was much to justify this view, but oftentimes accusations were made unfairly and insensitively. There were many desperate people in Japan after the war. The established religions seemed incapable of helping them. Social-action programs were almost nonexistent. In their desperation, great throngs of people braved the ridicule of their society and sought help in the New Religions. Among them, undoubtedly there were many who asked for bread and received a stone, but many others found what they fully believed to be a salvation equal to their need. Though scores of the smaller sects quickly passed away without having attained any real strength, many of the others still are growing. The very persistence of their appeal imposes an obligation upon all who would understand and attempt to influence Japanese society to comprehend the functions of these enduring New Religions in aiding the masses to cope with the world around them. Given the traumatic experiences of the Japanese nation, to what alternatives might the masses have turned if the New Religions had not been available?[62]

Classification of the New Religions

The effort to respond to this obligation to comprehend the functions of the New Religions is hindered considerably by the immense breadth and diversity of their phenomenological range. Thus far, we have attempted to gain some measure of control over these data by the qualified definition of the New Religions as "contemporary popular religious movements" and by the adoption of a long-range historical perspective that views them within the context of three and a half centuries of crisis existence. However, it remains to be asked whether it is possible to impose upon these sects still more precise systems of classification.

Presumably a number of additional typologies could be devised for this purpose. In my opinion, there are four particularly authentic and useful means of classification: (1) according to their relation to classical traditions, (2) according to their relation to the forerunners among the New Religions, (3) according to the "hope-discipline" scheme of sociologist J. Milton Yinger, and (4) according to the social roles that individual sects are playing. No one of these is sufficiently incisive or airtight to be used alone, but taken together they provide a comprehensive means of organizing the data. The first two categories are genealogical; the second two are functional.

RELATION TO CLASSICAL TRADITIONS

Since the religious history of Japan is dominated by Shinto and Buddhism, it is not surprising that most of the New Religions may be classified for various reasons as being either Shintoistic or Buddhistic. In some instances, the relation to one or the other of these traditions is deliberately maintained and openly advertised. For example, Omoto identifies itself as a Shinto sect, and Rissho Kosei-kai and Soka Gakkai claim to represent Buddhism, specifically the Nichiren tradition. In other movements, such as Tenri-kyo and Konko-kyo, which were arbitrarily classified as Shinto sects by the Meiji government, the relationship to a classical tradition is more circumstantial and tenuous. A few sects are identified with Christianity: *Tōitsu Kyōkai* (Light of Unity Church), *Genshi Fukuin* (Original Gospel Movement), and *Iesu no Mitama Kyōkai* (Spirit of Jesus Church).[63] Useful though it is, however, this method of classification has one very definite limitation: it is too arbitrary to comprehend adequately the amorphous folk character and syncretism that typify so many of the sects.

RELATION TO FORERUNNERS

In previously published English-language studies of the New Religions, the usual method of classification has been genealogical. For example, in a book by Offner and Van Straelen, *Modern Japanese Religions*, the specific movements selected for discussion are grouped in three categories: Tenri-kyo has a section all its own; Omoto, Seicho no Ie, Sekai Kyusei-kyo, and PL Kyodan are grouped together under the heading "Omoto-related Religions and PL Kyodan"; and Reiyu-kai, Rissho Kosei-kai, and Soka Gakkai are discussed as "Nichiren-related Buddhistic Religions." Similarly, Thomsen's *The New Religions of Japan*[64] includes a section on "The 'Old' New Religions," another on "The Nichiren Group," a third on "The Omoto Group," and a final catchall under the heading "Miscellaneous." This method is generally supported by the practice of Japanese sociologists of religion, many of whom seem to prefer the designation of Omoto as the original New Religion,[65] since it arose during the modern period and since many of the other sects can be regarded as offshoots from it or from some later sect, such as Reiyu-kai.

In general, this is a plausible and useful approach; certainly, lines of descent and indebtedness ought to be noted wherever they exist. However, this method of categorization also has some major shortcomings. For example, to designate an "Omoto group" is simply to classify certain movements in terms of their relation to one of their own number and thus to provide no external or historical frame of reference. Moreover, within that group, while it is true that there are or have been certain links with Omoto, it seems doubtful that knowledge of the Omoto relationship carries one very far in understanding the distinctive functions of the separate religious movements. Similarly, it is obviously correct to say that Rissho Kosei-kai and Soka Gakkai are Nichiren-related movements, but considering the very great differences between these two groups, one must wonder whether this is the most instructive method by which to classify them. The genealogical method, though indispensable, points toward the necessity of classification by function.

YINGER'S "HOPE-DISCIPLINE" SCHEME

In surveying the widespread occurrence of sectarian religious movements similar in character to the New Religions of Japan, sociologist J. Milton Yinger attempted to classify their varied activities "by ranging them along two variables: hope and discipline." Said he:

> On the basis of these two variables, one could describe four possible types of religious activity or of functional alternatives to religious activity. There could be movements which expressed neither hope nor discipline, others that expressed hope but not discipline, discipline but not hope, and both hope and discipline.[66]

To what extent is this scheme applicable to the Japanese situation? It seems to me that nearly all the New Religions, regardless of their lineage, fit into the fourth category—"both hope and discipline." Indeed, when we say of these various sects that they are movements that must be seen as a movement, it is the common occurrence of this union of hope and discipline that gives this utterance its greatest plausibility. In the next chapter, the conviction that this is so underlies the entire discussion of the recurrent characteristics of the New Religions; and, in turn, these characteristics are offered as evidence that in most instances of faith, the big acquisition is hope, and hope is sustained in large part by the discipline of the organization.

SOCIAL ROLES OF INDIVIDUAL SECTS

There is, in addition, another level at which the New Religions need to be classified. Whereas the diversity of the individual sects is largely incidental to their being considered together as a functional unity, their original similarity to one another also tends to lose significance the longer the sects persist as free and independent movements. In later chapters, by means of detailed examinations of five of the most prominent sects, we shall attempt to discover the distinctive new roles that each one plays, or may yet play, as it acquires greater stability and sophistication. It is now apparent that the New Religions of Japan not only reflect the immediate past history of that nation; they will also help shape its future.

Recurrent Characteristics
of the New Religions

THE MANY NEW RELIGIONS OF JAPAN are phenomena that must be treated as a phenomenon; they are movements that must be seen as a movement. The distinctiveness of the individual sects, though ultimately an important consideration, is at the outset secondary to their remarkable similarity. In character and function, each sect must be considered primarily as a factor in a widespread and significant socioreligious movement. Accordingly, the purpose of this chapter is to cite certain elements that recur so frequently in comparable forms that they may be regarded as the identifying characteristics of the New Religions considered as a single movement.

Charismatic Leadership

At the beginning of each of the New Religions there stands a founder or founders who claim to have received a new inspiration or revelation or to have discovered anew the truth or power inherent in something already familiar. Considered together, these founders (*kyōso*), both male and female, comprise a wide and interesting range of individual types; but there is at least one rubric under which virtually all of them can be classified: they are "charismatic personalities." That is, they are individuals whose very presence bespeaks personal power and authority and to whom, therefore, popular loyalty is given almost involuntarily.

Long accustomed to the occasional appearance of such persons, the Japanese have their own special term by which to designate them. They call them *ikigami* ("living *kami*"). In order to understand the significance of this term, it is necessary to refer again to the distinctive Japanese *kami* notion that there is no sharp differentiation of the human and the divine. According to this vague concept, it is admissible to say that all persons are *kami* or at least potentially so; however, ordinarily it is not considered appropriate to refer to a living person as *kami*. Rather, it is supposed that an individual becomes, or under certain circumstances *may* become, a *kami* only after his death. Exceptionally, however, there is a person who, by the general consent of those around him, merits acknowledgment that he is a "living *kami*."

From a technical standpoint, it can be said that the frame of reference within which the identity of an *ikigami* is determined probably is more dynamistic than theistic. That is, the primary consideration is the locus of power, not a question of ontology. Here the term *kami*, which in its wide range of meaning does sometimes denote "deity," probably is more nearly synonymous with "mana." Thus, an *ikigami* is one in whom certain elemental powers are concentrated. He is a power-charged person.

Because a correct perspective on this matter is necessary if we are to understand the essential character of religion in Japan, perhaps it is worthwhile at this juncture to sound a specific warning. When a non-Japanese, especially one from the West, considers the term *ikigami*, he is likely to envisage an image that is essentially misleading. An *ikigami* is rarely, if ever, regarded as "God become man" or "man become God" in any sense that is comparable to the metamorphoses that such figures of speech are likely to evoke from the viewpoint of the religious concepts of the West. Due to the vague notion of deity and the imprecise demarcation of the human from the divine in the Japanese religious orientation, the emergence of an *ikigami*, while remarkable, is nothing comparable to the once-for-all breakthrough described in most versions of the Christian doctrine of incarnation. It seems, indeed, that the appearance of an *ikigami* is considered a fortuitous extension of the hierarchical structure of society rather than a bridging action linking two disparate orders of being.

With possibly a few exceptions, the founders of the New Religions—and in many cases their successors—are regarded by their adherents as *ikigami*. In some instances, this very term is used; in others, various essentially synonymous honorifics are employed. But no matter the specific nomenclature, almost invariably the founders are seen as persons in whom remarkable powers reside.[1]

The ways by which these powers are manifested in the founders are quite diverse, but to a greater or less degree, they reflect one of the oldest and most durable features of Japanese religion, shamanistic possession, in which a deity commandeers the body of a chosen person for his dwelling place and begins to speak and act through that person to instruct and empower those who are attracted to this manifestation of his presence.

Among the founders of the New Religions, only a few examples of classic shamanism can be found. Probably the best known of these is the experience of Nakayama Miki (1798–1887), the peasant woman who in 1838 became the foundress of Tenri-kyo. In the literature of this sect, it is recorded that as Miki lay in a trance, those gathered around her heard a voice that said: "I am the True and Original God. I have a predestination to this Residence. Now I have descended from Heaven to save all men. I want to take Miki as the Shrine of God."[2] Thereafter, she spoke and acted by the power of the deity, Tenri-O-no-Mikoto.

One of the most notable examples of a shamanic type among those founders still living is Kitamura Sayo, called *Ogamisama*,[3] the foundress of Tensho Kotai Jingu-kyo, the so-called Dancing Religion. She is the only "preacher" for a movement that numbers approximately two hundred thousand adherents and has outposts even in the United States, both in Hawaii and on the mainland. Her followers regularly come from all parts of Japan and occasionally travel from overseas to hear her oracular sermons. Recordings of her messages are distributed widely among her devotees, and she herself has journeyed abroad several times to conduct preaching missions. Commenting on her sermons, she says that when she opens her mouth to speak, it is as if she has turned on a divine radio. The god within her body begins to speak. Thus there is no necessity for her ever to give any thought to what she is to say.[4]

In detail, the claims and experiences of other founders may vary considerably from these; still, as Hori Ichiro insists, they generally have as their base a "transformed" or "transfigured" shamanism. In almost every instance, some kind of mystical manifestation of power is offered as primary evidence of the validity of the religious mission.[5] This has long been a widely respected credential among the Japanese masses.[6]

Most of the founders also resemble one another circumstantially in that they were born to low social status, received little formal education, and experienced a full measure of personal adversity, such as ill health, poverty, and the frustration that comes from living in an oppressive social environment. Obviously, a founder's humble origin and experience of hardship help to establish and maintain his rapport with the masses. He knows their ways of thinking, the peculiarities of their speech, and their perennial grievances. Having lived as they live, suffered as they suffer, he can more convincingly cite his own experience of deliverance as evidence of the validity of his promises. But if his movement is even moderately successful, he is not likely to continue indefinitely to share the discommodities of his followers, nor do they expect him to do so. The general tendency (with some exceptions) is for the founders and/or their successors to become a new aristocracy, enjoying a standard of living that often is equivalent materially to that of the wealthiest and most prominent families in Japan.

Quite apart from the evident satisfaction that the leaders derive from the achievement of aristocratic status, this development is integrally important to the functioning of the New Religions. In the first place, it is significant for pragmatic or tactical reasons. As we shall see more fully in the next section, it is characteristic of the New Religions that they promise tangible results. To a considerable extent, the popularity of each movement is proportionate to the quantity of evidence it produces to prove that what it offers really works. Hence, the founder or his successor must project a success image that, at the very least, compares favorably with those of his rivals.

In the second place, this development is psychologically important to the believers. For the most part, it is *hope* rather than many very tangible rewards that they receive as a result of their faith. Certainly, with few exceptions, they do not expect that it ever will be their lot to ride in a chauffeur-driven automobile or to travel abroad, but they delight in participating vicariously in their leader's enjoyment of such luxuries.

In addition, the significance of the founders' emergence as new aristocrats may also be affected by the vicissitudes of the imperial system. This is an involved and subtle matter. At least two Japanese scholars view the New Religions as "by-products" or "stepchildren" of the imperial system.[7] By this they mean that the former totalitarian policies promulgated in the name of the Emperor created a religious void that the New Religions that arose in the early twentieth century tried to fill. In their relationships with the imperial government, the New Religions often manifested the ambivalent feelings of a stepchild. On the one hand, they disliked the imperial system and sometimes even opposed it; on the other hand, they were obliged to curry the favor of the imperial government. It is this ambivalence, together with the effect of the many years during which the Japanese people were conditioned to think of the Emperor as a divine personage and the center of their lives, that provides a basis for analyzing an interesting dimension of the current aristocratic status of the leaders of the New Religions.

In a sense, the Emperor himself was the head of a "new religion."[8] During the development of New Religions before World War II, the Emperor was at once both the chief rival and the paramount model of the founders. Some intimation of this ambivalence may be gleaned from one reason for the government's persecution of Omoto-kyo in 1921: the burial place of the foundress, Deguchi Nao, was completely destroyed because it resembled an imperial tomb.[9]

After World War II, when the Emperor renounced all claim

to divinity and his constitutional status was altered and when freedom of religion was guaranteed, the heads of the New Religions had an opportunity to become Emperor substitutes among a people from whose lives the lodestone had been removed. In many instances, consciously or unconsciously, they have essayed that role, with the result, according to Saki, that the image of the divine Emperor seems to be projected in the "living *kami*" (*ikigami*) of the New Religions.[10]

Evidence that this is so includes additional instances of burial places that simulate imperial tombs. Ideally located amid the scenic beauty of the Hakone area, the graves of Okada Mokichi and his wife, Yoshiko, of Sekai Kyusei-kyo, are one example. Another may be seen at the headquarters of PL Kyodan in Tondabayashi, where the tomb of the founder, Miki Tokuharu, seems unmistakably to be a stylized replica of an imperial tomb.

It must not be assumed, however, that Emperor substitutes are to be found only among the dead; they are much more importantly found among the living, although the evidence that this is so is not so obvious. It consists of innumerable clues that may be discernible only to an observant Japanese, such as one young Osaka housewife of my acquaintance. After seeing for the first time a copy of *PL Fujin* (a women's magazine published by PL Kyodan), she commented that an article on the training of the sect leader's small son was identical in tone with numerous articles in other women's magazines on the training of little Prince Hiro, son of the Crown Prince. In general, it is by such means as this that the image of the divine Emperor is projected anew in the persons of the leaders of the New Religions. Nevertheless, what we are discussing here is not necessarily something that has been foisted on the people; it is fully as much something that the people themselves have cooperated in fashioning. Among the dicta that many of the present devotees of New Religions heard in former years is this one: "Our country is one great family nation comprising a union of sovereign and subject, having the Imperial Household as the head family, and looking up to the Emperor as the focal point from of old to the present."[11] Even among those who have forgotten or who are too young to have heard these words, there are many who are emotionally conditioned to accept their essential spirit. Perhaps, therefore, in most of the New Religions, the "one great family" is no longer the nation but the community of believers, the "head family" no longer the imperial household but the family of the founder or his successor.

Despite the emergence of the leaders of the New Religions as new aristocrats or Emperor substitutes, the acclaim they receive comes almost solely from their own followers. In general, public opinion concerning them seems to be a combination of amusement, suspicion, and annoyance. It is alleged quite often that certain of them are or were mentally deranged or morally corrupt, and there can be little doubt that in some instances the accusations are justified. Though, to my knowledge, none of the charges of insanity has ever been substantiated by psychiatric examination, there have been several cases in which symptoms of mental illness do seem to have been altogether obvious.[12] In some cases, also, indisputable evidence of immorality or unethical practices has been adduced.

Particularly in the immediate postwar period, when the meaning of the newly promulgated provision for freedom of religion was still largely undefined, many charlatans saw their opportunity for licentiousness and quickly entered the "religion game." Some of the founders or would-be founders of New Religions soon were discovered to be black-market operators, tax dodgers, extortionists, sadists, and adulterers.

Perhaps the most publicized scandals were those involving Reiyu-kai and its president, Kotani Kimi. In 1949, in what became known as the First Reiyu-kai Incident, the headquarters were raided, because of suspected tax evasion, and a cache of gold bars and cocaine was discovered. The Second Reiyu-kai Incident, in 1953, involved charges of physical abuse of the president's maid, embezzlement of community-chest funds, political bribery, and black-market dealing in American dollars.[13]

It would be neither fair nor accurate, however, to leave the impression that the leadership of the New Religions generally should be characterized so unflatteringly. The gifts and capacities of some of these persons actually are quite considerable, and probably in most cases their commitment is as genuine and pur-

poseful as that of religious leaders anywhere else. Complexity of
motives is by no means a rare phenomenon in the history of
religions. This is to say that apart from those whose mental and
moral aberrations are habitual and irrefutable, the founders and
other officials of the New Religions deserve to be judged according to the fruits of their work.

Concrete Goals

In the middle of the sixth century A.D., as a part of the overture
that led to the introduction of Buddhism in Japan, the king of
Paekche in Korea sent to the Japanese court a commendation of
Buddhism that included the following claim:

> Imagine a man in possession of treasures to his heart's content, so
> that he might satisfy all his wishes in proportion as he used them.
> Thus it is with the treasure of this wonderful doctrine. Every prayer
> is fulfilled and naught is wanting.[14]

According to other anecdotes surviving from that same period,
Japan's initial response to the proffered foreign religion was, in
essence, to test whether this claim could be substantiated. For a
time, certain untoward occurrences made it appear that the
admission of Buddhism would result in tragedy, due to the anger
of Japan's own deities; but eventually the new religion was permitted to make a beginning, ostensibly because it showed signs
of possessing effective power.

Of course, the traditional accounts of the introduction of
Buddhism in Japan cannot indicate adequately the complex character of this event. Buddhism came as a part of the highly
respected culture of China and subsequently functioned as perhaps the most important civilizing influence in Japan. Yet it is
also clear that the pragmatism reflected in these accounts from
the sixth century was then and has continued to be typical of
much of the Japanese religious orientation. This is to say that
anticipation of concrete results—which is fairly common among
all religions, particularly at the folk or mass level—has been especially prominent throughout the religious history of Japan. It is

now one of the most conspicuous characteristics of the New Religions.

Toda Josei (1900–1958), the second president and the organizing genius of Soka Gakkai, described his religion as a "happiness-manufacturing machine" (*kōfuku seizōki*).[15] While to the spokesmen for most of the other sects such straightforward language might seem to be rather crass, in general their goals are no less concrete than those of Soka Gakkai. The activities and preachments of the New Religions are geared to the need consciousness of people who suffer. They are designed specifically for those who—to use a Japanese proverbial phrase—are "entreating *kami* in time of distress" (*kurushii toki no kami-danomi*).[16] To such persons, they promise happiness, defined almost invariably in terms of deliverance from suffering.

On one occasion, during a lengthy conference with three officials of Soka Gakkai, I proposed the following statement as a summary definition of happiness according to the views they had been expressing: "Happiness is living a life based on faith and thereby experiencing physical, economic, and social well-being." They agreed that this was an accurate and fair definition.[17] With allowances for some crucial differences of opinion concerning saving faith, this definition would probably be acceptable to most of the other sects as well. Not only in Soka Gakkai but also among the New Religions generally, the particular ills for which relief is promised are what Okada Mokichi (1882–1955), founder of Sekai Kyusei-kyo, called the "three great sufferings" (*sandaiku*): sickness, poverty, and tension in interpersonal relationships.[18] Each of these is antithetical to happiness.

At some stage in the development of each of the New Religions, the healing of sickness has had an especially prominent place among its activities.[19] In each one, the prospect of healing is or has been perhaps the most effective inducement in the effort to gather followers. In almost every instance, the founder himself is said to have experienced miraculous healing, usually in association with his receipt of "revelation." With this experience as an earnest, the promise is repeated again and again that similar healing is also available to others. To this, in turn, are added the testimonials of the "healed" believers. Every sect collects its "evidence" of healing and uses it as a major source of propaganda materials. Some groups are especially avid in its use; for example, the literature of Soka Gakkai and Seicho no Ie characteristically includes numerous case histories to create the impression that hundreds of thousands of their followers, some suffering from presumably incurable ailments, have been miraculously restored to health.

In considering the healing aspects of the New Religions, it is most important to be aware of their characteristic attitudes toward the nature and cause of suffering in general. Though they are variously embroidered in the doctrines of the different sects, basically these are Japanese folk perspectives overlaid with heterogeneous bits of occultism and scientism. Four notions, ideas deeply ingrained in the minds of the Japanese masses, are particularly evident. The first one, reflecting the Buddhist teaching concerning the karmic sequence of cause and effect, holds that for every situation—good or bad, but especially bad—there is a cause, which usually may be assumed to lie either in one's personal inheritance or in one's own behavior in this life. The second notion sees suffering as a warning from a deity or an ancestor that the afflicted person is remiss in the performance of duty. In the third view, the central item is a primitive dread of pollution, a factor that survives also in the rites of purification that invariably form a part of every Shinto ceremony. Through the normal contacts of life, as well as in exceptional events, a person accumulates impurities that eventually result in misfortune if they are not expunged. The fourth view is that a person's physical circumstances, including his environment, are in some way the reflection of his own mind or spiritual condition; thus, suffering, in whatever form, is nothing but a mental projection. In this instance, there is another echo of Buddhist teaching, namely, that the phenomenal world ultimately is unreal; but here too is a point where occult ideas from non-Japanese sources frequently are added. For instance, Taniguchi Masaharu, the founder of Seicho no Ie, has turned to the West and elaborated this doctrine by drawing on the teachings of Christian Science and New Thought.

These four notions, and others less basic than these, are manifested among the New Religions in numerous combinations and variations, but consistently in all of them there seems to be one point of agreement: although the cause of any specific misfortune, such as illness, may be quite obscure, it is in some sense personal and potentially identifiable—hence, the possibility is always present that a cause may be divined and effective action prescribed.

Divination and prescription are the special province of the New Religions. Each sect claims to have access to a source of remarkable power that makes possible an accurate analysis of happiness-inhibiting factors and a prescription for their removal. The methods they employ or advocate, though varying considerably in details, represent a rather narrow typological range. In some movements—for example, PL Kyodan—certain persons are supposed to have attained a clairvoyance that enables them to minister to their petitioners individually. At the opposite extreme, though in essence really not very far removed, is Soka Gakkai, with its blanket approach to all situations: failure to achieve happiness is the result of heretical faith and false worship; the solution is to adopt the one true faith and way of worship.

Prescriptions for overcoming adversity point to the need for one or a combination of the following: faith, ritual (including prayer or invocation), discipline, rectification of mental outlook, and contact with a power-charged leader.

Community Identification

One of the most common assumptions concerning the Japanese is that they are exceptionally adroit in masking their feelings. Though the stereotyped forms of this notion may be quite exaggerated, as in the wartime caricatures of a grinning but treacherous soldier or statesman or even in some of the current idealizations of the imperturbable Zen monk, the impression is not wholly incorrect. It is a fact that, characteristically, individual Japanese are reluctant to reveal their inner lives and to discuss their personal problems.

This reticence is rooted in the long-honored tradition (which also may be too easily caricatured) requiring that a Japanese observe the proprieties of every situation and, if necessary, stoically internalize his personal reactions. If he were remiss in practicing restraint, he had to expect some manner of ostracism; and if his personal honor had been seriously besmirched thereby, he sought escape through suicide or perhaps through entering a monastery.

Among the Japanese masses at the present time, it appears that this tradition is honored more in the popularity of stories and dramas in which it is the major theme than in its actual adoption as a pattern of behavior. Nevertheless, certain residual features of the former way of life are built into the structure of current Japanese society. If one suffers from frustration and anxiety, his problems may be greatly intensified by his supposing that he must suppress them. To be sure, in every complex society there are innumerable people who fight their personal battles in loneliness and virtual anonymity. If Japan's situation is distinctive, it is due to the fact that it offers relatively less incentive and fewer opportunities than do most other modern societies for a person to unburden himself to others. The following anecdotes suggest some of the typical problems that result.

In 1965, when for the second year in succession an abnormally cold spring had devastated the crops in northern Japan, there were twenty-one cases of suicide and infanticide, resulting in the loss of twenty-five lives. According to a newspaper report of these tragedies: "The hard-pressed farmers . . . had become desperate in many cases because of the absence of persons to consult."[20]

A young wife obliged both by tradition and by the housing shortage to live with her husband's parents may spend her days as the virtual servant of a demanding mother-in-law and receive from her husband very few words of affection or appreciation. Traditionally, it is expected that resignation should be her response. She rarely has any therapeutic outlet for her resentment and frustration.

Or consider the young man who comes from a rural area into a major industrial city. Because he is unskilled and inexperienced, he finds work only as a day laborer or the lowliest factory hand. Known by no one and knowing no one, he soon becomes dispirited and begins to spend his meager earnings on drink, dope, women, and gambling in an effort to escape reality.

One of the greatest needs in each of these instances is an

experience of community—an introduction to others who are similarly burdened, the discovery of people who care, the opportunity to hear and to be heard. In the "web society" of old imperial Japan, there was an intense consciousness of corporate identity, but who was the individual? Officially, in the latter days of that society, he was defined as "an existence belonging to a State and her history."[21] In the new democratic Japan, no clear new sense of national identity and purpose has yet arisen, and the individual knows not who he is. He must struggle in order not to be lost in the amorphous mass of his society, but with what and for what does he struggle?

The New Religions—those that arose before World War II as well as the more recent ones—have sought out the hopeless, helpless individual with a message of hope and a promise of help. Behind the message and the promise, perhaps the single most important boon that they have had to offer is the opportunity to belong to a community. In the days of totalitarianism, even though their own organizations were hierarchical and paternalistic and even though they sometimes cooperated with the ruling power, the New Religions were havens for "found" individuals from among the heavily oppressed. As such, they moved against the tide; in effect, they were movements of social protest. That this was so is indicated perhaps most clearly in the fact that the government sought to keep them tightly under control. In the postwar period, even though to many eyes certain features of the New Religions seem anachronistic or superstitious or undemocratic, the situation still obtains: these religious movements offer one of the few opportunities in Japanese society for the distressed individual to be identified with a community.

In any one of the more successful New Religions, the individual devotee is likely to find satisfaction in two dimensions of his community relationship. On the one hand, he is involved in a community whose very size, efficiency, and tangible monuments bespeak power and success. On the other hand, he may also be a part of a small, intimate cell group in which his repressions can find outlets and his loneliness be assuaged. The first of these will be discussed subsequently; the second is our immediate concern here.

In Saki's discussion of the New Religions,[22] it is possible to discern nine characteristics of the cell groups as they function in almost all the more noteworthy sects. (1) The groups are small, usually numbering from ten to twenty persons. (2) They meet several times a month for only one or two hours at a time. (3) Meetings are scheduled for the convenience of the members —usually during the day for housewives, at night for workingmen. (4) The atmosphere is always informal. (5) Discussion is intimate and open-minded. (6) There is opportunity for individual confession and repentance. (7) All participants are concerned with being mutually helpful. (8) The groups plan and evaluate most of their own activities. (9) The members of a group often participate together in various recreational and social activities.

Clearly operative within these groups are principles and procedures of group dynamics and a process of group therapy. As we shall note later, not all the functions and by-products of the cell groups are salutary or commendable, but the importance of at least one factor is irrefutable: they have given to thousands of frustrated and lonely people a "saving" sense of unity and mutuality within a new community.

Highly Centralized Organization

Throughout much of Japanese history, especially since the establishment of the Tokugawa shogunate at the beginning of the seventeenth century, social and political structures have tended to be rigidly stratified and strongly authoritarian. This tendency is also reflected in the highly centralized organizations of the New Religions.

Typically, a large religious movement maintains a national or, in some cases, an international headquarters, where for the most part the teachings are formulated and the principal program planning and policy making take place. The lesser administrative agencies are constituted at regional, prefectural, district, and local-community levels primarily for the purpose of disseminating and implementing whatever comes from headquarters.

To those working within such a system, the numerous prerogatives and lines of authority seem to be quite clear; however, an observer, even though he has before him a chart of the organization, likely will find much to confuse him. In every instance, it seems, organizational operations rest significantly upon the *oya-ko* ("parent-child") pattern, which in innumerable variations has governed relationships between individuals and groups in Japan since a very early date. Thus, operational efficiency depends largely upon conditioned responses and habits of mind—upon an ingrained sense of propriety and obligation—which could never be written into a constitution or bylaws.

A detailed delineation of the systems of organization employed among the New Religions is not important to this present study. Our concern is to note the actual or potential effects of these systems upon the Japanese people and their society. At this point, we can identify two: one is the attractiveness of such systems to large numbers of Japanese; the other is their possible infringement of democratic rights and processes.

The first of these reflects the fact that many Japanese want the sense of security that comes from submitting to authority. Fairly frequently, especially in major train stations throughout Japan, one may see large numbers of devotees on pilgrimage. Organized into squads or platoons lined up behind numbered banners, they keep their places and follow instructions in apparently complete docility and contentment. Such compliance, we may assume, stems mainly from previous orientation in a totalitarian society. Psychologically, this situation seems to be identical with that of the man just out of the army, whom Eric Hoffer describes as "an ideal potential convert" to a mass movement:

He feels alone and lost in the free-for-all of civilian life. The responsibilities and uncertainties of an autonomous existence weigh and prey upon him. He longs for certitude, camaraderie, freedom from individual responsibility, and a vision of something altogether different from the competitive free society around him—and he finds all this in the brotherhood and the revivalist atmosphere of a rising movement.[23]

There is also another aspect of this appeal that has a slightly more positive character. The New Religions attract vast numbers of people who have no distinctive status—no title or office or reserved privileges—in the society at large. Many are school dropouts; others have failed college-entrance examinations. But whatever the failure, which society may regard as serious, it becomes much less consequential for the person involved if within the extended chain of command of a religious movement he can find some place of responsibility. There, at least, he will have status. One such person of my acquaintance is a young woman who works as a domestic servant.[24] Poorly educated and married to a ne'er-do-well, she had experienced a dreary life until she joined Soka Gakkai. In her new faith she found new hope and purpose, and after several years she was made a class leader (*kumichō*), with responsibility for two other members. Thus, it became her task to offer these persons guidance in the faith and to invite them to discussion meetings. If she should succeed in converting still others, they too would become her responsibility; and if her group should grow large, she might be promoted to the next higher rank, squad leader (*hanchō*). To one who believes that Soka Gakkai is the most important association in the world, it is deeply satisfying to be given an office and title and to be able to anticipate an eventual promotion. Though society withholds this kind of fulfillment from most of its lowly ones, many of them do experience it within the New Religions.

However, in addition to providing comfort and status to many insecure people, the highly centralized, authoritarian regime that is typical of the New Religions may also infringe democratic rights and processes. This likelihood is especially evident in the lowest echelon of the system, the cell group, where paradoxically a person who has been "found" as an individual may easily be persuaded to forgo certain expressions of his individuality in order to preserve the general rapport. Neither his previous experience nor his new involvement is likely to incline him to struggle for his right to hold his own opinions. Thus, he tends to become blindly obedient, in most respects thinking as he is told to think and acting as he is told to act, without being aware that he has given up anything. The housemaid mentioned above, when asked whether Soka Gakkai members are instructed to vote for certain candidates, replied that they are not. However, she said, unless a candidate is approved by the president and other leaders, the members will not vote for him; for they know that their leaders are much more able than they to assess the qualifications of a candidate. Fundamentally, what we see manifested in this is, in the words of Vittorio Lanternari, "the desire of the faithful to 'separate' themselves from secular society and to establish another beyond its reach."[25]

There is, however, a potentially insidious type of relationship to a religious sect that is to a considerable extent involuntary. It is in some ways jointly a by-product of an authoritarian religious organization and an authoritarian social structure, but chiefly it comes from the latter. According to one steel-company employee, "If the social situation seems to obligate a person to become a member of a religion, he cannot refuse."[26] By this he meant that if one's employer is interested in the propagation of a particular religion, the employee may have no choice but to join. In the view of this informant, the prevalence of this kind of situation is one reason for the flourishing of Soka Gakkai.

I have also acquired data that indicate that certain employers serve the cause of Seicho no Ie in this manner. At a weekend youth retreat sponsored by this movement,[27] I was permitted to ask some questions of the young people. In response to the question, "How did you become acquainted with Seicho no Ie?" twelve of the fifty-three participants answered, "Through the company for which I work." Later, in a conference that included adult sponsors of this same gathering, an employer of more than three hundred people revealed his plan to send all of them, a few at a time—expenses paid and salary continuing—to Seicho no Ie retreats for inquirers. A benevolent and well-meaning man, he had no thought of coercing his employees, but how would the employees themselves understand their obligation in this matter?

There is probably no sure way to determine how prevalent these practices are among the New Religions; however, intimations of their presence are frequently found.

Construction Projects

The Higashi Honganji in Kyoto is a headquarters temple of the *Jōdo Shin-Shū*, the most popular Buddhist sect in Japan.

Founded in 1602, this great temple has been destroyed by fire four times, most recently in 1864. The construction of the present buildings, completed in 1895, was made possible by donations from the faithful throughout the country.

One of the treasures now customarily shown to visitors to the temple is a heavy rope made of human hair contributed by thousands of female devotees. In all there were fifty such ropes, which were used to draw the massive timbers required for the rebuilding of the temple. A flashback to this period is provided for us in Sugimoto Etsu's intriguing account of her childhood in a remote province of Japan.[28] She recalls that especially on the first and fifteenth days of each month (the regular holidays of the workingmen), there was great excitement in her town, as throngs of people laden with their gifts of many kinds of produce came in from the mountains and neighboring villages; but, above all, she remembers the hair. Nearly every woman contributed at least a few strands, and many of them cut off most of their hair—an act usually performed only by a widow. One young woman "cut off so much that she had to postpone her marriage for three years; for no girl could marry with short hair. Not a man of those days would be brave enough to risk the ill-omen of taking a bride with the cut hair of a widow."[29]

The assumption of so great a burden of support by the masses is not entirely typical, for at the time of the rebuilding of the great Honganji, Buddhism was out of favor with the government and thus was denied much of the rich patronage it had formerly received. Nevertheless, here we do have in focus some important features of traditional sectarian Buddhism and of the piety of the masses in Japan. Characteristically, each sect erected a headquarters temple that was intended to be the glory and delight of the faithful—the repository of all that they deemed most sacred, the subject of their dreams, the goal of their pilgrimages. For their part, the people responded with great loyalty and sacrificial devotion.

Another view of this phenomenon is presented by the novelist Osaragi Jiro in the form of the reverie of a Japanese repatriate trying to discover the true identity of his homeland after the war. Sitting in the city of Kyoto and gazing up at Mount Hiei, he muses:

It's incredible that they should have conceived of building a temple on such a high mountain a thousand years ago. It shows the power of religion, of course. Look at the Japanese today. They'd be completely incapable of any such grandiose scheme. Even now the temple looks superhuman, mythically vast, like some great dream of humanity, and they calmly set to work and made it real a thousand years ago, before the country was half civilized. They had no trucks and cables in those days, and they went to the top of that mountain to build a temple larger than any you can find on the plains.[30]

If the temple builders and the communities of loyal, self-giving devotees of former years have heirs in present-day Japan, perhaps they are to be found among the New Religions. Each of these sects, as it becomes sufficiently large and stable, begins to develop a headquarters. The most successful ones are engaged in astoundingly large and costly enterprises, supported almost exclusively by contributions of money and labor from their vast memberships. The context may not be precisely the same as in the old days, yet here again is the "power of religion," and here also is the capability to undertake a "grandiose scheme."

Perhaps the best known of these enterprises is their prototype, the Tenri-kyo headquarters near Nara—although in grandeur it is being superseded by the projects of some of the more recently popular movements, which we shall discuss in later chapters. For many years now, the reputation of the Tenri-kyo installation has been widespread, with the result that it regularly attracts large numbers of visitors, who generally are somewhat awestruck by the extent and quality of what is being wrought there. These ever-expanding facilities seem even more impressive when one realizes that the sect depends almost exclusively upon *hinokishin*, the "consecrated labor" of the devotees, for construction and maintenance. Their material accomplishments are remarkable, and it is obvious that the many busy volunteers whom one sees here are giving their time and labor with a genuine sense of joy and fulfillment.

This is no less impressively characteristic of what takes place at the headquarters of still other sects. One of my indelible memories of several visits to the headquarters of PL Kyodan is the sight of labor crews dogtrotting in formation to the site of their next task and of young people working to a cadence marked

by the bleats of a leader's whistle as they transported dirt by
means of shoulder poles and baskets. During the construction of
the Dōjō, Training Hall of Tensho Kotai Jingu-kyo, I watched
crews of people—who had come there at their own expense—
shoveling gravel for concrete, cleaning and sorting used concrete
forms, and smoothing and polishing wood for the interior decora-
tion. With their aid, what eventually arose in the remote paddy
fields of Tabuse is architecturally one of the most imaginative
religious structures in Japan.

Obviously, however, much more than voluntary labor is required for these often gigantesque undertakings. Money—lots of
it—is also needed. How are the New Religions financed? Because
their resources in some instances are so enormous, these movements sometimes facetiously are dubbed "religious *zaibatsu*,"[31]
recalling the immense financial trusts (*zaibatsu*) that dominated
Japanese economic life in the World War II period. For the most
part, financial support is provided by contributions from individuals and business firms and by profits from literature sales. But
is this support really voluntary? There are frequent allegations
that the New Religions are extortionate; but except for certain
flagrant examples, this is a very difficult matter to judge—especially for an outsider. From the outside, one cannot know in
detail either how or to what extent subtly defined relationships
and status concerns create a sense of obligation, or even a situation of covert pressure, within such a group. In view of the importance of such factors in Japanese society generally,[32] we
probably may assume that some element of compulsion often
operates within the tight web of relationships existing in these
sects; nevertheless, the more important fact still may be that
most of the devotees feel that they are getting or eventually will
get their money's worth.

In such devotion to the creation of a kind of heaven on earth,
there is, of course, a strong element of religious escapism.[33]
Here, in effect, is the holy city, new Jerusalem, not let down by
God out of heaven, but built up by men from the earth—a place
from which, hopefully, "the former things have passed away."[34]
Nevertheless, it would seem to be a mistake to suppose that the
motivations underlying these efforts are entirely pathological,

unless we also admit that the "edifice complex" now so prominent throughout the modern world is similarly a sign of aberrance. Also, for the devotees of the New Religions, construction projects are dramatic and tangible enterprises that challenge and inspire them. They provide diversion and an element of adventure in otherwise routine lives. When a project is completed, it stands before each person who contributed to its construction as a symbol of his own achievement and ownership. Grandeur becomes accessible, at least occasionally, to persons who are debarred from it in almost every other avenue of their existence.

Mass Activities

It is consistent both with general Japanese custom and with the other characteristics of the New Religions that many of the activities of these sects are undertaken en masse. Among the Japanese generally, there is a rather high degree of regimentation in many of their involvements—in schools, in business, and even in avocational pursuits. In part, as all detractors will point out, this is due to the survival of traditional patterns, but not only so; it also reflects the recognition that in a small, overpopulated land such as Japan, doing things together in an organized way often is the simplest and most economical way to do them. Among the New Religions, this general tendency is further enhanced by the adherents' strong sense of corporate identity and the authoritarian bent of these organizations.

Some of the most important mass activities among the New Religions are regular, ongoing enterprises such as pilgrimages and training programs. On just a normal day, for example, more than ten thousand devotees of Rissho Kosei-kai will convene for worship at the headquarters in Tokyo and then divide into small groups for discussion. Each day special trains carry many thousands of Soka Gakkai pilgrims to the Taisekiji, their great temple at the foot of Mount Fuji. At almost any given time at the headquarters of PL Kyodan, a large group of people will be in residence for the four-day training period that all members are expected to undergo.

Each sect also has a calendar of festive and memorial occasions that call for mass observances. Some of these may be times traditionally important in Japanese society, such as Buddha's birthday on April 8 and the fall and spring equinoxes. Others commemorate events that are significant only to a particular religion—for example, anniversaries of the founding of the sect and of the birth and death of the founder. Characteristically, each such occasion is celebrated by larger than usual local gatherings and by an especially large assemblage at the headquarters.

Some of the most impressive mass gatherings are special celebrations and rallies. The completion of a great new building is always an occasion for a grand spectacle. I was fortunate, in the spring of 1964, to be able to attend three such celebrations, sponsored respectively by Soka Gakkai, Rissho-Kosei-kai, and Tensho Kotai Jingu-kyo.[35] These gatherings, quite typically, included many invited guests, especially government officials, and received extensive coverage in news media.

Some of the largest groups also sponsor special rallies, often held in a large rented auditorium or stadium, in order to advocate a particular cause or to stimulate the enthusiasm of a certain segment of the membership, such as the women's division or the youth division. As we shall point out in more detail subsequently, Soka Gakkai in particular uses the device of the great mass rally most effectively, especially with its younger members. Their gatherings sometimes involve as many as one hundred thousand persons.

Closely related to these activities is the use of mass-communications media. In this regard, the Japanese are one of the most accessible populations in the world. They have one of the world's highest rates of literacy, they are second only to the United States in the total number of television sets in use,[36] and they have radios almost everywhere. Many of the New Religions make effective use of these media, especially publishing.

Syncretism, Mystery, and Novelty

In matters of religion, most Asians seem to subscribe in some degree to the principles of metaphysical monism and epistemological relativism. That is, they suppose that ultimately all things are one and that "saving knowledge" of essential truth, though always partial, can be acquired by many different means. The popular Japanese commitment to these principles is well expressed in this often-quoted verse:

Obscured by mists and shadows, many are the paths winding up the mountainside, but when the summit is attained, the pure beams of the full moon pour their radiance upon every wanderer alike.

The diversity originally comprehended in this perspective was provided mainly by the so-called three teachings (*sankyō*) imported from China: Confucianism, Taoism, and Buddhism. Along with these came the slogan "the unity of the three teachings" (Japanized as *sankyō ki-itsu*), which helped to prepare the way for their acceptance en bloc. Fairly successful efforts also were made thereafter to link Buddhism and the native Shinto through the creation of *Ryōbu Shintō* (Dual-aspect Shinto),[37] which resulted eventually in the undifferentiated folk faith called *shinbutsu* or *kami-hotoke* ("*kami*-Buddha") faith.

Though it certainly would ignore many fractious moments in the history of Japan to say that the Japanese have not taken religious differences seriously, it is nevertheless true that the clear preference of the masses has been an amalgamation of the various religions. Perhaps no one has spoken more clearly for this popular perspective than the so-called peasant sage, Ninomiya Sontoku (1787–1856), who once described his teaching as a "pill containing the essence of Shinto, Confucianism and Buddhism." When asked to define the proportions of the ingredients in his prescription, he replied: "One spoon of Shinto, and a half-spoon each of Confucianism and Buddhism."

Then someone drew a circle, one half of which was marked Shinto and two quarter-segments labeled Confucianism and Buddhism respectively. "Is it like this?" he asked. The old man smiled. "You won't find medicine like that anywhere. In a real pill all the ingredients are thoroughly blended so as to be indistinguishable."[38]

In view of the prevailing syncretic outlook of the Japanese, it is an anomaly, which we shall not attempt to explain here, that the proliferation of sects is one of the hallmarks of Japanese religion. This may be seen in the history of Buddhism in Japan, which is from one point of view the story of a splintering-off process. In the freedom of present-day Japan, the penchant for sectarianism is rampant in the development of the New Religions. It is another of the enigmas of this land that it maintains an atmosphere in which the lamb of tolerance and the lion of sectarianism may lie down quietly together.

Among the New Religions, certain sects prefer to identify themselves more or less specifically as Buddhistic or Shintoistic, but it is characteristic of these movements as a whole that they are to some extent syncretistic, both in the traditional sense that they stem from the popular *shinbutsu* faith and in their practice of adapting to their own views and purposes many elements from other sources. In some cases, a syncretistic orientation is almost wholly unconscious; in others, it is more systematically structured.

A clear example of the latter type is *Gedatsukai*, a movement that numbers perhaps forty thousand to fifty thousand adherents. It is said to be composed of "one way and three religions" (*ichidō sanshū*). The "one way" is Shinto; the "three religions" are the Chinese triad of Buddhism, Confucianism, and Taoism. In part, the adherents dramatize their manifold commitment in an annual three-day pilgrimage, which begins at Ise Shrine, the abode of the sun-goddess, Amaterasu; then continues to Kashiwara Shrine, dedicated to the legendary first Emperor, Jimmu; and finally culminates in Kyoto at the Buddhist temple Sennyuji, where thirty emperors and the founder of Gedatsukai are buried.

In Seicho no Ie, the syncretistic pattern is clear, although the founder, Taniguchi Masaharu, prefers not to describe his work in these terms. Rather, he speaks of "a movement reducing all teachings to one" (*bankyō ki-itsu no undō*), by which he means that he teaches the one truth that is common to all religions and philosophies. It is not for nothing, however, that outsiders jestingly refer to Seicho no Ie as the "department store of religions" (*skūkyō no depāto*), for it includes elements drawn from many of the world's religions, including Christianity quite conspicuously.

No matter the specific character of their syncretism, most of the New Religions, though they are rivals, are quite tolerant of one another and of other religions as well. There are, to be sure, some notable exceptions, such as Soka Gakkai and Tensho Kotai Jingu-kyo. The former, in particular, faithful to its legacy from the outspoken Buddhist prophet Nichiren (1222–1282), is notoriously intolerant of all other religions, which it brands unequivocally as "false religions." Such aggressiveness naturally arouses various forms of counteraction, but otherwise the New Religions are able to coexist fairly amicably and even, in some ways, to present a united front. This is most conspicuous in the cooperative efforts of more than a hundred sects that have banded together in the Union of New Religious Organizations (Shinshūren), but a number of other examples also could be adduced.

Even though the New Religions have many characteristics in common and generally are suited to coexistence in a laissez-faire environment, it would be a serious mistake to gloss over the apparently incidental differences among these sects or to suppose that their spokesmen do not consider them important. The New Religions *are* movements that constitute a movement, they *are* phenomena that must be considered as a phenomenon; nevertheless, it must also be seen that perhaps yet another general characteristic of these sects is the intention of each one to achieve uniqueness.

Each sect originated in a conviction that something distinctive and momentous had happened, and each one has developed through an endeavor to demonstrate the nature and significance of that occurrence. Oftentimes the result is quite superficial, being little more than the achievement of novelty for novelty's sake. Preoccupation with quaintness in nonessential matters is a common and engaging trait of the religions of Japan; but more often than not, it hinders real involvement in religious issues. It is easier and more pleasant to settle for something that is simply clever or ingenious, and much of the diversity achieved by the New Religions is apparent only in such options as architectural forms, dances, costumes, symbols, slogans, or gestures.

Nevertheless, there is another and deeper dimension to this quest for uniqueness. In each case, within an otherwise simple, perhaps even fatuous, doctrinal system and within a mishmash of rites and incantations, there is a mystery that somehow sparks it all. Therefore, when we inquire into the nature of the New Religions as a socioreligious movement, we must also ask, "What is the essential character of each sect?" At the level of basic attitudes and teleologies, whether these are explicit or implicit, conscious or unconscious, some of these sects, which are so much alike otherwise, begin to emerge as distinctive entities. Each one may be seen to be, in its own way, the source of a powerful influence that for better or for worse may affect the character of Japanese society and culture quite profoundly.

Though obviously it is impossible here to examine all the New Religions separately, each of the five chapters that follow is a summary description and analysis of a single religious movement. In each instance, an effort is made both to present the sect as an example of what is transpiring within a much larger socioreligious movement and to discern the distinctive thrust of the particular enterprise.

Konkō-kyō: A Functional Monotheism

OKAYAMA PREFECTURE is situated in southwestern Honshu, the main island of Japan. A favored area scenically, it looks out upon the portion of the island-dotted Seto Inland Sea that has been designated a national park. The climate here is mild, and local residents claim that the air is the clearest in Japan. The cities of Okayama are not metropolitan hubs, but neither are they satellites. Rather, they are characterized by the relatively detached involvement of places that lie "on the way" to major urban centers. Communication routes linking Kyushu, western Honshu, and Shikoku with Kobe, Osaka, and Kyoto and, beyond them, with Nagoya and Tokyo run through Okayama. Thus, while the principal communities of the prefecture regularly are in touch with the main centers of the nation, they also are sufficiently remote to escape being dominated by any of them. Altogether it seems fully appropriate that in this prefecture, thatched roofs are more in evidence than in most other parts of Japan, the manufacture of straw products is still an important industry, and a fairly lively folk-art tradition is still maintained. It seems ecologically right also that *Konkō-kyō*, a gentle, noncompulsive religion, developed here.

Occupying land that formerly was the homestead of the religion's founder, the headquarters of Konko-kyo are located just a few miles from the coast of the Inland Sea in a small town, which, in acknowledgment of the rise of this movement as its most significant development, has been renamed Konko-cho. Although the outposts and activities through which Konko-kyo may be approached are quite numerous and widespread, throughout Japan and even abroad, the most appropriate introduction to this religion is to begin at the headquarters.

Ideally, perhaps, one should begin by attending an early-morning service if one wishes immediately to savor the essential atmosphere of Konko-kyo. For this purpose, it is most convenient for the visitor to spend the preceding night at an inn in the town, for he will want to reach the headquarters precinct by about 3:45 A.M. Once there, he finds a broad, dimly lighted courtyard, at one end of which a number of people are standing quietly, facing in the direction of a portal at the far end of the area. If only because of the numinous quality of the predawn, perhaps every person there feels, in some degree, the mysteriousness of the moment. In addition, one may sense on the part of the gathered devotees a restrained anticipation of the forthcoming rites. It is not expectation of imminent ecstasy or miracle. Rather, it is anticipation of the foreknown—of that which, like the dawning of the day, is predictable yet also inexplicable and indispensable. As the day surely will dawn and renew the world, so one is coming who represents both in person and in office the continuing renewal of the essential relationship between man and the divine.

At about 3:55, a lantern bearer appears. A few paces behind him comes the awaited personage, the *Kyōshu* (spiritual head or patriarch), followed in turn by two bearers of votive offerings and, finally, his special assistant. With dignity but without pretension, this five-man procession crosses the courtyard, via a paved walkway, to the worship hall, near which the people are waiting. Unseen attendants within the building open the doors to admit the patriarch and his entourage and then close them again immediately after their entrance. The worshipers, all of whom have been waiting outside, now enter the hall by another door.

The worship hall is a rectangular room (approximately thirty feet wide by fifty-four feet long) with traditional *tatami* (straw mat) flooring. At one end of the hall are two altars. The larger one, centered against the end wall, is dedicated to the deity, Tenchi Kane no Kami; the other, positioned to the worshipers' left of the central altar, is dedicated to the spirits of the founder and the succeeding two patriarchs and of the ancestors of all the believers. This "chancel" area is separated from the rest of the hall by a low portable railing.

As the worshipers enter the hall, the altars are concealed from their view by portable screens; but as soon as all have seated themselves on the *tatami*, the screens are pushed back to reveal the *Kyōshu*, bowed low before the central altar. The worshipers clap their hands, bend forward until their foreheads rest on their hands on the floor, and then begin to pray in silence. This period of silent prayer, which lasts about twenty-five minutes, is followed by a second period of approximately five minutes, during which the *Kyōshu* bows before the altar of his predecessors and at the conclusion of which he rises and goes to the *kekkai*, his special seat at a low desk just within the chancel and to the right of the congregation. At this juncture, the assistant to the *Kyōshu*, taking a position in front of the people and facing the altars, leads the worshipers in chanting ritual prayers (*Norito*), a recitation that requires approximately twenty minutes.

This regimen of prayer ends at about 4:50 A.M. At its conclusion, many of the worshipers leave the hall and go to the nearby tomb of the founder; others go immediately to the quarter of the room near the *Kyōshu* to await their turn for *toritsugi*, the quintessential event or moment in Konko-kyo.

The Toritsugi *Way*

The dictionary meaning of the term *toritsugi* is "intermediation." In popular speech, various forms of this word are used in reference to many quite commonplace interpersonal relationships. As employed within Konko-kyo, however, this term has acquired a reserved and somewhat mystical connotation. Though usually rendered as "mediation" or, perhaps preferably, "intercession" in

the translation of Konko-kyo documents, the word has in fact
become essentially untranslatable. It embodies the basic theological tenets of this religion. It signifies the ineffable mystery
underlying this faith. Whoever understands *toritsugi* also understands Konko-kyo, for Konko-kyo preeminently is the "*toritsugi*
way."

Each day, from before dawn until about 5 P.M., the *Kyōshu* is
accessible to all who come to him for *toritsugi*. The petitioners
sit within the worship hall to await their turns and then approach
the *Kyōshu* without having to be marshaled by a secretary or any
other aide. Each one bows low as he comes before the *Kyōshu*
and then describes the problem from which he seeks deliverance,
whereupon the *Kyōshu* makes a note of the name, age, and
problem of the individual and propounds a solution for his
difficulty.[1]

So far as an eyewitness can tell, this is all that transpires in
toritsugi; but from the standpoint of the Konko-kyo faith, such a
description is quite superficial and is partly misleading as well.
This meeting, we are assured, is not to be construed as a man-
to-man counseling relationship. Rather, it is the coming of a man
to Kami[2] and of Kami to a man—a two-way relationship that is
fulfilling to both. For his part, the petitioner with a problem
approaches *toritsugi* openly, already mentally prepared to accept
without question the guidance that will be proffered. The
Kyōshu, who is wholly committed to conveying his best understanding of Kami's will to the seeker, hears the problem and, so
far as possible, endeavors to share the burden. In this attitude,
he joins the petitioner in prayer, seeking a solution to the problem; and thus the *Kyōshu* and the seeker are united in one way
of the two-way process. Knowing beforehand that Kami desires
to help this person, the *Kyōshu* attempts, to the fullest extent
possible, also to identify himself with Kami and thereby to let
himself be used in effect as a bridge by which man and Kami
are enabled to meet. Thus, man is saved and Kami is served.

Actually, no effort is made within Konko-kyo to state precisely
what happens in *toritsugi*. It is, after all, a sacramental rite that
not only provides an occasion for Kami and man to meet but
also betokens the surpassing richness and complexity of the basic

divine-human relationship upon which *toritsugi* depends. Even though this relationship is acknowledged to be beyond the limits of human description, its nature, nevertheless, can be intimated. For this purpose, two special formulas are employed: *Aiyo kakeyo* and *Ujiko atteno Kami, Kami atteno ujiko.*

The first of these (*Aiyo kakeyo*) seems to have no intrinsic meaning. Apparently it is simply a rhythmic chant formerly used by laborers to coordinate their efforts. As employed in Konko-kyo, however, the term signifies a principle and a relationship of *mutuality* that tends toward the fulfillment of all parties involved. The second formula (*Ujiko atteno Kami, Kami atteno ujiko*) also utilizes words for which there are no direct equivalents in English; however, it is possible in this case to render the sense of the statement: "Solely because of the devotee, Kami is manifest; solely because of Kami, man has being." The key word here (and perhaps also currently the key word in Konko-kyo theology) is *atteno*, a grammatically obscure form of the verb "to be" (*aru*). This term in the present instance denotes a concept of *mutually contingent being* that is presumed to underlie the divine-human relationship. Without the believer, Kami cannot manifest himself; without Kami, the believer cannot find his existence. An apt analogy is said to be the relationship between parents and their child: because the child exists, there are parents; because of the parents, the child exists. Without the one, the other does not exist, and vice versa.

The nature of this relationship of interdependence between Kami and man was revealed originally to the founder, who was assured that if he would begin *toritsugi*, the condition would be created by which "Kami would be assisted and his children also would be saved" (*Kami mo tasukari ujiko mo tachi yuku*). By accepting this commission, he proved the soundness of the prediction. He devoted the remainder of his life to *toritsugi*, and he has been succeeded by his son, grandson, and great-grandson in this commitment. While *toritsugi* preeminently is the function of the founder and his successors, it is also practiced in all Konko-kyo churches, where, for up to twenty hours a day, ministers are available for this essential rite. Let us repeat: Konko-kyo is the "*toritsugi* way," a faith, religion, and total way of life based upon *atteno*, existence conceived as involving and requiring the mutually supportive quests of Kami for man and man for Kami.

The Founder and the Founding

In order to trace the origin and implementation of these distinctive features of Konko-kyo, we must go back to the experience and teaching of its founder, Kawate Bunjiro (1814–1883), a peasant whose life spanned one of the most tortuous yet significant periods in the history of Japan. The early nineteenth century was an especially inauspicious time to be born a peasant, for as feudalism deteriorated, the life of the peasants steadily became less predictable and more disadvantaged. In the middle of that century, the isolation of Japan, which had been maintained effectively for two and a half centuries, suddenly was ended, and the nation was convulsed by the ambivalence of its responses to the prospect of living in close association with the outside world. Shortly thereafter, imperial rule was restored, and the latter part of the century was devoted to the rapid modernization of the nation. All these developments form the backdrop for considering the life of Konko-kyo's founder, and problems resulting from them were often reflected in the specific hardships (*nangi*) that he came to interpret as manifestations of Kami that incline man to turn Kami-ward.

Except for the fact that even in childhood the founder was conspicuously pious, there was little in the first forty years of his life to presage his eventual career. The family into which he was born possessed in full measure the typical peasant virtues of industry and frugality, but they had little else. When their son was twelve years of age, they permitted him to be adopted by the more prosperous, but childless, Kawate family in the neighboring village of Otani, the present-day Konko-cho.

Probably all the people among whom the young Bunjiro was reared took for granted the proximity of numberless *kami* and regularly based their decisions on the results of divination by astrology or other means. Yet so inordinately concerned with religious matters was he that even among these universally religious people, he was nicknamed Shinjin-bun, the Pious One. He was constantly alert to the necessity of propitiating various *kami*. He possessed an ascetic's readiness to assume a sacred vow or impose a strict regimen upon himself. While he was still a young man, he made the especially meritorious pilgrimages to the Grand Shrines of Ise and to eighty-eight designated Buddhist temples. In retrospect, it appears that had it not been for two other balancing traits—common sense and a sensitivity to the needs of others—Kawate's penchant for religion might have led to a complete personal breakdown (as it very nearly did anyway) instead of to the development of a theopathy.

With the death of his adoptive father in 1836, Kawate became the head of the household, and shortly thereafter he married. During the next two decades, in spite of extraordinary diligence in religious activities, he experienced a great deal of hardship and sorrow. Three of his children died; the community was ravaged by a smallpox plague; he lost all his cattle; and, as the climax, in 1855 he was afflicted by a severe throat ailment from which it appeared he would not recover. This illness, however, proved instead to be the occasion for integrating and redirecting his life.

Kawate was stricken in his forty-second year, which, according to Japanese folk tradition, is in the life of every man a critical year (*yakudoshi*) and likely will be an unlucky time unless various precautions are taken. With his usual punctiliousness, Kawate had endeavored to observe all the rites and taboos that were prescribed as safeguards in that critical period. Yet at some point, he was sure, he must have failed, for the severity of his illness clearly suggested that he had incurred the anger of one or more *kami*. He suspected that it was Konjin, a malevolent and greatly feared deity,[3] whom he had offended, and presumably it was this deity who finally did speak to clarify the nature of the offense and to bestow healing upon the offender.

To be the medium of this revelation, the *kami* chose a brother-in-law of the suffering man. Speaking through him, in an unnatural voice signifying *kami* possession, the deity accused Kawate of having committed an offense when, some time previously, he had remodeled his house. Threatened with imminent

death, Kawate left his bed and began to pray fervently. Pleading
that he had sought earnestly to fulfill all the requirements but
acknowledging that, due to his human limitations, he could not
be perfect, he begged forgiveness for his shortcomings. Apparently he was adjudged to have been wholly sincere, though technically remiss; therefore, he was forgiven, and his health gradually
was restored.

From this time, Kawate's entire life began to change. His com-
pulsive, almost frenetic concern with being right with the *kami*
gradually gave way to a sense of having been found by deity.
Whereas previously fear and dread had characterized his devotion to the *kami*, he began to experience for the first time a *kami*
consciousness in which he received repeated assurances of divine
favor. He could not be certain concerning the specific identity
of the *kami* who seemed to be preempting his whole being, but
he knew him to be of a benevolent nature. Gradually, during a
period of several years, he relented to the *kami*, until at length,
late in the year 1858, he experienced fully the visitation of divine
favor. Very quickly thereafter, people from the surrounding area
began to come to him in great numbers to seek his mediation of
the divine will for their lives. In the following year, 1859, on
October 21, Kawate received an oracle commissioning him to
undertake full time the service of the deity who addressed him.
His acceptance of this charge is regarded as the founding of
Konko-kyo. On November 15, having set aside a room in his own
home for this purpose, he began the practice of *toritsugi*, which
was to be his almost daily occupation until his death twenty-four
years later.

As in the case of all profound religious experience, the experience of the founder of Konko-kyo is enigmatic and paradoxical.
It is significant that for a long while, Kawate and those about
him were uncertain concerning the identity of the *kami* who was
manifesting himself. Initially it was assumed that it was Konjin,
since he was regarded as the most irascible of the *kami*; but this
identity was never clearly established, so that for several years
the deity was invoked by various names, some of which seemingly were devised experimentally. Such impreciseness, of course,
was due in part to the innate indeterminateness of the Japanese

kami "theology"; yet, in this instance, something more crucial seems also to have been involved. It was as if the founder had received a revelation of deity which did not fit any of the known *kami* and which, moreover, seemed also to transcend the whole *kami* concept. Eventually this deity was given the name Tenchi Kane no Kami,[4] an appellation by which no deity previously had been known. Yet, significantly, the deity himself was not seen as a new deity; rather, he came as the *one* Kami uniting all the myriads of *kami*.

Momentarily leaving aside long-range theological implications, we can see in Kawate's experience the integration of a life that had been fragmented by pathological involvement in a multitude of religious endeavors. Motivated largely by fear, he had learned well the folklore of his community and was regularly attentive to the omens revealed by divination. Provided with such knowledge, he had gone from this *kami* to that *kami*, from this shrine to that shrine, seeking always to fulfill every obligation and to take every precaution lest he become the victim of the *kami*'s displeasure. But, as in the case of Martin Luther and of so many others in the history of religion, when his whole frantic effort had collapsed about him, the miasma of superstitious and magical concerns began to clear. A new dimension of faith was discovered, a new person emerged.

Perhaps it is recognition of this development that prompts present leaders of Konko-kyo to insist that the experience of their founder was not shamanistic; that is, he was not "possessed" or "indwelt" by deity. Technically, one might challenge the accuracy of this assessment, for certainly the context of the initial divine visitation, at least in terms of the background and expectations of Kawate and his household, was shamanistic. Even so, it must be acknowledged that while the initial experience seems to fit that pattern, there apparently was present within it a distinguishing quality that led to a new breakthrough. The resulting perspective actually included elements of protest against and reform of the old orientation. The ultimate effect, as seen from within Konko-kyo, seems to have been a kind of victory for both Kami and man: *Ujiko atteno Kami, Kami atteno ujiko.* Because of man (a particular man), Kami was indeed made manifest. Deity tran-

scended the ignominy of demonic associations and was elevated
to the position of dignity that essential benevolence merits. On
the other hand, man (a particular man) found his existence.
Delivered from fear and desperation, man achieved wholeness
through his trust and faith in a benevolent deity to whom he felt
himself related as a child to his parent.

In the understanding of the founder, his experience did not
signalize a radical innovation: "Tenchi Kane no Kami is a Kami
who exists from of old; he is not a Kami created in the middle
of man's history."[5] Yet the experience did have an archetypal
character: "Konko Daijin is the first to have received the favor
of Kami. All people can receive the divine favor as Konko Daijin
has."[6] Furthermore, as a result of this experience, it had become
necessary to repudiate certain aspects of the old life: "By consulting the directions and days which are to result in good fortune, they dishonor Kami."[7]

The ministry of intercession undertaken by Kawate Bunjiro
was immediately attractive to the rural people of Okayama Prefecture. The reasons are not difficult to ascertain. In the first
place, the man himself seemed to merit the confidence of others.
He was a man of the soil and had experienced the hardships
common to peasant life. His personal life was characterized by
severe austerity and indubitable sincerity, probably the two principal virtues in the rural system of values. Perhaps most important
of all, he was an insightful man, genuinely capable of understanding human problems and of giving helpful advice concerning them. Most of the people who came to him had no difficulty
in believing that they were in the presence of an *ikigami*, a "living
kami." In 1868, the year of the Meiji Restoration, Kawate claimed
to have received Kami's permission to call himself honorifically
Ikigami Konko Daijin (literally, "Living *kami*, Metal Luster,
Great *kami*").[8] Soon thereafter he applied to the town office to
change his name. The office refused to accept the full appellation
but did agree to register him officially as Konko Daijin, his surname thus becoming Konko and his given name Daijin.[9]

In addition to the personal charisma of the founder, there
must have been something attractive also in the quality of the
teaching and of the community of faith that was forming in

response to it. The ministry of Konko Daijin basically was continuous with the traditional folk faith, yet it seemed also to possess a freshness and a specific relevance that inspired new hope. At a time when social, economic, and political structures were changing, the peasant class needed the stability that only familiar traditional resources could give; simultaneously, they needed to be given a sign that the old resources really were still availing. Not a radical innovation but an effective renewal was their need. It was this that Konko Daijin seemed to give.

However, perhaps more than either the founder or his followers were aware, something importantly new also was being developed: a concept of a dynamic faith, relevant and effective amid changing conditions, instead of the static faith of rigid traditionalism. The novelty of this factor was recognized in at least two quarters at a fairly early date. On the one hand, certain reactionary groups and individuals, including some religious functionaries and governmental officials, viewed the new movement with apprehension and sought various means by which to harass it. On the other hand, there were those in still another segment of society, the rising class of businessmen of the early Meiji era, who thought they saw in Konko-kyo something that was relevant to the new, ill-defined socioeconomic role that they were essaying. It happened, therefore, that people began to come out from Osaka by ship and, landing at Okayama or Tamashima, to seek guidance through *toritsugi* at Konko-cho. Thus, the founder, himself a farmer whose followers theretofore nearly all had also been farmers, had to meet and give appropriate guidance to people of a different environment and social class. The fact that he succeeded in gaining followers from among these persons served as an earnest that the faith was broadly relevant, and the extension of influence into the urban environment had a very significant, though not always salutary, influence upon the development of Konko-kyo. That the original perspectives of Konko Daijin frequently were distorted in this transmission is clearly indicated by the fact that fairly soon, among the people engaged in industry and commerce in the Kansai area, the deity of Konko-kyo was being referred to as "the god of moneymaking" (*kane-mōke no kamisama*).[10]

Relation to Shinto

Discussion of the distinctiveness of Konko-kyo necessitates raising the question of the relation of this movement to Shinto. For many years (1900–1946), Konko-kyo was registered with the government as one of the thirteen officially recognized sects of *Kyōha Shintō* or *Shūha Shintō* (Sectarian Shinto or Religious Shinto), and even now it is voluntarily a member of the Sectarian Shinto Alliance (Kyōha Shintō Rengōkai). Furthermore, in many externals, it manifests a real affinity to Shinto. Its ceremonies, the garb of the officiants, the altar furnishings, and the food offerings to the deity are in the traditional Shinto pattern. Also, the massive ferroconcrete Festival Hall in the headquarters precinct, though in many ways modern in design, has a distinctively Shintoistic cast, accented by the typical projections (*chigi* and *katsuogi*) decorating the roof ridge. Still, without additional commentary, these data can be quite misleading if one wishes to understand more thoroughly the essential character and function of Konko-kyo.

The first time that I asked one of its priests concerning the appropriateness of classifying Konko-kyo as a Shinto sect, he replied that if a religion originating in Japan must be classed as Shinto, then Konko-kyo is Shintoist; however, the Kami worshiped in this religion is not a *kami* of old Shinto.[11] It has since become apparent that this is a perceptive observation, both in its avoidance of a categorical response and in its inclusion of a very important distinction. It cannot be said unequivocally either that Konko-kyo is a kind of Shinto or that it is not. At the same time, no matter this ambiguity, it is important to see that Konko-kyo has a distinctive quality of its own. The elucidation of both dimensions of this matter requires additional historical review.

It is probably safe to assume that Kawate himself cared little for religious labels. His original orientation was in the Japanese folk faith, which even yet is most conspicuously characterized by the blending of Shinto and Buddhism, an undifferentiated syncretism aptly described as *shinbutsu* ("*kami*-Buddha") faith. The fact that in 1867 he applied for and was granted status as a Shinto priest might seem to belie the assumption that he was indifferent to distinctions; actually, it may serve to confirm it. Apparently this action was taken for wholly expedient reasons. Kawate saw in the changing political order a threat to the freedom of his ministry. By regularizing his status, he sought to avoid unnecessary interference from the emerging pro-Shinto imperial government; however, he seems never to have shared the government's ulterior purposes in favoring Shinto. It is extremely doubtful that the founder of Konko-kyo was at all jealous concerning the identification of his movement with Shinto.

Nevertheless, the movement eventually was so identified, though largely by fiat; but, here again, the extenuating circumstances must be understood in order to assess the importance of this development. The effort of the Meiji government to control the various religions was thwarted in part by the existence of a number of popular religious groups, technically called *kō*. Each *kō* was an organization "established by laymen . . . for the express purpose of worshiping some god in the Shinto pantheon or some awesome force in nature."[12] In 1882, the government created the category Sectarian Shinto (*Kyōha Shintō*) and began the registration of what eventually amounted to thirteen recognized Shinto sects, all but one of which, so it is said, developed out of the *kō*.[13] In retrospect, it seems that this action was rather an unimaginative and imperceptive contrivance on the part of the government at a time when they were committed to the ideal of *saisei itchi* (the unity of worship and government) but were obliged by circumstances to grant at least a modicum of religious freedom. Among these thirteen sects there was considerable diversity, but they had at least one thing in common: proselytism leading to individual personal commitment. This was the factor that constituted a threat to governmental purpose and policy, and it could be tolerated only if it could be confined within limits where surveillance was possible. The effort to achieve this condition resulted in the creation of a clumsy classification that has since rendered even more difficult the naturally complex task of analyzing the religious life of the Japanese people.

In 1900, Konko-kyo became the eleventh organization to be registered as a sect of Shinto.[14] Presumably, it might have qualified for this distinction because of its devotion to the god Konjin; however, as we have noted, there was initially so much uncer-

tainty concerning the identity of the deity who claimed Kawate
Bunjiro for his mediator that finally he was called Tenchi Kane
no Kami, a name that did not appear in the literature of Shinto.
Therefore, in order to acquire legitimacy, Konko-kyo had to
adopt some recognized Shinto *kami*. To make this accommodation, the sect employed a device similar to the Indian avatar
concept, which long before had been invoked to categorize the
native Shinto *kami* as manifestations of Buddhist deities. They
accepted three deities (the *kami* of the sun, the moon, and the
earth, respectively) and declared these to be *manifestations* of
Tenchi Kane no Kami. Thus, Konko-kyo became acceptable as a
sect of Shinto, and so it remained until 1946, when, free at last
to be what it wished to be, it dropped the extraneous deities and
became an independent religion.

What, then, is the relation of Konko-kyo to Shinto? If the term
Shintō is a synonym for "indigenous Japanese religions" (and in
some ways it certainly is), then Konko-kyo may appropriately be
called a Shinto sect. So to label it is by no means a serious viola-
tion of the integrity of Konko-kyo; at the same time, neither is it
an important contribution to a clear definition of the essential
character of this movement. The clue to that definition seems to
lie in the fact that the Kami of Konko-kyo is not one of the
yao-yorozu no kami (myriads of *kami*) of traditional Shinto.
Rather, he is the "Parent-God of the Universe." From the time
of the founder to the end of World War II, there was developing
within Konko-kyo a sufficiently broad and profound concept of
deity to provide a basis for both an intensive personal ministry
and a diversified program of social outreach. In the freedom of
the postwar period, this concept continually is being refined; and
many of the people of Konko-kyo, sustained by their theocentric
commitment, are attempting to stem the rapid advance of secularization by the claims of religious faith.

Organization and Program

October 21, 1859, the date on which Kawate Bunjiro received
his oracle, is considered within Konko-kyo as the founding date
of the religion. However, it was not until 1885, two years after

the death of the founder, that steps were taken to effect an actual organization. From the beginning of the movement, the central activity had been *toritsugi*, the mediation or intercession made possible through Kawate. It was therefore natural that the emergent organization should be keyed to this ministry and should make a clear provision for the succession of leadership in the office of *Kyōshu*.

Eventually, four rules were adopted and written into the constitution (*Konkō-kyō Kyōki*) to govern the selection of the *Kyōshu*. (1) The candidate must be a descendant (either male or female) of the founder. (2) He must already be an ordained minister in Konko-kyo. (3) He must be elected by the nationwide group of the heads of Konko-kyo churches. (4) His election finally is contingent upon his willingness to accept the office. Thus far, the line of succession has flowed invariably from father to first son, but it is not mandatory that the principle of primogeniture be followed.

The founder himself held the office of *Kyōshu* for twenty-four years. His son, who succeeded him, served for ten years. The third *Kyōshu*, grandson of the founder, took office at the age of fourteen and continued in that role for seventy years until his death on April 13, 1963. His remarkably long tenure spanned an epoch of wrenching change in Japanese society—a period that included the Sino-Japanese War (1894–1895), the Russo-Japanese War (1904–1905), the two world wars, and the immediate post-surrender agonies following World War II. It is impressive to discover that, having dealt with the manifold problems of people during so long and turbulent a period, he left as his legacy the recognition of change as a fact of modern life and a determination to find and demonstrate the continuing relevance of faith within that circumstance.

The present *Kyōshu*, great-grandson of the founder and the fourth person to hold this position, took office on July 9, 1963, at the age of fifty-three. Unlike any of his predecessors, in the process of achieving maturity he had a broad range of contacts away from the rather isolated setting within which, probably for the remainder of his life, he will receive those who come to him for *toritsugi*.

In the town of Konko are quartered six agencies that are

integral to the organization of Konko-kyo: (1) the headquarters for all the religious and general affairs of the sect, (2) an institute for the training of ministers, (3) an institute for doctrinal study and research, (4) an institute for general education, including a kindergarten, middle school (junior high), and high school, (5) a library, and (6) an agency for propagation through literature. All these agencies are under the authority of the *Kyōshu*, although he is most directly concerned with the religious affairs. Administratively, the second-ranking official, called the *Kyōkan*, assumes the major responsibility for supervising and coordinating these varied enterprises. In general, Konko-kyo appears to be less rigidly centralized than most of the other New Religions.

To attempt a detailed description of the organization and program of Konko-kyo lies beyond the scope of this treatise; however, a brief consideration of selected activities that center in certain of the headquarters agencies may help to give a more adequate over-all impression of the character of this movement.

TRAINING PROGRAM FOR MINISTERS

The Konko-kyo Institute (*gakuin*) provides three different courses realistically designed to accommodate students at different levels of academic preparation and competence. At the top level is a one-year course open only to college graduates. Another course, of two years' duration, is provided for high-school graduates. Finally, a special one-year course, described as "deliberately easy," is available for those who have only a middle-school education.[15] While a student is enrolled in one of these programs, his lodging, meals, and tuition are provided free of charge, but other expenses, such as clothing and books, he must bear himself. When he has completed his studies, normally he will return to the local church from which he has come, either to serve on the staff of that church or to be assigned to a mission church that it is sponsoring.

Two features of this training program, namely, the graded courses of study and a large percentage of female candidates, call for additional commentary here. The provision of graded courses signalizes the important fact (which also is manifested in many other ways) that Konko-kyo is striving continually to attain a higher level of sophistication. At the same time, a preponderance of ministerial candidates in the third-level course indicates, along with other evidence, that Konko-kyo still appeals primarily to people of modest educational attainments. In view of the rural origin and relatively short history of the movement, this latter circumstance is not at all surprising; but, by the same token, the urgency of the drive toward greater sophistication acquires added significance.

Noting the large percentage of women among the ministerial trainees provides an occasion to remark also on the generally important role played by women in Konko-kyo. In contrast to many of the traditions of Japan, this movement accords a relatively favored status to women. This fact is a source of considerable pride and satisfaction to the leaders, who nevertheless are inclined to assign all credit for this circumstance to their founder. He, it is said, emphasized the importance and dignity of the woman's place in the family, treated women with respect, and in matters of status made no distinction between male and female. The result is that the membership of Konko-kyo includes more women than men, and there are more female ministers in this movement than in any other Japanese religion.[16]

DOCTRINAL RESEARCH AND STUDY

The Japanese characteristically have had no penchant for systematic theology; however, in Konko-kyo, considerable interest in this direction is developing. From the very outset, there was inherent in the experience and ministry of Kawate Bunjiro a distinctive concept of the nature of deity and the divine-human relationship, and much of the continuing vitality of Konko-kyo has stemmed from this orientation. However, until the post-World War II period, there had been little concern with producing a summary theological statement. This is readily understandable on at least two grounds. In the first place, so long as the movement had to comply with governmental prescriptions, theological formulations tended to be mere contrivances, designed specifically to make the mandatory accommodations without obliterating the movement's own fundamental perspectives. In the second place, the general religious orientation of the Japanese people requires no clear statement of doctrine. The Japanese tend to place small reliance upon verbal communication but to have much confidence in experience. Accordingly, heretofore the devotees of Konko-kyo have been thoroughly immersed in a kind of "theology of experience"; although, paradoxical as it may seem, they have been enjoined all the while to have faith according to "reason." The apparent contradiction, however, exists only in the English rendering, not in the Japanese context. There are several Japanese words that may be translated as "reason." The one used in this instance is *dōri*, a term whose suggestiveness can be understood only through an analysis of the two Chinese characters by which it is formed. The first of these, meaning "way," is the intriguing *tao* of Chinese philosophy and religion. It is also the *tō* in *Shintō* and the *dō* in *jūdō* (an art of self-defense) and *Bushidō* ("the way of the warrior," or Japanese chivalry); and it occurs in many other compounds as well to denote a "way," a basic orientation, a total involvement that underlies and is prior to all concerns for technique and results. The second character, *ri*, alone means "reason," but also it may be translated as "justice," "truth," or "principle." In many of the compounds in which it occurs, it signifies orderliness, naturalness, that which is. For example, it is the key component in the word for "physical science," *rigaku*. Thus, when we approach the faith orientation of Konko-kyo through the term *dōri*, we can see that the principal emphasis is placed upon living, not thinking, one's way into the truth; yet the whole enterprise is to be safeguarded by "reason" (or, perhaps better, "common sense" or the logic of life and action) lest it result in blind faith or fanaticism.

For most of the adherents of Konko-kyo, this theology of experience is all that is required; but among the leaders, especially since World War II, there has been a growing concern for a more adequate theology. This concern is expressed most directly as the need to understand more fully the uniqueness of Konko-kyo in order that its continuing relevance to rapidly changing conditions can be discerned and demonstrated. Consciousness of this need stems very largely from the problems incidental to expanding institutionalization and sustained exposure to Western thought and culture.

A concrete example of the type of quandary underlying this theological concern was brought to my attention in an extended conversation with the *Kyōkan*,[17] the second-ranking official and chief administrator of Konko-kyo. Throughout much of our conference, he was "thinking out loud" concerning an issue with which he was then struggling. A group of American delegates who had come to headquarters for the fall festival had stayed over to agitate for a guaranteed income for the Konko-kyo ministers in the United States. To the *Kyōkan*, this proposal seemed to call for a radical innovation that would threaten the very basis of Konko-kyo. "If it comes to this," he said early in our discussion, "Konko-kyo need not propagate in the United States." No Konko-kyo minister ever has had a guaranteed income. He lives from day to day on what people contribute as they come for *toritsugi*. To forsake this principle seemed to this official almost tantamount to forsaking the faith. Yet, as we discussed this matter in the fullest detail, it became evident that the mere preservation of tradition was not the issue, for this man was fully committed to the necessity of modernization and even a certain amount of compromise. "But," said he, "the more we are inclined toward modernization, the more we see the necessity of recovering the essential nature of our faith. Modernization and essential affirmation are not opposites but must stand side by side." His real fear seemed to be that the "essential affirmation" has not yet been made with sufficient clarity and cogency to support the widespread involvements of Konko-kyo. Unless this lack is remedied, he felt, efforts at modernization and compromise can result only in the perversion of the faith. As still another spokesman for Konko-kyo states the issue: "Because the idea of God is the very kernel of faith, and also the basis of any anthropology, so long as the idea of God is undefined, the raison d'être of life will also remain undefined."[18]

Here, in essence, is the concern that has led to the establishment of the Institute of Doctrinal Research, dedicated to the development of a well-formulated theology for Konko-kyo. Many of the methods and categories employed by the researchers therein are adaptations from Western philosophy and theology. For example: "Konko-kyo's God can be said to be both *transcendent* and *immanent*."[19] Also, an apparently useful device is the comparative study of Konko-kyo and Christianity, with a view to demonstrating the uniqueness of the former. Thus, it is said that whereas in Christianity the relationship between God and Christ is *ontological*, in Konko-kyo the relationship between Kami and Konko Daijin is *functional*.[20]

Nevertheless, the reigning perspectives still are Japanese, and while much of the Institute's work is ingenious and intriguing, it also leaves one wondering whether Japanese religion either requires or can accommodate an "intellectual love of God" that is comparable to the dimension of Western theological enterprise that may be so designated.

Somehow it seems that the more authentic endeavor of Konko-kyo theologians is their current perusal of a newly opened resource that is uniquely their own: the notes compiled by the founder as he received people for *toritsugi*. "Confessional secrecy" requires that during the lifetime of a *Kyōshu*, only he will have access to his notes and that, for a respectful time thereafter, they will be kept from all eyes. Now, however, the notes of the founder, though still not accessible to the public, may be examined by those who are legitimately engaged in doctrinal research. In support of the effort to define more clearly and fully the essential character of Konko-kyo, this could prove to be a very rewarding enterprise. It remains to be seen whether the essence of this faith, no matter the clarity of its formulation, can be brought under the reign of reason, other than that called *dōri*, without its being desecrated. Perhaps Konko-kyo has yet to discover that one of the greatest pitfalls of modernization is theological gamesmanship.

PROPAGATION THROUGH LITERATURE

Konko-kyo differs from most of the other successful New Religions in that it is not driven by the necessity to propagate. It conducts no house-to-house visitation and holds no mass rallies for the purpose of propagation. The fundamental religious activity, *toritsugi*, is not aggressive but passive. Kawate Bunjiro sat each day in his mediation room and received all who came seeking his ministry. This example of the founder provides the basic pattern for his direct successors as well as for the Konko-kyo clergy in general. Anyone may go to the headquarters or to a local church and avail himself of a minister's service in *toritsugi* or hear a sermon expounding the faith of Konko-kyo, but no one is likely to be sought out and importuned to accept this faith.

However, like most of the other New Religions, Konko-kyo does engage in extensive publishing activity, one purpose of which is evangelistic. In addition to books and pamphlets, the publishing agency issues at least four periodicals that have the dual purpose of providing religious nurture for members and enlisting the interest of nonmembers. These include a newspaper published three times a month and distributed to all who request it, a monthly magazine for young people fifteen to thirty-five years of age, another monthly for still younger readers, and a quarterly journal for general circulation. This outreach through literature is greatly augmented by the publication of about one hundred additional magazines by individual churches.

The Konko-kyo Church of Izuo

From the headquarters in Okayama Prefecture, let us move now to a local Konko-kyo church in Osaka, Japan's second largest city, whose name is virtually synonymous with mercantilism. In the endeavor to understand Konko-kyo, this should be tactically a good move, for let us recall that while this religion originated as a peasant movement, its constituency began to change after 1868 as merchants from Osaka began to affiliate with it. Subsequently, laborers from urban areas were attracted. Now persons of the lower middle class, often associated with medium or small business enterprises, seem to constitute the major portion of the membership. The church to be considered here, the Konko-kyo Church of Izuo, is fairly representative of Konko-kyo at work among such people within an urban setting.

Izuo Church was founded in 1927 by Miyake Toshio, its present

chief minister. Though seemingly poorly located in a section of
the city that is predominantly industrial, the church has spacious,
well-tended grounds and buildings and is able to attract and
minister to people from a wide area. The total membership is
approximately sixteen thousand persons. Graded according to
socioeconomic strata, about eighty percent of these are middle
class, fifteen percent are lower class, and five percent are higher
class (here defined as employers of two hundred and fifty or
more people).[21] To serve so large a constituency, the church
maintains a staff of nineteen ordained ministers, who are assisted
in innumerable ways by a "devotees-for-service group" (*Shinja
Shūdan*), thirty-eight volunteers who, without remuneration,
assume much of the routine responsibility for the church program
and property maintenance.

As in all other Konko-kyo churches, the membership of Izuo
Church consists of three categories of believers. In ascending
order, these are the *kyūshinja*, the *shinto*, and the *kyōto*. The
first of these, the *kyūshinja*, are "inquirers" or "seekers of faith,"
who manifest their interest and intention to believe by attending
services regularly or at least frequently. If at the end of about
one year, such a one is approved by the chief minister, he may
be officially registered as a member. Izuo Church has approximately eight hundred *kyūshinja*. The second category is composed of *shinto* (literally, "laymen" or "believers"), a term not to
be confused with the Shinto religion. These are persons who,
having been approved for membership, are listed on the church
roll and voluntarily receive *toritsugi* for guidance in every aspect
of their faith and life. This generally is the largest of the categories (about ten thousand in Izuo Church) and includes many
of the most devout followers, preponderantly women whose
families have not accompanied them into this faith. The highest
category, the *kyōto* (literally, "believers" or "adherents"), consists of heads of families. To qualify for such a listing, a person
must first give evidence, acceptable to the chief minister, that
he has achieved an exemplary state of spirituality; he must also
agree to let the church conduct all his family ceremonies, such
as weddings and funerals; and his faith must be publicly con-
firmed through a special ceremony (*Kikyō Shiki*) in the church.

Thereafter, he and his family are privileged to participate in ancestral rites that are reserved for this category of members. Following his death, his family may designate a successor who— again, subject to the chief minister's approval—will become a *kyōto* in his stead. The rolls of Izuo Church list more than one thousand *kyōto*, but since each one represents an entire family, the total number of persons involved in this category is approximately five thousand.

The program of Izuo Church is planned with the needs, interests, and circumstances of its members clearly in view. The schedule for worship, from Monday through Saturday, calls for four services daily: at 6 A.M., 9:30 A.M., 2 P.M., and 7:30 P.M. On Sunday, only the two morning services are held. This schedule has been devised specifically for the convenience of working people, who comprise the majority of the membership. While all services are well attended, the early-morning service is regarded as the most important and attracts the largest congregations. Each service includes prayer and a sermon. In addition, one or more of the ministers are available for *toritsugi* during twenty hours each day.

The church also sponsors a variety of groups, differentiated on the basis of such factors as sex, vocation, special interest, residence, and age, to provide opportunities for comradeship and cooperative endeavor for everyone. These include associations for women, youth, students, children, and widows and widowers, as well as Boy Scouts, Girl Scouts, and a choir.

Some of the most devout members of Izuo Church also cooperate in helping to establish believers' associations (*Kōsha*) in various localities, often at a considerable distance from the church. In rare instances, a *Kōsha* develops to the point where it can be incorporated as a new church with its own ordained minister. One such case is the Tokiwadai Church in Tokyo, to which the younger son of the chief minister of Izuo Church has been assigned as pastor. On May 16, 1964, I was present at Tokiwadai Church for the *Senza Sai*, the service of the enshrinement of the deity, for which occasion about forty or fifty persons (both ministers and laymen) made the long trip from Osaka, most of them by chartered bus. The sermon was delivered by the Izuo minister, who is known to the Tokyo congregation as Oya-sensei (Parent-teacher). This occasion provided a good example of two important characteristics of the New Religions generally, the *oya-ko* ("parent-child") pattern of organization and responsibility and the strong feeling of mutuality among believers.

During the course of a year, many special services for the membership and rallies for the various associations are held in Izuo Church. One great annual occasion is a festival on January 24 celebrating the anniversary of the church's founding. Other major rites are observed in common with other Konko-kyo churches. The most important are the spring and autumn festivals (celebrated in Izuo Church on April 25 and October 25), dedicated respectively to the deity, Tenchi Kane no Kami, and the founder, Ikigami Konko Daijin. As I can attest from having witnessed them, these ceremonies are quite impressive in their dignity and solemnity.

Services are also held at the times of the spring and autumn equinoxes. Traditionally in Japan, the week in March and the week in September that include the respective equinoctial days as their middle days are periods of special significance within Buddhism. Called *higan* (literally, the "farther shore," in reference to the journey of the dead), these two weeks are occasions for holding memorial services for ancestors. For the sake of its own members, many of whom formerly were Buddhists and most of whom, in any case, share the typical Japanese sense of reverence for ancestors, Konko-kyo has adopted this function of the Buddhist temples. Therefore, on the equinoctial days, a memorial service is held honoring the ancestors of the *kyōto* families. For these services, only the secondary altar, dedicated to the ancestral spirits, is used.

Izuo Church, true to the spirit of Konko-kyo, is concerned with problems of social welfare and world peace. One of the basic tenets of this religion is that the whole of mankind constitutes a single *ujiko*. This word *ujiko* traditionally designates a kind of Shinto parish, a relatively small community of people united in their common dependence upon and loyalty to a local patron deity (*ujigami*). Konko-kyo has expanded this concept to its ultimate limit by affirming that all people are the children of

Kami's family and ought, therefore, to be concerned for one another's well-being. Indicative of this interest within Izuo Church are two activities: a home-industry program and special efforts in behalf of world peace.

The home-industry program is an effort to help impoverished people, many of whom are incapable of working full time or on a regular schedule, to earn at least a little income. The building that formerly housed Izuo Church is made available without charge to a group of about two hundred such people, who use the premises to work for various industries on a subcontract or piecework basis. Such tasks as wrapping candies, making bags, and packing pastries are performed here. Anyone needing money may participate. Only about ten percent of the workers are members of the church. This program is said to be the largest and most profitable for the workers of all such enterprises in the city of Osaka.

The cause of peace and world brotherhood is especially attractive to the chief minister of Izuo Church. He is active in several organizations devoted to these ends, most notably the World Federalists, and has traveled abroad with delegations of religionists seeking to promote goodwill and understanding. This interest is reflected most directly in the program of his church in the scheduling each year of one week of special emphasis on "World Peace Through World Brotherhood" and another week devoted to "Enhancing the Spirit of World Federation."

Reflections

In Konko-kyo we see a religious movement that, now in the early years of its second century, is achieving significant maturity. Inevitably it must face many additional crises of adjustment, but in the face of these, there are at least three factors—flexibility, openness, and modesty—that seem to augur favorably for Konko-kyo as a long-lived, though perhaps not dramatically prominent, movement.

Organizationally, it appears to be quite stable and resourceful, and certainly it is much less highly centralized and domineering than many of the other New Religions. Though the sect retains strong reflections of traditionalism in its doctrines, rites, and interpersonal relations, it is relatively free of such so-called superstitions as magic and divination.

Theologically, Konko-kyo perhaps can be currently described as a functional monotheism. Its concept of deity tends to integrate the pluralistic outlook common to Japanese religion, yet it does so without negating that outlook and resorting to the kind of categorical claims that often result in exclusivism and intolerance. It is a concept that, being primarily derived from and sustained by experience, permits flexibility, updating, and openness to others.

PL Kyōdan: An Epicurean Movement

F ROM ABENOBASHI STATION IN OSAKA, a half-hour journey southward via the Kinki-Nippon Railway brings one to Tondabayashi, from which it is only a short taxi ride to the wooded, hilly area called Habikino, where the headquarters of *PL Kyōdan*, "Perfect Liberty Order," are located. Since the approach to this precinct is an upgrade, the buildings are not fully visible from the townside; but as one nears the brow of the hill, he sees on the right a long embankment covered by an abstract mosaic and on the left a large abstract sculpture—two foretastes of things to come.

As the hill is crested, the exquisite Renseikaikan, the sect's training hall, rivaling in plushness the Tokyo Hilton, suddenly appears, and a view of the whole extensive "Holy Land" (*Seichi*) begins to unfold. In the foreground are baseball fields, adjacent to which there are, on one side, an outdoor altar surmounted by a tall column bearing the letters "PL" and, on the other side, a gigantic Quonset building with the letters "PLY" (standing for PL Youth association) inscribed across the front. Further away, beyond small artificial lakes, other intriguing structures may be seen, and providing a background for it all are the rolling fairways of three fine golf courses. Many Japanese, who are fond of twitting the New Religions anyway, like to call this one the *gorufu shūkyō* ("golf religion"); but in this whole panorama, the golf courses must be seen, along with all the other installations, preeminently as symbols of the modernity to which PL Kyodan, probably more avidly than any other new religious movement, aspires. It is this commitment that also accounts for the sect's having adopted the English words—or, perhaps more accurately, the American words—"Perfect Liberty," for its name.

From such an introduction as this, even if it were extended to include a more careful scrutiny of the headquarters and an opportunity to attend one or more services, a newcomer could not be expected to guess how this sect is related to the religious traditions of Japan. Even for the person well acquainted with Japan, this would be a poser; for while there is an unmistakable Japanese touch to almost everything, nowhere does one see any of the customary symbols of Shinto or Buddhism. Almost all the architecture is modern, and some of it is quite novel and imaginative. Only one building, the Women's Hall, is built entirely in the traditional Japanese style, and it is religiously nonsuggestive. For the most part, the plentiful examples of art—sculpture, mosaics, calligraphy, paintings, flower arrangements—are abstract and avant-garde. Vestments worn on ceremonial occasions are apparently original and unique to this sect. Overall, it seems, those who design and execute the accouterments of PL Kyodan are motivated primarily by certain contemporary aesthetic standards, not by the motifs of traditional Japanese religions. Yet, this sect is importantly a product of the Japanese experience, both religiously and otherwise; and before we can adequately assess the meaning of its present commitment to modernity, we must identify and describe the character of its heritage.

The Antecedents: Tokumitsu-kyō *and* Hito no Michi

Previously in this study (Chapter III), we noted the rise and fortunes of PL Kyodan's two predecessors, Tokumitsu-kyo and Hito no Michi. Thus, we should be somewhat prepared to grasp what is meant when it is said that the tradition formed by the succession of these three sects constitutes an "important phase in the spiritual history of the Osaka merchants."[1] Let us review why this is so and, in the process, endeavor to identify those elements in this tradition that survive in some significant form in the present.

It may be recalled that Kanada Tokumitsu (1863–1919) was a relatively prosperous Osaka cutlery dealer who, in 1912, at the urging and with the sponsorship of some of his fellow businessmen, became the leader of a religious fellowship that flourished during the economic boom of the World War I era. Here we must add further information concerning his religious background and his methods of work.

Kanada's preparation for his leadership role was an almost lifelong interest in various occult religious traditions and disciplines. He was particularly attracted to *Shingon-shū*, an esoteric sect of Japanese Buddhism, whose headquarters on Mount Koya he is said to have visited more than one hundred times. Also, he was a highly ranked member of *Mitake-kyō*, a mountain sect, which was listed as one of the thirteen approved Shinto sects. Through both these contacts, he was exposed to an essentially syncretistic and magical religious orientation, which is clearly reflected in his own teaching. Reality, he taught, is the manifestation of Buddha and Kami, who actually are one all-pervasive deity, symbolized by the sun. This deity is called Dainichi Nyorai,[2] in the terminology of Shingon Buddhism and Amaterasu-O mikami according to Shinto usage. Since human beings all are imbued alike with the nature of this deity, they should live as equals.

Ideologically, Kanada's doctrine held considerable appeal for busy merchants. It eliminated the necessity of assessing rival truth claims, and it bound into a unit all the supernaturalism, humanism, and nationalism that somehow had to be accommodated in their workaday world. But perhaps even more than as a teacher, Kanada was appreciated as a practitioner of occult arts. We have already taken note of his popularity as a purveyor of stock-market tips and business advice, but he was also renowned as a healer. During the period of World War I, he developed a technique known as *ofurikae* ("transfer")[3] by which he was supposed to be able to heal any illness by absorbing it into himself. This was essentially a novel implementation of folklore. The notion long had been common among the masses that certain of their deities, especially the bodhisattvas Jizo and Kannon (the patron of women and children and the goddess of mercy, respectively), were willing to suffer vicariously for their faithful devotees. Instances of the miraculous transfer of human afflictions to the images of these compassionate deities are related in numerous folktales.[4] Presumably, then, it was this residual folk faith that underlay Kanada's practice, but by being dramatically personalized, it was given fresh relevance within the merchant community. As we shall see, this practice in a modified form still survives in PL Kyodan.

In 1916, a Zen priest named Miki Chojiro (1871–1938) and his teenage son, Akisada (b. 1900), became devotees of Tokumitsu-kyo in an effort to find relief from recurrent hardship. The elder Miki had been born to a merchant family, but because of the failure of his father's business, he had been sent as a boy to a temple of the Obaku Zen sect to be trained for the priesthood. Each of the temples to which he was assigned as a priest was so small that he found it necessary to conduct some kind of business enterprise on the side. At forty years of age, with a sick wife and three children, he quit the priesthood and moved to Osaka in the hope of finding an adequate means of supporting his family. In the following year, 1912, his wife died, and some time thereafter he began to visit Kanada. Apparently, when Miki and his son committed themselves to full-time service in the new movement, he had been Kanada's disciple for two or three years. Having become teachers in Tokumitsu-kyo, both father and son were given new names, Tokuharu and Tokuchika, respectively.

As the war boom faded, so did Tokumitsu-kyo; and after the death of Kanada in 1919, the movement was never strong again. However, a line of continuity already had been established through Miki Tokuharu. Presumably, Kanada had considered his work to be incomplete. Expecting twenty-one revealed precepts, he had received only eighteen. Therefore, when his death was imminent, he had said to Miki: "If you will plant a *himorogi* tree at the site of my death and tend it, eventually you will meet a person of true faith who will know the three remaining commandments."[5] Miki planted the tree and visited it daily for five years. In the final months of this regimen, between September of 1923 and October of 1924, he had three mystical experiences in which new insights were revealed to him. After the third of these, Miki realized that he himself was the one whose coming Kanada had foretold. With a literary group (which had been organized by his son Tokuchika) as a nucleus, Miki formed a new sect, proclaiming it as the successor to Tokumitsu-kyo. With forty-nine of his followers, he made a pilgrimage to Ise Shrine on October 29, 1924, to report the formation of the new movement to the sun-goddess and to request divine recognition of the practice of *ofurikae*. Approval was indicated miraculously when a "divine wind" (*kamikaze*) lifted the curtain before the altar and suspended it horizontally for five minutes. In order also to be legally sure, the organization was registered under *Fusō-kyō*, one of the recognized sects of Shinto. It was not until 1931 that the name Hito no Michi was adopted. Meaning "the way of man," this name signified the movement's principal concern for that which actually is effective in human life.[6]

The new movement was almost immediately a success. Its teachings reflected—hence in turn appealed to—the conservative humanism of the merchants. Emphasis was placed upon peaceful and faithful family relationships, industriousness, and the concrete rewards of virtue. The latter point was underscored by playing upon the verbal coincidence that the word for "virtue" (*toku*) and the word for "profit" (*toku*), though written with different characters, are phonetic homonyms. This kind of word game is a delight to the Japanese and, as in this instance, may easily be assigned occult significance.

In 1930, the practice of *asamairi* ("morning visit" to a sacred place) was begun. This was an early-morning meeting consisting of a sermon, liturgy, confessions or testimonies, and a free breakfast of rice and soup. Symbolizing the virtue of an early start each day and combining the characteristics of the family system and mass mobilization, this was a very effective instrument. Only slightly modified, it is continued still as one of the principal features of PL Kyodan.

The ill-starred effort of Hito no Michi to cooperate with the militarist government in the 1930's has already been described (Chapter III). When it became evident in 1936 that his avowed loyalty to official purpose was to be rewarded by persecution, the elder Miki retired and passed the leadership of the movement to his son, Tokuchika. Two days later, Miki Tokuharu was arrested. In the following year, the government ordered the dissolution of the movement; and in 1938, while free on bail, the elder Miki died. Subsequently, Miki Tokuchika attempted to refute the charges against Hito no Michi, but his efforts were futile, and in May of 1945 he was incarcerated in Kosuge Prison, where he remained until his sentence was declared void by the Occupation authorities.

The Founding of PL Kyōdan

Shortly after his release from prison on October 9, 1945, Miki Tokuchika began to be importuned by many of the former Hito no Michi people to reconstruct the movement. Principally because of physical disabilities resulting from imprisonment, he was reluctant at first to accede, but finally he relented. However, rather than reassume the burden of all that would be associated with the old name, he thought it best to choose a new name more in keeping with the mood of the times. Hence, he called it Perfect Liberty Kyodan.

Initially there was some indecision as to whether the organization should be launched as a cultural movement or as a religious movement; however, since there already was evidence of a widespread response to seemingly "new" religious appeals, it was decided that PL Kyodan would be a religion. Emphasis was placed upon modernizing the life of middle-class urban people and upon the enrichment of personality through self-expression. The fact that the movement had suffered persecution during wartime actually turned out to be a boon in the new era. It won the sympathy of some rebellious and resentful persons, and many old ghosts could be laid by the explanation that formerly much that was false had had to be taught because there had been little freedom to teach the truth. Thus, this newly refurbished movement had little difficulty in appearing to identify itself with the temper of the new day.

To be sure, their efforts to attract young people through the sponsorship of dance parties and other "modern" activities elicited some rather caustic criticism. There were those, for example, who

said that such meetings had the "atmosphere of a colony"
(*shokuminchi-teki fun-iki*).[7] This was an especially biting accu-
sation, for just after the war a "colony" (*shokuminchi*) meant
a community that had sprung up around a United States military
base. Characteristically brassy, it featured bars, girls, and gaudy
souvenirs. To allude to this atmosphere in describing PL Kyodan
was to allege that the sect had adopted only the superficial and
tawdry trappings of modernity. Nevertheless, that which repelled
some charmed others, and soon the movement was growing
rapidly.

In September, 1946, the first headquarters for PL Kyodan were
set up in Tosu, Saga Prefecture, on Kyushu, the southernmost
island, far away from Osaka. In 1948, the headquarters were
transferred for a brief time to Hamamatsu and then, in 1949, to
Shimizu in Shizuoka Prefecture, about midway between Tokyo
and Kyoto. Finally, the organization "returned home" to Osaka
in 1953 and moved into its present headquarters, Daihonchō, at
Tondabayashi in 1955.

Chiefly responsible for the prosperity of this organization is
Miki Tokuchika, a man who has the appearance of "a managing
director of an Osaka trading company."[8] Not a mystic or con-
templative, not a fanatic or visionary, he is essentially an active,
highly skilled organization man. To his followers he is known as
the *Oshieoya* (Teaching Parent or Master Teacher), the voice of
authority at the apex of a highly centralized *oya-ko* ("parent-
child") organizational structure. At his urging, the community
also continues to venerate his two predecessors, who have been
assigned official titles suggestive of their respective roles in shaping the total tradition. Kanada Tokumitsu is called the *Kakurioya*
(Hidden Founder or Parent), and Miki Tokuharu, whose tomb
is one of the principal shrines within the headquarters area, is
known as the *Kyōso* (Founder).

Twenty-one Precepts for Conduct in Life

Twenty-one precepts formed the basis of the teaching of Hito
no Michi. Eighteen of these had been inherited from Tokumitsu-
kyo; three had been revealed to Miki Tokuharu. PL also has

twenty-one precepts in its basic creed, but while at certain points the influence of the earlier movements is still reflected, the present list differs from its predecessors. The new formulation is believed to have been revealed to Miki Tokuchika at Hiroshima in 1947.[9] In retrospect, an outsider might see in it also signs of an understandably impetuous and exaggerated reaction to the total regimentation from which the Japanese people had just been delivered. The precepts are as follows:

1. Life is art.
2. The whole life of the individual is a continuous succession of Self-Expressions.
3. The individual is a manifestation of God.
4. We suffer if we do not manifest ourself.
5. We lose self if we are swayed by our feelings.
6. Our true self is revealed when our ego is effaced.
7. All things exist in mutual relation to one another.
8. Live radiantly as the Sun.
9. All men are equal.
10. Bring mutual happiness through our expression.
11. Depend on God at all times.
12. There is always a way peculiar to every name.
13. There is one way for men, and there is another for women.
14. All things exist for World Peace.
15. Our whole environment is the mirror of our mind.
16. All things make progress and development.
17. Grasp the heart of everything.
18. At every moment man stands at the crossroads of good and evil.
19. Practice at once whatever your first inspiration dictates.
20. Attain the perfect harmonious state of mind and matter.
21. Live in Perfect Liberty.[10]

One or another of these rather vague epigrams seems usually to be the subject of the homilies delivered at most PL gatherings; however, by far the most important of them all is the one that heads the list: "Life is art." This is the PL motto and the order's most distinctive and incisive doctrine. It holds that each individual is a unique personality who by right ought to be happy. Happiness is achieved when the individual is able to express perfectly that which he is, basically and uniquely, as a person. This is possible when the individual sees that life itself is art and

that each person is potentially an artist. Art no longer need be
regarded as the province of the few. It is not just what the
musician does with notes and rhythms or what the painter does
with colors and brushes or the sculptor with marble and chisels;
it is what any person can do, using the medium appropriate to
his own life. Real living is expressing one's own personal qualities
in his daily work, just as the professional artist expresses his
personality in art forms. As Miki himself has said it: "When one
sets one's whole mind on washing or sweeping or any other work,
one's true personal quality is expressed in it. Then, those works
have been elevated to art."[11] Every person knows that happiness
and satisfaction result when he has done his best in anything.
These qualities will reign in his life when, with consistent diligence, he expresses his own personality perfectly in everything.
Then he will have achieved what PL calls "artistic life."

The Ministry of Restoration

Life can be beautiful and happy, but it is not always so, for
these intended issues of life sometimes are aborted by illness,
poverty, strife, or other forms of suffering. How do these arise,
and how may they be dealt with?

The source of life and all things is known in PL as Mioya
Okami (Parent Deity). The true "self" of man—the "self" that he
must express perfectly in his actions—is the manifestation of deity.
If one forgets that this is so and begins to lead a life based only
on ego-consciousness or willful self-interest, he disrupts the natural process that leads to the intended fulfillment. Though he is
at perfect liberty to make such expression as he chooses, if his
art degenerates into mere artifice or artfulness, then he will be
afflicted by various troubles.

Most people who suffer do not understand the cause of their
suffering. They pray for relief, but they remain unaware that the
suffering itself is one part of the answer to their prayer—a non-
verbal communication from deity. PL calls this experience *mishi-
rase*, that which is "known to deity." Suffering, then, is the
warning of deity that something is wrong in the thinking of the

person concerned. Beyond this, however, deity does not reveal to man directly the details of his problem. To receive this part of the communication, one must seek the counsel of the *Oshieoya*, or one of a very few other spiritually qualified persons, who will issue a *mioshie* ("teaching") identifying the cause of the trouble and specifying what must be done to rectify it.

Those who are able to discern the causes of personal misfortune are called *Oyasama* (literally, "parents" or "ancestors"). In addition to the *Oshieoya*, there are, at the present time, fifteen such persons, including Miki's wife, his daughter, and his adopted son. By faithful dedication and sustained discipline, so it is said, these persons have achieved a stage of "Conformity to God"[12] that makes their ministry of restoration possible. Though, theoretically, this advanced spiritual state is attainable for any PL follower and all are urged to aspire to it,[13] the *Oyasama* are not likely ever to be very numerous.

Though theirs is the essential ministry, the *Oshieoya* and the *Oyasama* are not usually accessible to the members for personal conferences. Each suppliant describes his symptoms on a form provided for that purpose and submits it for diagnostic examination. Then a typewritten copy of the diagnosis and prescription (*mioshie*) is sent to him by way of a PL teacher who, in a personal interview, explains the meaning of the communication.[14] A large clerical staff at the headquarters is kept busy handling the great volume of correspondence this ministry entails.[15]

There is one phase of this ministry of restoration that only the *Oshieoya* can perform. This is "vicarious suffering," which in Tokumitsu-kyo and Hito no Michi was called *ofurikae* but which in PL Kyodan has been renamed *tenshō*. Not surprisingly, this is perhaps the vaguest aspect of PL doctrine and practice, for it depends most directly upon the indefinable but exalted *ikigami* character of the *Oshieoya* and lies closest to the ineffable mystery that vindicates the faith. From what little is said concerning this matter, it appears that principally it is a kind of buffering action available to the believers in two kinds of situations. In the first place, it is clearly an emergency measure. If one suddenly is afflicted by trouble and there is no time for him to go through the usual channels to receive a *mioshie*, he may, then and there, call upon the *Oshieoya* to assume his burden temporarily until he can seek restorative counsel. In the second place, it has an intercessory character. If one has applied for and received a *mioshie* and has been obedient to its instructions and yet the "warnings" persist in spite of it all, then "it is the Patriarch [*Oshieoya*] and not the follower who is responsible to God for the warning."[16] Each month, as a part of the thanksgiving service (described in the next section), there is a ceremony in which the *Oshieoya* renews his commitment to accept vicariously the afflictions of others and the believers transfer their responsibilities to him.

Liturgical Life and Symbols

PL Kyodan is a liturgically oriented community. That it should be so is thoroughly consistent with its other characteristics, such as its tightly controlled organization, on the one hand, and, on the other, its endeavor to live so as to feel the rhythm of things as they are. Among the liturgical provisions made by this sect are rites and prayers—usually brief and simple but sometimes also cryptic—for use on many occasions. For the most part, the occasions are those that in traditional Japanese society customarily are celebrated by Shinto or Buddhist rites. In place of these, or in addition to these, PL offers its own. Some are "rites of passage" or life-cycle rites—for example, the thanksgiving ceremony for a newborn baby, the naming ceremony, the coming-of-age celebration, the wedding, and the funeral. Others, though related to these, are adaptations of popular traditions, such as the celebration of seventh, fifth, and third birthdays (patterned after the Shichi-go-san Matsuri, Seven-Five-Three Festival, held on November 15 at Shinto shrines) and the celebration of sixty-first birthdays. Still others are seasonal or occupational. The total list is long and inclusive,[17] and we shall not attempt here to survey it in its entirety. For the purposes of this study, it should be sufficient to examine only three ceremonies: (1) the daily morning worship, (2) the monthly thanksgiving service, and (3) the annual summer festival.

MORNING WORSHIP (ASAMAIRI)

Daily early-morning assembly is one of the practices of Hito no Michi that continues to be a conspicuous feature of PL Kyodan. At 5 A.M. in the summer and at 6 A.M. in the winter, a service is held at the headquarters and in all the larger branch churches. The atmosphere of this service is relatively informal, although the procedure is standardized. It begins with the singing of the PL hymn, followed by the recitation of the *Shikiri*, a prayer of "commitment" or "dedication," which perhaps is the most important part of PL worship, whether public or private. Then, there is a period for testimonies, when any believer may edify the congregation by telling of his own experience. This is followed by a sermon delivered by a PL minister. The meeting then is closed with the singing of the PL hymn. From its inception, one of the attractive features of this assembly has been a simple breakfast after the service; but whereas formerly it was served free of charge, now the partakers of the meal usually are asked to pay a small amount.

The early-morning worship also is combined occasionally with a specific work project. For example, prior to the 1964 Olympic Games, which were held in Japan, some PL devotees participated in a "movement to beautify the nation" (*kokudo bika undō*). Each Sunday morning they met at 5:30 and for one hour worked together in cleaning up some public facility, such as a railway station, a park, or a rest room. Thereafter, they held their morning worship and ate breakfast together.[18]

THANKSGIVING SERVICE (KANSHASAI)

In the evening of the twenty-first day of each month, thanksgiving services are held simultaneously at the headquarters and at all branch churches. The one such service that I attended at the headquarters (on December 21, 1963) was held in their lavish new festival hall. It was an occasion of dignity and beauty. The service began with the entrance of twenty-four ritualists (*saishi*), wearing black-and-white uniquely tailored vestments. With one of their number presiding at the altar, they led the ritual service, accompanied musically by an organ and an excellent girls' choir. At appointed times, the congregation joined in, reciting in unison the prayer of commitment and the creed (*PL Shikiri Kotoba*). About midway through the service, the *Oshieoya*, accompanied by six *Oyasama*, all gorgeously appareled, entered and in stately procession went to the dais. There, in a rite previously mentioned, the *Oshieoya* stood before the altar and took upon himself anew the burdens of his followers. This done, he and his entourage left the hall, and the service of prayer was resumed. The chief ritualist, taking a large scroll to the altar, read several prayers of gratitude and commitment. Then from out of the congregation, several individuals, representing different sections of the PL organization, went forward to participate in a rite of dedication. When the congregation had united once again in the *Shikiri* prayer, the ritualists withdrew and the brilliantly colored stage curtain was closed to signal the end of this phase of the service.

When the curtain was opened again after a brief interval, the chairs used by the ritualists had been cleared away and a large pulpit had been set in the center of the platform. Slowly, from behind the pulpit, the *Oshieoya*, standing on a section of the platform equipped as a lift, arose through an opening in the floor and stepped forward to the pulpit to address the congregation. He had changed his garb from the rather ostentatious ceremonial robe to a high-collared, double-breasted black coat and matching trousers, an ensemble similar to the uniform worn by all PL members when "on duty." He proved himself to be a very capable public speaker with a refreshing sense of humor. At the conclusion of his sermon, he stepped back onto the lift, and when there was an awkward delay in the beginning of its descent, he stamped his foot and then laughed with the congregation as he disappeared. The curtain was drawn again; the people sang the PL hymn and then began to disperse. Each month as this service is being conducted, the same order, except for one inevitable variation, is followed in all the branch churches. During that period in the headquarters service when the *Oshieoya* publicly renews his covenant, the worshipers in the branch churches simply engage in silent meditation. Also, in the branch churches, the period following the liturgical service is devoted first to individual testimonies and then to a sermon by the local leader.

FOUNDER'S FESTIVAL (KYŌSO-SAI)[19]

Among the many colorful annual festivals sponsored by religious bodies in Japan, the PL Founder's Festival, held each
August 1, has become one of the most spectacular. Commemorating the death of Miki Tokuharu and perpetuating his prayer for
world peace, this festival features a magnificent three-hour display
of fireworks, synchronized with symphonic music and the "dancing waters" of illuminated fountains.[20] The rites that are climaxed
by this spectacle center in the *Seiden* (main sanctuary), a large
white-marble, almost Grecian structure, flanked on either side by
two outwardly matching modernistic buildings and facing a
reflecting basin in which the fountains are located. While the
Seiden accommodates only the officiants, its interior is open to
the view of the people gathered on the spacious grounds. The
exhibition of pyrotechnic art is in effect a sacrifice or a votive
offering. When the *Oshieoya* has completed the liturgy for the
occasion, he himself fires the first rockets by remote control from
the altar. The setting is ideal for what follows. The golf courses
and the wooded hills beyond them, the reflecting basin and the
small lakes, the white *Seiden* and the other unique structures
dotted about the area all "react" to the brilliant display overhead
and help to make of this an unforgettable occasion for all who
witness it—and, so it is said, there are sometimes about a quarter
of a million people who do so.[21]

In association with PL liturgy, we should also comment briefly
on the symbolism of the order. For this purpose, our previous
discussion of the prominence of solar imagery in the teachings of
Tokumitsu-kyo and Hito no Michi again becomes relevant. While,
to my knowledge, the teachers of PL Kyodan, unlike their predecessors, do not speak of the sun as the most apt symbol of the
supreme deity, there are reasons for supposing that it is still
appropriate so to regard it. For instance, above the main entrance
of the training hall, there is a splendid mosaic that suggests the
whirling sun and the dissemination of solar energy. This is indicated also by the two most distinctive symbols of the order: the
emblem (*Omitama*) and the gesture (*Nisshō*).

The *Omitama* ("divine spirit"),[22] the official emblem of PL, consists of a jewel from which twenty-one rays emanate; thus, it symbolizes both the presence of deity and the precepts revealed by deity. Worn as a lapel pin, it is the badge of membership in the sect. Rendered large, it is displayed decoratively in various ways in and on PL buildings. In a worship hall, it is mounted above the altar with a light behind its crystal center.

In the devotional practices of a number of Japanese religions, traditional and modern, gestures or hand symbols have a conspicuous place.[23] PL worship, both individual and corporate, includes a ritual called *Raihai* ("worship"), consisting of several prescribed postures and gestures culminating in the *Nisshō* ("sun design"). To form this symbol, both hands are opened, palms forward, fingers apart and extended, then a circle is formed by touching thumb to thumb and forefinger to forefinger and the hands are lifted just above the head; thus, the circle seems to describe the solar disk and the three extended fingers on each hand suggest the sun's rays. By this means, according to the explanation of a young PL teacher, "the individual signifies his belief that he is a child of God."[24] It is not surprising that a Japanese journalist should report that this is done "in order to show that the Sun is with the person."[25]

Organization and Activities

Several times we have remarked in passing that the organization of PL Kyodan is tightly knit and highly centralized and that, in its present form, it is principally a reflection of the work and personality of Miki Tokuchika, a remarkably skillful organizer and administrator who also has been quite successful in projecting himself as an authority figure. The consequence is a movement that features attractively an intimate fellowship and opportunities for new experiences—combined, however, with unquestioning obedience. In traditional Japanese terms, this is essentially the *oya-ko* ("parent-child") pattern of relationship. Though it is rooted in antiquity, this pattern still is very common among Japanese social institutions; and while it may be argued, sometimes very persuasively, that such a relationship is the best one

possible for a land so seriously overpopulated as Japan, the fact
remains that it is anything but modern.

As the Teaching Parent (*Oshieoya*) of the extensive PL
"family," Miki, together with his conjugal family, lives in luxury,
immune from accountability and criticism within the order. Apparently (as we saw in Chapter IV), there is an effort in certain
PL literature to develop toward Miki and his family the same
kind of attitude that some other publications still encourage
toward the Emperor and the royal family. That is, the leader's
immediate family is seen as the paradigm for all other primary
families as well as for the total life of the one combined "family"
he leads.

One of the most important privileges reserved for the *Oshieoya*
is the sole authority to choose his own successor. The order
assumes that inevitably he will cast his mantle upon the person
who has the highest gifts and graces for the position; however,
there is no constitutional regulation to govern the decision in any
way. Miki long since has named the one who will take his place.
He is Miki Tokuhito, an adopted son of the *Oshieoya* and a
graduate in Oriental philosophy from Waseda University. In
1959, the *Oshieoya* announced his decision and, in an elaborate
service of investiture, conferred upon his chosen successor the
title *Tsugioya* (Next Master).

Communication from the *Oshieoya* to the membership is simple
and swift. District directors throughout the country receive the
word directly from the top. They pass it on to their group leaders,
who in turn relay it to the unit leaders, each of whom then is
responsible for the instruction of the five families in his charge.
This chain of command must always be responsive and reliable.
It is reported that careful precautions are taken to ensure that
collusive relationships between teachers and local members do
not arise, and allegedly this accounts for the frequency of the
sudden transference of teachers from post to post.[26]

FINANCES

The vertical character of the PL authority and organization is
nowhere more evident than in its system of money raising. When

a person joins the movement, he is given containers (*hōshō-bukuro*) for use in submitting his contributions. He is encouraged to think of all money as having been given by deity and to see it as his duty to return, with thanksgiving, some portion of it to be used for the purposes of deity. Preferably his contributions will be made monthly. Without any local accounting, the contribution is sent directly to the headquarters, where it is dedicated and sanctified in the monthly thanksgiving service. Out of the headquarters treasury, which is thus supplied, funds are allocated for the payment of teachers and the needs of the branch churches. The remainder belongs to headquarters.

TEACHER TRAINING

There are three grades of teachers (*hokyōshi*) in PL Kyodan. To become a teacher, one must be recommended by specified minor officials and be approved by the *Oshieoya*. He then is trained at headquarters and through apprenticeship in branch churches. Requirements for the lowest grade are easily met if the applicant gives evidence of sincerity and wholehearted application. To achieve the higher grades and the more responsible appointments, proportionately more thorough preparation is required. The principal activity of the teachers in branch churches is said to be personal guidance or counseling. However, if the report is accurate that one teacher may be called upon to counsel from fifty to a hundred people in a single day,[27] we may question whether the term "counseling" is appropriately applied to what takes place. Generally, so it seems, personal interviews are occasions for dispensing precepts or for relaying to a suppliant a *mioshie* from headquarters. The simplistic doctrine that one's total experience and environment are just the reflection of one's own mind limits the possibility of depth counseling.

In the spring of 1963, the *PL Kyōkō* (teacher school or seminary) was begun in order to develop a higher-quality, more systematic program of "ministerial training." This agency provides a two-year program, open only to male applicants who are college graduates. Others, including women, may still qualify as teachers by the older means; but this program reflects a special effort to enlist bright, attractive, gregarious young men who, in top positions of leadership, can perhaps make PL more appealing to Japan's sophisticated middle- and upper-class citizens. In addition to their instruction in the history, doctrine, polity, and liturgy of PL, these young men are trained in a wide variety of skills that will mark them as well-furnished men in modern Japan. A part of this preparation is in traditional Japanese arts, such as poetry, calligraphy, flower arranging, tea ceremony, and dancing. Much of it is in more modern enterprises: automobile driver training, social dancing, public speaking, English conversation, and golf. Also, instruction in common medical knowledge and counseling, in addition to occasional field trips to major industries, helps to give a pragmatic orientation to their whole experience. Some, perhaps most, of these young men may look forward to additional training or experience abroad.

OVERSEAS OUTREACH

In 1957, on the occasion of my first visit to the headquarters of PL Kyodan, I was told that while the order was interested in international outreach, it was as yet too young and small to support a foreign missionary program. At that time, it was estimated, there were perhaps only about fifty believers among Japanese emigrants abroad. By 1963, when next I inquired, overseas churches with their own attractive buildings had been established in Honolulu, Hawaii, in Los Angeles, California, and in São Paulo, Brazil, with constituencies apparently numbering several thousand. From reports printed in the PL newspaper, *Geisei Shimbun*, it appears that youth activities, which are chiefly recreational, are especially popular in these outposts. Efforts at propagation now also are being made in other areas of the world, notably Europe and southeast Asia.

SPORTS

Among the general public, perhaps PL Kyodan is best known for its three fine golf courses. Also, the baseball and *kendō* (Japanese fencing) teams of the PL high school are consistently among the best in their class. Other sports as well are emphasized. This stress on athletics is thoroughly consistent with the PL teaching concerning the importance of developing strong, healthy bodies; it also is another bid to be identified with the popular aspects of modern Japanese life. Japan has become extremely sports-conscious. Baseball is played and watched by millions of people throughout the country. Thousands of businessmen have become obsessed with golf, which also, due to the scarcity of courses and the expense of playing, is a status sport.

MEDICINE

Healing is one of the principal activities of PL. Since illness, along with other forms of suffering, is understood to be a warning from deity that something in one's thinking is amiss, its cure is primarily a function of the order's ministry of restoration. However, PL does not ignore the field of medicine. At the headquarters, there is a small hospital (subsequently to be replaced by a much larger one), staffed by qualified medical doctors, all of whom are PL members. These doctors are chiefly interested in psychosomatic medicine and are regularly engaged in research in this field. In this connection, PL claims to have discovered during the 1940's that pressure and frustration are causative factors in heart disease and stomach disorder.[28]

THE ARTS

An article in a popular Japanese magazine suggests that the full slogan of PL Kyodan should be " 'Life is art'—and art is religion."[29] This is at most only a mild exaggeration, for there is much to indicate that, above all else, PL is a patron of the arts. It is significant, for example, that its *leading* publication is a monthly journal entitled *Geijutsu Seikatsu* (*Life of Art*), devoted to the whole range of the arts—Japanese and foreign, classical and modern—but containing no articles on specifically religious subjects. This, incidentally, is a first-class art journal, employing leading writers and including many excellent color photographs. Also, among the myriads of publications issued by the New Religions, it is one of the very few that can be found regularly on the newsstands.

Furthermore, as we have stated, there are works of art almost everywhere at the PL headquarters, but identifiable religious motifs are almost entirely absent. Throughout the headquarters, many of the decorative touches have been provided by one of Miki's closest friends, Teshigahara Sofu, an avant-garde artist, who is *not* a member of PL. Perhaps best known as the headmaster of Sogetsu-kai, one of the three largest schools of Japanese flower arranging (*ikebana*), Teshigahara also specializes in abstract sculpture, mobiles, painting, and calligraphy. Examples of his work at the headquarters are so numerous that they seem to represent the norm for PL taste in these media.

We have noted the emphasis placed upon the arts in the program of ministerial training. PL sponsors still other artistic endeavors. Varied and numerous, these include painting and sculpture exhibits, *kabuki* dramas, dance festivals, and music concerts.

Reflections

What is the real character and meaning of PL Kyodan's commitment to modernity? In the style of its external trappings, this sect is ultramodern; in the patterns of human relationship that it exemplifies and fosters, it is generally conservative and at times even reactionary. What are the factors in this enigma that must be sorted out if one is to understand the nature, appeal, and long-range significance of this movement? It is premature at this time to hope to answer these questions definitively, but it may be possible to make a few observations that will contribute to their clarification.

To many outside observers, the authoritarianism and paternalism of the *Oshieoya* must be disturbing. Most so-called progressive Japanese also would find them objectionable. Yet when considered within the context of contemporary Japanese society, these traits of the PL leader are not really inordinate. The fact is that Miki Tokuchika exemplifies the successful executive type in present-day Japan. It is no mere happenstance that his fellow religionists have elected him to the highest posts in their interfaith associations,[30] for among them he is the administrator par excellence. Actually, his closest counterparts are the heads of commercial, industrial, and governmental enterprises. With them he shares essentially the same ethics, many of the same methods, and the same view of society and the nature of man. Though the way of life over which these men preside may be viewed by many—both Japanese and non-Japanese—as anachronistic, it is indisputably true that for a large proportion of the Japanese people, this is the very way of life in which they feel most comfortable and secure. They would be most reluctant and fearful to leave this behind, even though, almost unanimously, they are also attracted to modern ways.

But what can we say about PL's obsession with modern, largely avant-garde art? Art as a kind of religion is in itself nothing new in Japan. The Japanese are a feeling people, for whom, through many centuries and in many circumstances, art has been a means of spiritual fulfillment and/or escape from reality. Much of the well-deserved reputation of the Japanese as an artistic people rests upon this circumstance; but if we are to see its relation to our present concern, we must also be quite clear that Japanese aesthetic taste is not uniform. Indeed, there are two diverse aesthetic traditions prominent in Japanese art: one we may call the "art of poverty," the other the "art of abundance." The former was developed by and among a people who "had been denied the luxury of really satisfying their human desires, so they . . . suppressed them and found ways to enjoy poverty." It reflects "the taste of a people who had learned to bear the meagerness of their lives by cultivating a fondness for simple things."[31] A single flower or branch in the *tokonoma*, the suggestiveness of a few brush strokes in *sumie*, the primitive design and unpainted wood of Ise Shrine—these are products of this tradition, which uses understatement and restraint to isolate the uncluttered simplicity which alone seems to have meaning in a cluttered life.

By contrast, the other tradition finds beauty in the unrestrained proliferation of ornamentation. Its motto is this famous line: "Never say *kekkō* ["magnificent"] until you have seen Nikko." Its best examples are the buildings of Nikko, gorgeous beyond description, erected by the Tokugawa rulers at the height of their power and dedicated unashamedly to the glorification of man. Essentially the same taste was also regnant in the bourgeois culture that emerged during the Tokugawa period, when the merchant class, controlling much of the nation's wealth but living a socially precarious existence, turned to hedonism in order to salvage what they could of their material gain. The bold and sensual character of this life was reflected in the arts of the new urban society, especially in the *kabuki* and *bunraku* (puppet) dramas; and the arts, in turn, though brilliant and dynamic, became chiefly a source of entertainment rather than enlightenment.

The artistic taste of PL Kyodan, a merchant-oriented community, belongs principally to this latter tradition. Fed, if not by abundance, then by the aspiration to abundance, it wants a blossom on every stem. To a very significant extent, this sect is an epicurean movement that values the enjoyment of lavish beauty and of "gracious living" as a high level of religious achievement.

What, then, is the essential function of PL Kyodan? Is it perhaps to serve as a kind of halfway house in which one who finds comfort and security in a life of obedience can feel at home but which is also a sort of never-never land wherein one can share without risk in the excitement of a new world?

Seichō no Ie:
Divine Science and Nationalism

In the vicinity of Harajuku Station in Tokyo, there are three distinctive establishments that are intimately associated with the national life and character of Japan: the Meiji Shrine, the imperial railway station, and the Togo Shrine. By far the most famous and impressive of these is the Meiji Shrine, named for and dedicated to the most illustrious of all the Japanese emperors (reigned 1868–1912) and situated in the midst of one hundred and seventy-nine beautifully wooded and landscaped acres. Overlooking this reservation and standing near the public station is the large covered train platform reserved exclusively for the use of the Emperor and his family on those rather infrequent occasions when they journey outside the capital. Removed from these two by only a few hundred yards is the Togo Shrine, dedicated to Admiral Togo Heihachiro (1847–1934), one of the most renowned heroes of the Russo-Japanese War. Adjacent to this shrine stands the large red-brick building that serves as the headquarters of *Seichō no Ie*, "House of Growth."

Despite the proximity of these other three institutions, the headquarters of Seicho no Ie are in a relatively quiet, largely residential sector of Tokyo. Furthermore, although the headquarters building is itself an architectural novelty, it is situated rather inconspicuously. The front of the structure is not fully visible from any of the main thoroughfares, and from most of the angles from which it can be viewed by passersby, only the building's cylindrical tower and its red-and-white Japanese flag are likely to be seen. Thus, in certain respects, it might appear that Seicho no Ie has selected its site and erected its headquarters with less regard for the distinctive and the dramatic than have most of the other successful new religious movements. This may indeed be the case; however, for reasons that will become apparent, it seems significant that, whether by design or by chance, the headquarters of Seicho no Ie are located within a *de facto* complex of national symbols that call to mind two formerly dominant aspects of Japanese life and character: the unique status of the Emperor and the incomparable virtue of loyal service to the nation.

If one approaches this headquarters building from the front, his attention certainly will be attracted by a large white statue mounted on a pedestal above the main entrance. It is a standing male figure, bearded and robed, with a halo about his head. In his left hand he holds a scroll, and his right hand, forefinger extended, is upraised in a teaching gesture. This figure is said to represent God or the Eternal Christ, but many observers have been heard to remark that, except for the beard, the countenance is that of Taniguchi Masaharu, the founder of Seicho no Ie.

Taniguchi and the Truth of Life

Taniguchi Masaharu is a man of arresting appearance. He wears his hair long, in a fashion which used to be quite common among Japanese scholars but which nowadays is to be seen only occasionally. He has a sensitive face, the natural paleness of which is accentuated by a mustache and a very high forehead. His voice is refined and well modulated. For his public appearances, he often wears a formal kimono. Withal, his manner is self-possessed and dignified.

The image of himself that he apparently wishes to project is that of a scholar and a mystic. In the publication by-lines and advertisements of Seicho no Ie, he is listed as a PhD; however, so far as I have been able to ascertain, he actually holds no earned academic degree of any kind. As a writer, though, he produces an almost unbelievably prodigious quantity of work. He is credited with having written more than three hundred books, and he contributes regularly to the five monthly magazines that his sect publishes. According to his own claim, this literary outpouring is largely the product of divine inspiration. "Of course," he says, "the pen in my hand writes the spiritual teachings . . . , but once I sit at my desk to write . . . , I am no longer the ordinary 'I.' Holy spirit comes over and inspires me."[1] He represents himself, therefore, as a medium of revelation and thus feels constrained to say: "I am not the founder but the finder of the spiritual truth of Seicho no Ie."[2]

As seen by the followers of Seicho no Ie, Taniguchi is an exemplary man of remarkable talent and power. As have so many among them, he has experienced intense personal hardship and anguish, but unlike themselves, his superior determination and his love of pity have enabled him to overcome it all. They see in him a man who has progressed spiritually to the point where he is in fact the recipient of divine revelation and the instrument of divine power. He displays more than just a scholar's insight in his ability to distill the essence of truth from all the great repositories of revelation and to present it in easily understood expositions as the way and the power for living in the modern world.

Taniguchi's critics (and they are numerous) see him rather differently. The charge they make most frequently is that he is an obsessive refugee from reality and an unmitigated opportunist. They see him, furthermore, as a pseudoscholar, who admittedly is a clever and active writer but whose proficiency in dealing firsthand with great ideas and literature is limited almost entirely to skillful name-dropping. He is, in his detractors' judgment, an unoriginal man whose principal indebtedness is to the work of second-rate authors.

What are the foundations in fact of the conflicting appraisals of this man? The career of Taniguchi is so replete with confusion

and even lurid incidents as to seem almost improbable. Yet, for
the most part, it has not been left to critics and gossipmongers
to ferret out the sometimes shocking details in order to piece
together the story. As if to offer his own "deliverance" as proof
of the promises he makes to others, Taniguchi has written his
own "confessions" and published them, prominently, in the *Seimei
no Jissō* (*Truth of Life*), the scripture of Seicho no Ie.[3] This is a
story compounded of five principal ingredients: (1) a person of
sensitive temperament with an inquisitive mind and a literary
gift, (2) a social environment that is restricting and threatening,
(3) a succession of traumatic personal involvements that create
anxiety and bewilderment and encourage escapism, (4) the discovery of other persons in similar predicaments and of one's own
power to speak to them persuasively and comfortingly, and
(5) exposure to a book that says what one has sought to say (and
even more) and that prescribes a way by which one may become
a teacher and a "great philosopher."

Taniguchi was born in 1893 in a village near Kobe. He was
adopted, at the age of four, by his aunt and her husband and
was reared in their household as their second son. At the age of
nineteen, after only a mildly presageful childhood and youth,
he enrolled in the literature department of Waseda University in
Tokyo to major in English literature. For much of the next two
decades, his life was a turbulent one.

Taniguchi entered the literature department of the university
in defiance of the wishes of his family but with the support,
nevertheless, of an allowance from his aunt. While there, exposed
for the first time to the works of such men as Schopenhauer,
Tolstoi, Oscar Wilde, and Nietzsche, he became virtually intoxi-
cated with ideas, which he was incapable of reducing to order
but which impelled him to want to "write" some drama in his
own life. In this mood, he began a love affair with a seventeen-
year-old daughter of a stevedore. This led to ugly and embarrassing showdowns with both their families. Taniguchi's aunt
discontinued his allowance, and eventually he deserted the girl.
In retrospect, he has admitted to cowardice, but he has also
rationalized his action by saying that love alone does not make
life. His scholarly analysts insist that this was but one in a series

of crucial experiences in which Taniguchi, "beaten by realities," had to retreat from them to seek refuge elsewhere.[4]

Thus, in 1914, his university career aborted, Taniguchi found employment in a cotton-spinning company. Trying hard to better himself, he also enrolled in a night school and acquired a side job as a translator. Soon, however, he became involved simultaneously in affairs with two girls, one a prostitute and the other a niece of one of his company superiors. From the prostitute he contracted a venereal disease, and he began to fear that he had communicated it to the other girl. Tortured by guilt and the fear of being fired, he passed through a period of excruciating anxiety, during which he sought help, unsuccessfully, from a man noted for his cures by hypnosis. Ultimately his own physical affliction was cured by medical treatment and surgery; but in his concern for the girl, he began to study spiritual healing in the hope that, without her being aware of it, he could heal her also. In this way, it appears, he began to console himself by self-deception. He denied the fact of contagiousness. It was, he decided, only a way of thinking.

This episode ended with his being rebuffed by both girls. Chastened, he turned from the love of women to the love of laborers and, for a while, worked diligently for their welfare. He rose quickly to a supervisory position; but he did not really enjoy this role and, after a quarrel with a superior, left the factory.

For some time thereafter, Taniguchi's principal interest was in spiritualism, which he studied under several auspices. In 1917, his quest took him to Omoto-kyo. Here his literary talents soon were recognized, and he was employed as a writer and editor for publications of the sect. Still troubled by a sense of guilt for his former profligacy, he adopted the role of an ascetic penitent, referring to himself as "the St. Francis of Omoto." One may wonder, however, how deeply he was committed to achieving absolution, for it was not long until he was attracted to two women, employees of Omoto, and began to court both of them. In this instance, though, the long-range result was salutary. In 1920, he married one of them, Teruko, in a ceremony that was attended by Deguchi Onisaburo, the head of the sect.

Was Taniguchi's entrance into Omoto chiefly an attempt to

escape reality and find refuge in mysticism? Perhaps it was. At least it seems evident that this action was less a commitment than an experiment; although, to be sure, this Omoto interlude did contribute significantly to the shaping of his eventual career. When he entered this sect, he seems already to have been wedded to the idea—which was sharpened there and later became his fundamental dogma—that illness is a creation of mind and therefore can be healed by mind. While there, he also began to form another basic conviction to which Omoto teaching contributed, namely, that sin and divine punishment are unreal. Nevertheless, Taniguchi's own sense of indebtedness or loyalty to the sect itself seems never to have been very strong. Soon after the First Omoto Incident, in 1921, Taniguchi withdrew from the sect to avoid having to face persecution.

In that same year, Taniguchi and his wife moved to Tokyo. This was the beginning of what was to be for them a long period of struggle against the demoralizing effects of social unrest, natural catastrophe, ill health, and poverty. Already, however, Taniguchi had developed a tendency to counter all misfortunes with a determined optimism, saying in effect that these untoward realities were not really real. Then, rather suddenly, he discovered that there was a market for such an attitude.

It was a time of economic depression, and Taniguchi found that many hard-pressed people, especially students and company employees, were reading religious literature and getting together for discussions of "life," in the hope of finding some means of relief. For people such as these, he wrote and published an essay in which he set forth what he himself had been thinking. Probably to his considerable surprise, the piece sold so well that for a while he was able to support himself from its proceeds.

In this essay the foundation of the later Seicho no Ie philosophy was being laid. On the one hand, it was a diatribe against all doctrines of sin and judgment; on the other hand, it was an appeal for stressing the brighter side of life. The material, he said, is only the shadow of the mind. To escape from suffering, one begins with his own wish and then realizes it through the power of mind. Interestingly, in fashioning these concepts, Taniguchi thought himself to be under the influence of the philosophers Bergson and Hegel. Although a qualified critic might regard this purported lineage as, at most, rather tenuous, it is important to note in passing that just such an appeal to the authority of renowned personalities and literature was to become one of Taniguchi's most characteristic devices.

In 1923, after fleeing from the great Kanto earthquake that devastated Tokyo, Taniguchi took his wife and infant daughter to live with his adoptive parents in Kobe. Relations in the home were tense, and poverty was a continuing problem. However, it appears that by that time, Taniguchi was pointed so clearly in the direction that his subsequent career was to assume that each experience of the next six years somehow contributed to the launching of that career. His daughter became ill, but because there was no money for a doctor, Taniguchi treated her himself, with unanticipated success. He attended a seance of a spiritualist medium, and while he knew that the whole show was faked, he was much surprised and impressed by the eloquence of the medium. He discovered a book entitled *The Law of Mind in Action*[5] that seemed to say what he wanted to say. In it, so he thought, he had found a viable combination of Christian theism and Buddhist pantheism; here also he had further proof for his contention that he who grasps the principle of mind can rule over the material. It was also during this period that the writings of Sigmund Freud, newly translated and circulating widely among the Japanese, came to Taniguchi's attention.

Considering all these factors, those who see Taniguchi as an opportunist contend that he found his "mission" then in the exciting possibility of creating a marketable product by joining the principle of mind over matter to the emergent popular psychologism.[6] On the other hand, the orthodox explanation is that in 1929, Taniguchi received the divine message that the material does not exist—there is only *jissō* ("reality"), the divine life of the mind, the original and essential character of man. Immediately thereafter, so it is said, he proved himself able to control his own fate. Desperately needing employment, he decided to sit thinking that a good job awaited him. Having sat thus for a month, he saw a notice that an oil company had an opening for a translator. He got the job, which paid a large salary, and suddenly it seemed that the world had turned for him.

While working for this company, in March of 1930 Taniguchi

began publishing a magazine, in the first issue of which he announced the beginning of Seicho no Ie. Describing the critical, even desperate, character of the situation then current, he promised blessings for mankind in the form of happiness and victory over illness and poverty. The purpose of the new enterprise, he said, would be to study the principles of mind and apply them to practical life. The new magazine was immediately popular. In June, Taniguchi organized a chapter of ten subscribers and opened the way for a large-scale organization by promising direct guidance from headquarters to all such groups of ten or more.

When his magazine was well established, Taniguchi gathered the first several issues and published them together as the initial volume of *Seimei no Jissō* (*Truth of Life*), his magnum opus (which subsequently has grown to more than forty volumes and ranks as one of Japan's all-time best sellers). Thus launched as the head of a new enterprise, Taniguchi left the oil company and returned to Tokyo, where he began to solidify the organization of Seicho no Ie.

Seichō no Ie *and Chauvinism*

Seicho no Ie was begun in 1930. The decade that followed was a time of rapidly escalating militarism; the burgeoning of patriotic societies[7] overshadowed the rise of new religious organizations, and the government was ever watchful for ideological criminals. Though there were many small sects in existence even then, theirs was a precarious status. Only a few of them, by devising acceptable patterns of accommodation to the purposes and policies of the militarist regime, were able to prosper. Seicho no Ie was one of these. However, it must be made clear that the importance of this datum does not lie in this one movement's support of the war effort. Virtually all Japanese religious groups eventually cooperated in that cause to some degree. Rather, according to a team of Japanese university professors, its significance lies in the quality of Taniguchi's own personal involvement. He was, they say, "the most remarkable of the fascists."[8] This is a serious charge. What is the history of the matter?

Seicho no Ie has been a religious movement since its inception; however, during the more than three decades of its history, its official status has been altered repeatedly either by Taniguchi's design or with his consent. This seeming vacillation is in part a record of opportunistic decision intended to gain certain tactical advantages in the diverse circumstances under which the movement has functioned. It is also in part the result of forced compliance with governmental directives, which at times laid down the only conditions under which any organization might exist at all. On both counts, however, the history of Seicho no Ie is a remarkable chronicle of expediency.

Originally, Seicho no Ie was organized as a publishing company under capitalistic management. The "believers" initially were "subscribers." They were free from all obligation to make financial contributions to the movement, but if they wished to do so, they could invest in the company and receive dividends from it. By drawing only a regular salary, Taniguchi and the other officials of the new venture placed themselves in a position from which they could criticize the established religions for fleecing people of their money.

In 1936, Seicho no Ie was re-registered as a *kyōka-dantai*, a term which is sometimes translated as "religious organization" or "social organization" but which seems to carry a connotation of "suprareligious" or "spiritual" and to suggest enlightenment by essential truth. By the time of this revision, Japan was deeply involved in warfare to expand and consolidate its territorial holdings on the Asian mainland, and one of the principal problems constantly confronting the militarist government as it pursued this course was to maintain the morale and support of the Japanese populace. By redefining their organization as a *kyōka-dantai*, the leaders of Seicho no Ie seemed to indicate their willingness to cooperate with the government in the task of "edifying" the people. In ways that we shall note subsequently, they actually proceeded to do so.

With the promulgation of the Religious Bodies Law (Shūkyō Dantai Hō) in 1939, the Japanese government moved to gain absolute control over all religious organizations—to make them, in effect, service and propaganda agencies of the militarist effort.

In 1941, Seicho no Ie officially became a religious organization under the provisions of this law and was thus subject to supervision by the Minister of Education. One of the stipulations of this law was that responsibility had to be concentrated in the hands of a single leader who was approved by the government.[9] It would appear that Taniguchi was the very type of man whose presence in such a position would have been especially gratifying to the militarist leaders.

"The self-assurance of popular chauvinism," says Richard Storry, "rested on the belief that Japan possessed exceptional spiritual advantages, outweighing more material factors not in her favour."[10] This belief could be fed by Taniguchi's teachings with little or no accommodation. Furthermore, at the very time when the rapid production of large quantities of essential goods was required, Seicho no Ie was able to advance among small and medium-sized factories, there to be a spokesman for improved efficiency and to promise a reduction in accidents and sickness. It is said, for example, that in one cotton-spinning company in Tokyo, placing a copy of the Seicho no Ie magazine in every room of the plant proved to be very effective in decreasing anti-war sentiment and activity. Such effective cooperation no doubt redounded also to the benefit of Seicho no Ie, for the movement was permitted to propagate even in the Japanese-occupied areas of the Asian mainland. In 1942 and 1944, Taniguchi himself visited the groups that had been organized in Manchuria.

There were times, indeed, when Taniguchi's fervor seems actually to have exceeded that of the militarists themselves. One such instance was his undertaking a slogan campaign to offset what he considered to be a defeatist attitude on the part of the army. According to Taniguchi's own account of this matter,[11] people were singing, at the insistence of the army, a song that was ordaining their defeat:

> *Umi yukaba mizuku kabane*
> *Yama yukaba kusamusu kabane.*[12]

> If you go to the sea, you will become a
> corpse left in the water;
> If you go to the mountain, you will become
> a corpse covered by grass.

Presumably the purpose of such a song was to inculcate a stoical attitude toward death; but to Taniguchi, who believed firmly in the power of words, it was the song of doom, for, he insisted, whatever is expressed in words will be realized. Therefore, he began to compose counterslogans, such as, *Kōgun hisshō, hisshō seikan*, which means, "The Imperial Army always will win and, having won, will return alive." By the end of the war, Taniguchi claims, he had prepared by his own hand fifty thousand copies of this slogan, which he distributed among the members of Seicho no Ie; however, at the same time, he says, seventy million people in Japan and thirty million in Manchuria were singing the army's song. Therefore, since the power of his winning word was inferior to that of the losing word, Japan had to lose the war.

In the postwar years, Taniguchi has tried very hard to explain his active support of the war effort in such a way as to avoid any stigmatization that would be permanently damaging or embarrassing, and for the most part he has succeeded. He defends himself by declaring that Seicho no Ie had never taught that the war was a righteous or holy war but that since Japan was in fact at war, it was only normal that he and his organization should do their utmost to help their country to win. His actions, therefore, were simply the natural response of a loyal citizen, not that of the militarist he is accused of having been. Indeed, he insists that anyone can see by examining his slogan campaign that his standpoint actually was the opposite of that of the militarists. This may seem to be a quaint bit of casuistry, which becomes all the more remarkable when considered in the light of the following claim:

> If the whole of the Japanese nation had become members of Seicho no Ie at an early date and had been praying for victory, then I think Japan would have won the war. I do not say this without proof. The proof is that, at the end of the war, all of the military ships which had not been damaged had members of Seicho no Ie on board.[13]

Perhaps it would be more reassuring to hear him say that if the nation had turned unreservedly to Seicho no Ie, the war could have been avoided altogether; for as the explanation now stands, it comes at least dangerously close to implying, despite his earlier disclaimer, that the war was potentially a holy war—

that divine sanction for victory could have been achieved if the
right people had been in charge.

At the end of World War II, because of their conspicuous
support of militarism, Taniguchi and some of his staff were purged
by the Occupation authorities. In effect, this meant only that
they were debarred from being directly associated with a publishing enterprise; they could still legitimately be affiliated with
a religious organization. Consequently, even though the popularity of Seicho no Ie did decline rather sharply in the surge of
antimilitarist resentment immediately after the war, Taniguchi
was able to hold his enterprise together during the Occupation
by complying with certain legal technicalities. Thus, in 1946, the
publishing interests were incorporated as a separate company,
called the Kyōbunsha. Taniguchi and his purged colleagues
gathered together the remaining interests and organized a specifically religious movement, the *Seichō no Ie Kyōdan*, which
was incorporated under the Religious Corporations Ordinance
(Shūkyō Hōjin Rei, 1945) and its successor, the Religious Juridical
Persons Law (Shūkyō Hōjin Hō, 1951). Through this agency,
Taniguchi was able to continue to function as a "religious"
teacher throughout the period of the Occupation.

Predictably, the end of the Occupation, in 1952, was the signal
and the occasion for significant changes to be made in Seicho
no Ie. Of course, its publishing activities were quickly resumed;
even more important, steps were taken to alter the definition and
public image of the organization itself. The term *kyōdan*, which
had identified Seicho no Ie as a specifically "religious" movement, soon was dropped from the name, and the movement later
was withdrawn from membership in the Union of New Religious
Organizations (Shinshūren). These were revealing developments.

The name was changed because, in the view of the leaders,
the term *kyōdan* seemed to restrict the organization too severely
or exclusively to the religious sphere; whereas its actual goal was
and is to attract people on the basis of a much wider appeal.
Possibly even some who have ill feeling toward religion may
nevertheless be attracted to Seicho no Ie.[14] A similar motivation
also lay behind the withdrawal from the Shinshūren. The leaders
wish to avoid being typed as just another in a group of religious

sects. Rather, they prefer to advertise Seicho no Ie as a "truth" movement that transcends all sectarian religion. This perspective is spelled out by Taniguchi himself in the following ways:

> The reason why Seicho no Ie has quit the Shinshūren is not in order to identify itself as being different from the other *shinkō shūkyō*, but in order to make it clear that Seicho no Ie is the scene of truth, preaching the truth common to every sect and every religion. The world in general has tried to classify Seicho no Ie in a particular category of *shinkō shūkyō*.[15]

> Seicho no Ie has left the Shinshūren because it is not a religion. Rather it preaches the truth common to every kind of religion. If Seicho no Ie belongs to the group of *shinkō shūkyō*, it identifies itself with a group which is separate from the established religions such as Buddhism and Christianity. If Seicho no Ie belongs to the *shinkō shūkyō* group which confronts the established religions, then it cannot preach the truth that all religions are one.[16]

In retrospect, it is obvious that the withdrawal of the Occupation forces meant more to Seicho no Ie than just the end of mildly troublesome regulations. Its greater significance lay in the fact that for the Japanese people, this event psychologically was a very important juncture, following which there began to develop among them a marked tendency toward a reactionary mood. Nothing else could have been of greater benefit to Seicho no Ie. Immediately it began to regain strength rapidly.[17] Disavowing identification as a religion, therefore, was essentially a move to exploit this new opportunity. Subsequently, as the reactionary mood has continued to grow, a reactionary line has become increasingly prominent in the pronouncements and program of Seicho no Ie, and the organization has identified itself with nearly all the ultraconservative causes.

Early in this chapter, we indicated that Taniguchi's detractors see him as a chameleonlike, unprincipled opportunist. Their evidence, we must agree, is impressive. During wartime, he seems to have been an excessively vigorous advocate of militarism and Emperor worship. During the Occupation, he lent his support to democracy. In more recent years, with the marked increase of conservative reaction, he is becoming a kind of patron of resurgent patriots, who at last are recovering their self-respect and love of country. This pattern of vacillation—if such it is—has been followed also at every stage by the organization he heads.

Perhaps, therefore, the case should be closed and Taniguchi dismissed derisively from any further consideration; but if there is any lesson that one should learn from the history of religions, it is this: always take at least a second look at the work of the persuasive man who is discredited because of his opportunism, for sheer opportunism is rarely the key to the durability of a religious movement. Accordingly, we shall now examine Seicho no Ie more carefully in terms of the four characteristics that are thought to be its most important ones: (1) "a religious body linked with real life," (2) "a movement reducing all teachings to one," (3) propagation through literature, and (4) extensive social activity.

"A Religious Body Linked with Real Life"

As its history indicates, Seicho no Ie stands ready to assume almost any configuration that will enable it to flourish in apparent relevance to the conditions of its environment. Therefore, it denies that it is a religion (for such a label seems prejudicial to its cause) and chooses rather to speak of itself as "a religious body linked with real life" (*Jisseikatsu to musubi-tsuita kyōka-dantai*). In part, this is perhaps a candid acknowledgement that this organization wants always to be able to claim the advantages both of being a religion and of not being one. At the same time, as we shall attempt to show, this characterization does describe quite well both the basic orientation and the far-ranging interests of this movement.

In its every aspect, Seicho no Ie is dominated by the mind, the voice, and the presence of its founder and president, Taniguchi Masaharu, who is essentially a charismatic religious personality. Together with the members of his family—Teruko, his wife; Emiko, their daughter and only child; and Seicho, whom the Taniguchis adopted and who is the husband of their daughter[18]—he lives above the organization as its medium of revelation and power. This entire "holy family" is surrounded by a mystic aura.

The organization of Seicho no Ie, being highly centralized and hierarchical, is fairly typical of the New Religions as a whole. The preeminently authoritative body is the Hombu (headquarters), with offices in Tokyo. Thereafter, in descending order, are the regional, prefectural, and local administrative agencies. The movement also has gone abroad—carried there chiefly by Japanese emigrants and Taniguchi's lecture tours—and has established centers in such major cities as Honolulu, Los Angeles, Vancouver, São Paulo, and Mexico City.[19]

More than any other New Religion thus far, Seicho no Ie appeals to middle- and upper-class Japanese, including a fair number of intellectuals. Perhaps in part this accounts for the fact that its constituency is somewhat less closely knit than those of other movements. Many of the sect's followers are principally interested in the ideas and special causes that it espouses and have relatively little need to be identified with an intimate community—although let us hasten to add that Seicho no Ie is fully prepared, along with the other sects, to meet this need where it exists. Not infrequently, a member of Seicho no Ie is simultaneously a member of an established religion, such as Buddhism or Christianity. Seicho no Ie is quite happy to have it so, since the sect sees itself not as a religion but as a religious body teaching the truth that is common to all religions. Indeed, one of its avowed purposes is to make better Buddhists of Buddhists and better Christians of Christians.[20]

Individually, the constituency of Seicho no Ie is divisible into three groups: members, subscribers, and inquirers. The members are those who make regular monthly financial contributions to headquarters. These are still further differentiated and ranked according to whether they give 100, 200, or 1,000 yen per month.[21] Those in the latter two brackets also help support the local branch, since one-half of their contribution is returned for local use. The subscribers are those who purchase annual subscriptions to one or more of the five monthly magazines published by Seicho no Ie or who regularly buy them as they appear. The inquirers are those who may attend meetings and read the literature but have not yet become formally either members or subscribers. Because of the inquisitiveness and hopefulness elicited by the varied appeal of Seicho no Ie, this group seems always to be fairly large. Such persons are assured of a continuing welcome, and it appears that in all gatherings where inquirers are presumed to be present, considerable care is given to presenting the teaching at a level sufficiently elementary to enable any newcomer to understand it.

The local branch, called the *sōai-kai* ("mutual-love society"), includes the local adult male members plus three associations constituted on the basis of sex or age: (1) Shirahato-kai (White Dove Society), the women's association, (2) Seinen-kai (Youth Association), post-high school to thirty-five years of age, and (3) Kokosei-renmei (High-school Students' Movement). In addition to their involvement in local activities, the constituencies of these three associations also have opportunities to participate in training sessions, rallies, and conferences organized at the prefectural, regional, and national levels. There is a sustained effort throughout the entire organization to increase dedicated activity at the local level and, at the same time, to promote a sense of unity and loyalty on behalf of the total movement.

While the principal teachings and much of the program of Seicho no Ie are handed down from headquarters, their dissemination or implementation depends to a considerable extent upon the cooperation and initiative of local followers. Perhaps again reflecting the somewhat higher sophistication of its adherents, Seicho no Ie must rely upon obedience relatively less and upon persuasion relatively more than most of the other New Religions. This is evident at several points. For example, instruction throughout the movement is provided by two orders of teachers: the "headquarters teachers" (*hombu kōshi*), about seventy full-time staff members who are appointed by headquarters, and the "local teachers" (*chihō kōshi*), more than three thousand part-time volunteers. The former are itinerant experts available wherever and whenever their services are needed, but much of the effectiveness of the movement depends rather upon the motivation of the local teachers. Another instance is the movement's reliance upon local sponsors for its radio broadcasts. Every Sunday morning, a radio program featuring an address by Taniguchi is broadcast from the Tokyo headquarters, but this program could not be heard in many localities in Japan if it were not for the sponsorship of local business firms whose executives are supporters of Seicho no Ie. Also, the provision of adequate training facilities seems to depend mainly upon local planning and initiative. One of my own most memorable experiences in association with Seicho no Ie was attending a weekend youth retreat (March 7–8, 1964) in the Hanayama Training Center near Wakayama. These excellent facilities, completed only a short time previously, had been constructed by local businessmen, one of whom was the principal speaker for the two-day program.

Among the most important regular local activities are the daily early-morning service for meditation (*shinsōkan*) and the monthly meeting of the *sōai-kai*. The early-morning service, usually scheduled at six o'clock, is especially important to the most devout believers. It consists principally in a form of meditation that Taniguchi has adapted from an Omoto practice. Called *shinsōkan* (literally, "divine concept contemplation") and defined by Taniguchi as "prayerful meditation," this is a means by which the believer may realize his oneness with deity. The technique is not easily mastered. It begins with the assuming of a prescribed posture. The devotee sits on his feet on a cushion; his head and upper body are erect; the palms of his hands, fingers pointing upward, are pressed together lightly in front of his face; his elbows are extended; his eyes are closed. At first, a person can remain thus for only a few minutes; but with patience and practice, he not only will increase his endurance but also eventually will achieve a kind of hypnotic state of spiritual empowerment. By this means, it is claimed, many healings and other remarkable transformations are effected.

The monthly meeting of the local association (*sōai-kai*) frequently is held in the home of one of the members. One such meeting that I visited in a large home in Nigawa was attended by about seventy-five people. The speaker on this occasion was a university professor from Osaka. Though he spoke for more than two hours, his lecture was so vivid and liberally interspersed with anecdotes and humor that no one seemed to grow restless. His presentation was followed by a number of personal testimonies, relating stories of illness and family tension that had been cleared up through accepting the teachings of Seicho no Ie. These were surprisingly frank utterances. The meeting was concluded with a period of informal fellowship and the serving of refreshments.

Through all its activities, Seicho no Ie wishes to demonstrate the usefulness of its teachings. In a flattering tribute to the movement, former Prime Minister Hatoyama Ichiro characterized the *Seimei no Jissō* as *kindai ningengaku*, "modern anthropology" or "modern human science"—teachings that actually lead people to happiness, help them to establish their homes in harmony, and advance social welfare. From Taniguchi's standpoint, the Prime Minister could scarcely have chosen a more apt designation.[22]

While Seicho no Ie promises relief from all human problems, it gives major attention to the healing of physical illness. Over and over again, Taniguchi reiterates the thesis that underlies his diagnosis of sickness, and many of his books are little more than collections of the case histories and testimonials of those who have been healed through his ministry. Man, he says, is the child of the deity (God or Buddha) and is therefore originally and naturally pure. The phenomenal world (that is, man's environment and bodily existence), since it is only the manifestation of one's mind, originally is free from all illness and unhappiness, and it remains so just as long as one's mind stays uncorrupted. However, with the rise of unnatural thoughts, unnatural conditions are manifested phenomenally—among them, illness and disease. By becoming obsessed with the apparent "reality" of these manifestations, the mind proceeds to proliferate them still further. Thus, it is the belief that disease is infectious that makes it so, and it is the fear of disease that renders disease fearful.[23]

The way to be healed, therefore, is to correct one's wrong ways of thinking and thus remove the cause of those symbolizations or reflections of mind that the world calls illness. While the range of possible mental aberrancies certainly is vast, "lack of gratitude" is considered to be basic to all the rest.[24] Hence, developing and interiorizing an attitude of gratefulness, both *to* and *for* all persons and things, are in most instances the surest ways either to cure an illness or to prevent its arising. Accordingly, the watchword among Seicho no Ie devotees is *Arigatō gozaimasu,* "Thank you very much." It is used, apparently in almost any circumstance, as a greeting or a countersign; but it also has essentially the force of a magical incantation (though no teacher of Seicho no Ie would consent to this terminology), for another of the hallmarks of this movement is the doctrine of the "power of words" (*kotoba no chikara*): whatever is expressed in words will be manifested.

"A Movement Reducing All Teachings to One"

Seicho no Ie insists that it teaches the truth that is common to all religions, and it acknowledges that salvation is available in any religion. What, then, is Seicho no Ie's own reason for being? It is, on the one hand, to rekindle the vanishing lights of the various religions, in which long familiarity with sources of truth has led to the neglect or distortion of the truth itself. It is, on the other hand, to extend the awareness within each religion that sources of truth exist in all religions. Therefore, Seicho no Ie appropriates and uses expressions of truth from Buddhism, Christianity, Shinto, and other sources.[25] In so doing, it not only testifies that all have the truth but also bears witness to each that its teaching is unnecessarily limited if it is based only on its own sources.

Because of the eclectic composition of Seicho no Ie doctrine and literature, its critics and hecklers sometimes refer to it as a "department store of religions" or a "religion of excerpts." Spokesmen for the organization itself prefer to speak of it as "a movement reducing all teachings to one" (*Bankyō ki-itsu no undō*)— a movement dedicated to rejuvenating all religions and pointing all mankind anew to the one "Eternal Reality":

When the Christians discover "Christ" not in the material form of Jesus-the-flesh but in the Eternal Divinity who said "Before Abraham was, I Am," when the Buddhists discover Buddha not in Gautama-the-flesh but in the eternal Gautama that told Ananda "All Buddhas in the past are my disciples," when the followers of Seicho no Ie discover Seicho no Ie not in the house where Taniguchi-the-flesh lives but in the Seicho no Ie of Eternal Reality which declared that "All religions will be rejuvenated by Me," religions will no longer have to quarrel on their spheres of influence.[26]

Taniguchi depends upon intuition or spiritual perception to guide him in identifying and interpreting the truth that is expressed in the scriptures and traditions of the various religions. He is principally attracted to Buddhism and Christianity,[27] but he also wishes to be acknowledged as an authoritative interpreter of the Japanese classics, particularly the *Kojiki* and the *Nihonshoki*, eighth-century compilations of Japanese myth and history, and the *Norito*, old Shinto ritual prayers. At this point, Taniguchi's universalism and nationalism are joined, for he seems to be committed a priori to finding all essential truth prefigured in the *authentically* Japanese way of life that is reflected in the ancient classics.

Propagation Through Literature

"In Seicho-no-Ie the word is . . . the training hall for the soul's salvation or the treating room for various diseases."[28] Thus does Taniguchi sum up his reliance on the printed word to accomplish quickly and directly the salutary goals that under other auspices are sought by utilizing special facilities and burdensome techniques. For this reason, he suggests, "it may be appropriate to call Seicho-no-Ie 'literature' or 'art' instead of calling it 'religion.' "[29]

As we have noted, this movement began as a publishing enterprise, and except for the period of the Occupation, the distribution of literature consistently has been its principal means of both reaching and extending its constituency and of financing the organization. In addition to a constant flow of books and tracts—most of them authored by Taniguchi, whose average output is about a book a month—Seicho no Ie publishes five monthly magazines: (1) *Seichō no Ie* (*House of Growth*), (2) *Hikari no Izumi* (*Fountain of Light*), (3) *Risōsekai* (*Ideal World*), a magazine for youth, (4) *Shirahato* (*White Dove*), a magazine for women, and (5) *Seishingaku* (*Mental Science*). Behind this massive output, there is more than just a routine intention to propagate ideas. There is, again, what appears to be an almost obsessive commitment to a belief in the "power of words." Many are believed to be healed or enlightened simply by reading Seicho no Ie publications.

Extensive Social Activity

In their material and economic recovery and development since World War II, the Japanese people have performed near miracles. Yet even as they rejoice in their growing prosperity, they generally are haunted by a sense of failure and misgiving in the face of their ineffectiveness in coping with moral degeneracy. The rapid increase in juvenile delinquency, the corruption of sexual morality, the extremely high incidence of abortion, the continuing high rate of suicide, the chaotic and often lethal traffic conditions, and the over-all increase in all forms of criminality are forcing many Japanese to acknowledge that the stability of their tension-packed, highly competitive society is being seriously undermined by the lack of any real sense of moral responsibility. The one thing that they lost in the war and have been unable to recover, to reconstruct, or to replace is an acknowledged center of value reference by which to determine their identity as persons and the rightness and appropriateness of their choices.

Within Seicho no Ie, this whole problem has become almost a matter of proprietary concern. It is axiomatic that the way of life that it teaches is the original and authentic form of existence for Japan. Therefore it offers to the nation the guidance and the motive power that it needs both for reordering itself internally and for establishing its place in the larger world. However, many Japanese are heedless, and many have been misguided by radical and subversive influences. The result is a task of propagation so urgent and so difficult that the usual method—that is, seeking the salvation of individuals one at a time—must be supplemented by large-scale united action. Therefore, Seicho no Ie is engaging in extensive social activities in an effort to purify society and to influence the alignment of political power.[30]

The social activities essayed by Seicho no Ie are ambitious and far-ranging. From the humanitarian standpoint, the most impressive is their campaign for a higher regard for human life. They see Japan's high rate of suicide, its frequent traffic accidents (including numerous major disasters involving public conveyances), and its annual abortion rate of two million to three million cases as evidence of a growing disregard for human life. The most serious of these, they think, is abortion; hence, they are concentrating on a major effort to make people aware of its evils and to collect signatures petitioning for the revision of legislation governing its practice.[31]

Another major concern is educational reform. In Taniguchi's opinion, the nation's educational system is being subverted by the leftist-dominated Nikkyōso (Japan Teachers Union). Its members, he says, are "like spies of another country." They oppose the displaying of the national flag and the singing of the national anthem. They expose children to shameful historical facts instead of emphasizing the good. As a result, says Taniguchi, the Japanese people are being cut off from their historical foundations. They are losing a sense of history, without which they will become a "race of tramps."[32] In an attempt to counter this influence, Seicho no Ie has organized another association of teachers, the Union of New Educators (Shinkyōikusha renmei).

As one goes beyond these two areas to trace the still wider scope and implementation of Seicho no Ie's social concern, one soon discovers that it encompasses nearly all the evidently reactionary causes. Perhaps the most prominent are the following: (1) revision of the constitution, (2) revival of the celebration of National Foundation Day (Kigensetsu), and (3) increased use of the national flag (*Hinomaru*) and the national anthem (*Kimigayo*). Each of these involves, in one way or another, an effort to return to the symbols and value orientations of the pre-1945 period.

REVISION OF THE CONSTITUTION

Since the end of the Occupation, proposals to revise the so-called MacArthur Constitution of 1947 have been heard from many quarters; and for much of this time, the advisability of doing so has been under consideration by the government. The issue, however, is highly controversial and provocative of emotionalism. This is due in large measure to the prevalence of two irreconcilable views concerning the nature of the document itself. On the one hand, there are those who are convinced that the constitution was forced on the Japanese by an outside power at the time when they were helpless in defeat. To these persons, the constitution seems to be a denial of Japan's right to determine the political structure of its own corporate existence. On the other hand, there are those who regard this document as a joint product, worked out by responsible representatives of both Japan and the United States and reflecting the Japanese wishes then current for the future course of the nation. Unfortunately, the documentary evidence adduced in support of each of these views seems to be inconclusive, and the only persons who could have revealed what really happened went to their graves without having done so.[33]

Obviously, the former of these views is linked with the conservative position that also favors a general revision of the constitution in order to eliminate residual "foreign" obstructionism.[34] This basically is Taniguchi's stand, though he goes even further and demands that the present constitution be totally rescinded and that the Meiji Constitution of 1889 be revived with such emendation as may be necessary to fit it for use in the modern period.[35] Among other things, this would involve the restoration of the sovereignty of the Emperor, who now is defined only as "the symbol of the State and of the unity of the people," and would result in the reestablishment of the "ideal political system," for the people once again would be united harmoniously as members of a single family with the Emperor as their head.[36]

REVIVAL OF KIGENSETSU

National Foundation Day (Kigensetsu) formerly was celebrated throughout Japan on February 11 to commemorate the ascension to the throne of Jimmu Tenno, the legendary first Emperor, an event that, according to reckoning based on mythology, occurred in 660 B.C. Because of its close association with ultranationalism, the celebration was banned during the Occupation and has not yet been reinstated as a national holiday. However, in the early 1950's, rather inconspicuously and apparently spontaneously, a few people here and there, carrying Japanese flags to the Shinto shrines, resumed the celebration on a small scale. Some of these celebrations evolved into lively rallies agitating for the official revival of the holiday, and the Jinja Honchō (Shrine Headquarters) soon began to press the cause determinedly.

In a public-opinion poll conducted by the Japan Broadcasting Corporation (NHK) in 1956, eighty-five per cent of the persons questioned were in favor of restoring Kigensetsu as a national holiday.[37] It seems reasonable to assume that most of these respondents were simply expressing the feeling—which perhaps most other Japanese would share—that it is natural for a nation to commemorate its founding and that, at any rate, it would be good to have another day off from work. When the issue has been approached on an ideological basis, however, opinion has been sharply divided. For the most part, history scholars, led by Prince Mikasa, younger brother of the Emperor, have opposed the revival on the grounds that it would be resurrecting fictitious history.[38] Others, including the most reactionary voices, consistently demand that the celebration be revived and reject all compromise proposals that, as a precondition to revival, would divest the holiday of its jingoistic flavor.[39]

In this controversy, Seicho no Ie sides with the latter. On February 11, 1964, I attended a rain-hampered celebration at Kashiwara Shrine (which is dedicated to Jimmu Tenno and hence is the principal locus for Kigensetsu activity) and was quite interested to see there a group of ten people displaying a large Seicho no Ie banner to publicize their movement's espousal of the cause. Such support is based on Taniguchi's teaching that the tradition of the founding of Japan by Jimmu Tenno is historically sound.[40]

USE OF THE NATIONAL FLAG AND ANTHEM

For many Japanese, since the end of the war the national flag and national anthem have served only as reminders of their nightmarish experiences under militarism. For most such persons, these symbols never again can be made to suggest national unity and purpose. They now fulfill these functions chiefly for the nostalgic or unreconstructed elders. Among the youth of the postwar period, such effort as has been made to acquaint them with the flag and anthem and to instill a sense of respect for them has been countered rather effectively by the stubborn opposition of the Japan Teachers Union (Nikkyōso), which until 1963 actually forbade its members to use the flag and anthem among their students. At that time, the union voted to leave the matter to the discretion of its individual members.[41]

The necessity of recovering a salutary sense of patriotism is now widely acknowledged, even among Japanese moderates, some of whom are also supporting efforts to promote the display of the national flag. Here again, however, the program of Seicho no Ie seems to be linked with the far right. The National Hinomaru Union (Zenkoku Hinomaru Rengōkai), Seicho No Ie's organization to encourage the use of the flag, was refused admittance to the reputedly moderate Council for the Display of the National Flag (Kokki Keiyō Kyōgikai) on the grounds that it was an ultrarightist group.[42]

In this instance, it is not the cause but the manner of its espousal that brings on this stigmatization, for in urging the use of the flag as the symbol of the country, Taniguchi hopes to make it signify a very specific understanding of the "true" meaning of the state and of loyalty to it. On this matter, he is considered to be reactionary, though, to be sure, he is not fully condemned by his own words on this subject. For example, consider the following:

> Our Japanese flag has a circle on it. This expresses the ideal mission of the Japanese race. A circle has everything in it without corners. We make a circle when we make the motion of embracing all. Thus the flag symbolizes the spirit of Japan which envelopes everything.[43]

These words seem innocuous enough, but they are ambiguous. Read within the context of current Japanese endeavors, these words may seem somewhat maudlin but otherwise unthreatening. However, if they should be thrust back into the thoughtway of the *Kokutai no hongi*, formerly the "bible" of Japanese fascism, they would fit there also, and their meaning in that context would be profoundly insidious. With Taniguchi's personal history as an ultranationalist and with his characteristic "both-and" approach, just what is the significance of his interest in the flag and other patriotic symbols?

It is among the members and through the agency of its Youth Association that Seicho no Ie works hardest to awaken interest in patriotism; therefore, it is there in particular that we must look for data that will help clarify questions concerning the real nature and significance of this effort. At a youth retreat that I attended in the spring of 1964, I was allotted a period of about twenty minutes during which I could ask questions of the young people themselves. One question I asked was this: "What aspect of Seicho no Ie doctrine and practice is most appealing to you?" Of the three options given them—love of country, filial piety, and recovery from illness—love of country was chosen by 77.4 per cent (forty-one persons out of a total of fifty-three).

Subsequently, I interviewed some of these young people individually to inquire into the content of this statistic. Their thinking on this matter was quite uniform. It was only natural, they said, for a Japanese to love his country; but since the war, patriotism had often been regarded as outmoded and expendable. They confessed to having been quite confused concerning this problem until they found a workable perspective in the teachings of Taniguchi, who told them that it is in first loving one's own country that a person becomes able eventually to love the whole world. Significantly, although they acknowledged that they were working for causes that are also supported by the rightists, they did not think of themselves as being rightists. Apparently, in their minds, the devotion of Seicho no Ie to the cause of universal truth is an adequate safeguard against a return to chauvinism.

In general, then, it would appear that in the opinion of my young informants, love of country is somehow pivotal both for domestic restoration and harmony and for the extension and preservation of world peace. This notion was especially prominent in the comments of their earnest and articulate presiding officer, a thirty-four-year-old schoolteacher. As he understands the doctrine, it is not an abstract theory of patriotism, nor does it advocate a love of country that is restricted to the Japanese nation itself. Rather, love of country is a necessary first step which works initially to reestablish the ties between a Japanese and his own father or ancestors but which then carries him successively from love of family to love of the community, the city, the nation, and all mankind. Thus understood, the teaching is eminently practical. For example, this young man said, if a man learns to love his nation and to love his neighbors, he may put his love into practice by caring for a boy who is tending toward delinquency. Not by speaking loudly and enthusiastically in the presence of his fellow believers but by living his faith in his community does one give evidence of his true faith.

Reflections

To find fault with the idealism and the enthusiasm of these earnest young people would seem picayune and unnecessarily alarmist. Certainly there can be no question concerning the im-- portance of patriotism for the Japanese. This need is obvious. There is perhaps no reason either to impugn the sincerity or good faith of any of the other Seicho no Ie efforts. Even so, there is an issue here that is not so clear-cut as it may appear to be from the testimony of these young devotees. The question concerns the appropriateness, wisdom, realism, and practicality of trying to resuscitate particular traditions and symbols that, for the most part, can now be appreciated only by those persons of middle age or above who have not rejected them outright and by younger persons who have undergone indoctrination based on the reinterpretation of Japanese mythology. The situation that is feared by many Japanese—even by many who would like to see a general bolstering of national pride and self-confidence—is the return of brainwashing with mythological doctrines and interpretations of history. Thus, their response is something less than enthusiastic when Taniguchi calls for the acknowledgment of such ancient classics as the *Kojiki* and the *Nihon-shoki* as the authoritative sources for defining the Japanese national character. Because of language reforms, most Japanese educated since the war cannot even read this literature. If they acknowledge it to be their authority, they must depend on another, such as Taniguchi, to tell them what it means. Japan has been down that road before.

Risshō Kōsei-kai:
Buddhism of and for Laymen

Iғ A vɪsɪᴛoʀ ғʀoᴍ ᴀʙʀoᴀᴅ is interested in religion and has useful contacts in Tokyo, it is likely that he will be taken to visit the headquarters of *Risshō Kōsei-kai*, a Buddhist lay association, in Suginami-ku in the northwest section of the city. Since the mid-1950's, several hundred such persons have gone there and been cordially received. One of the principal attractions since 1964 has been the splendid and costly Daiseidō (Great Sacred Hall), which is proclaimed to be the largest structure for religious purposes in the East. However, if the sample of opinion to which I have access is an accurate index, the feature that through the years has been most impressive to foreign visitors is the sight of thousands of earnest devotees divided into small circles for group counseling.[1]

From shortly after 9 ᴀ.ᴍ. until 3 ᴘ.ᴍ. daily, except for occasional holidays, this counseling takes place. The activity is called *hōza* (truth-sitting).[2] Each circle usually consists of ten to twenty members, predominantly women, plus a leader. The purpose of the gathering is to discuss personal problems and to seek solutions for them in the religious resources of Buddhism as understood and expounded by Rissho Kosei-kai. Within an atmosphere of mutual trust and concern, troubled people reveal their difficulties to one another with a frankness that seems very un-Japanese. Problems that some more propriety-minded Japanese would die rather than reveal are laid out and explored with remarkable candor in these groups. Seemingly nothing is too intimate or personal to be discussed. One's own illness or that of a family member, strained family relations, financial crises, behavior of children, juvenile delinquency, a philandering husband, and sexual incompatibility or inadequacy—all these and many other problems are eligible topics. The almost daily gathering of thousands of people in these *hōza* circles surely must be one of the world's most dramatic instances of applied group dynamics. Whence does it come?

The Founders

In 1938, a young man named Niwano Nikkyo (1906–   ) and a woman seventeen years his senior, Naganuma Myoko (1889–1957), withdrew from Reiyu-kai and, with only about thirty followers, organized a society called *Dai Nippon Risshō Kōsei-kai* (The Great Japan Society to Establish Righteousness and Foster Fellowship).[3] Though seemingly oddly matched, these two persons formed a very effective team. Myoko Sensei (as Mrs. Naganuma was called affectionately) was a shamanic type. Though ranked as only the vice-president (*Fukukaichō*) of the society, she was in fact its real spiritual leader during its early period. Niwano, the president (*Kaichō*), was the capable organizer and systematizer.[4] Thus complementing each other, they led a movement that grew steadily during the war and then expanded with amazing rapidity immediately thereafter. Subsequently we shall analyze that development further, but here let us introduce the cofounders more adequately.[5]

Niwano Nikkyo (whose given name originally was Shikazo) was born in 1906, the second son of a farming family in Niigata Prefecture. While still a youth, he went to Tokyo, where, during the early 1920's, he was employed first by a rice merchant and

One in a long series of matching buildings at the headquarters of *Tenri-kyō* at Tenri City, near Nara.

View of the main sanctuary of *Tenri-kyō*. Man in foreground wears *happi* coat with sect name on back. Lanterns are displayed for festivals.

Festival hall of *Konkō-kyō* at the headquarters in Okayama Prefecture.

Patriarch (*Kyōshu*) of Konkō-kyō engaged in mediation (*toritsugi*).

Great Sacred Hall (Daiseidō) of *Risshō Kōsei-kai* in Tokyo on the day of its official opening, May 15, 1964.

Training hall (*Renseikaikan*) of *PL Kyōdan* at the headquarters in Tondabayashi, near Osaka.

Worship hall of *Sekai Kyūsei-kyō* at the "Paradise" at Atami, a seaside resort south of Tokyo.

Tombs of Okada Mokichi and his wife, founder and second leader respectively of *Sekai Kyūsei-kyō*, in Hakone.

President Ikeda Daisaku and aides watch mass performances at *Sōka Gakkai* Culture Day rally at Koshien Stadium, near Osaka.

President Niwano Nikkyo of *Risshō Kōsei-kai* eulogizes co-founder Naganuma Myoko on the seventh anniversary of her death, in Kosei Cemetery near Tokyo.

Young people of *Seichō no Ie* engaged in meditation (*shinsōkan*) *at* Hanayama Training Center in Wakayama.

Devotees of *Tenshō Kōtai Jingu-kyō* laboring voluntarily to help build the training hall (*Dojō*) in Tabuse.

Members of *Risshō Kōsei-kai* at a memorial service for their foundress. The prayer formula (*Daimoku*) is inscribed on chest bands.

Children in prayer at the tomb of the founder of *Gedatsukai* in Sennyuji, a Buddhist temple in Kyoto.

Kitamura Sayo (*Ogamisama*), foundress of *Tenshō Kōtai Jingu-kyō*, leads followers in prayer during rites celebrating completion of headquarters building in Tabuse.

Ecstasy dance (*muga no mai*) of *Tenshō Kōtai Jingu-kyō*, the so-called Dancing Religion.

then by a charcoal dealer. During this time, too, he developed what was to be a continuing interest in occult arts and even joined a divination society.[6] Subsequently inducted into the navy, for three years he was subject to the stern Japanese military discipline. After his discharge, he opened a small pickle shop in Tokyo and married. Though he was diligent in his work, the early 1930's was not a propitious time for small businesses, and Niwano's little shop did not prosper. While he was thus burdened with financial cares, his second daughter became seriously ill. It was during this critical period that he was converted to Reiyu-kai, which, as we have indicated, was the most successful of the New Religions during that time of rising militarism and imperialism.

One reason for the popularity of Reiyu-kai was its sponsorship of the small discussion groups called *hōza*. The group with which Niwano became associated was led by an extraordinarily gifted and learned man who was well versed in Chinese classics and the *Lotus Sūtra*. Stimulated by this man's lectures, Niwano became deeply committed to his new faith and began to spend most of his spare time in propagating it. This engagement was an important factor in his decision to close his pickle shop and become a milkman, for, he reasoned, in this latter occupation he would have opportunities for propagation even while making his deliveries. In this supposition he was correct. The tightening pressures of that ominous time were acutely perturbing to the class of housewives who were his customers. So readily did they respond to his advocacy of Reiyu-kai that he sometimes enlisted as many as twenty new members in a single day. Among the customers whom he converted was Mrs. Naganuma, who became for Niwano "both a patroness and a shaman."[7]

Naganuma Myoko (originally called Masa) was born in 1889 to an impoverished family in Saitama Prefecture. Left motherless at the age of nine, she was the ward of relatives until she was sixteen, when she was adopted into the family of her older sister, an ardent devotee of Tenri-kyo. Under her sister's influence, she also joined this sect and remained within that faith until her conversion to Reiyu-kai about three decades later. Though she had never been physically strong, at the age of twenty she joined the migration of young women going to Tokyo for factory work;

but after five years, illness forced her withdrawal from this employment. Soon thereafter she married a barber, whose dissolute habits she endured for eleven years. After leaving her husband and then suffering the loss of her three-year-old child, she worked as a maid for two or three years. At the age of thirty-nine, she married a man who was only twenty-three. Together they established a good business selling ice in the summer and baked potatoes in the winter. However, though their business was prosperous, Masa's health remained chronically poor, despite frequent prayers offered in her behalf by Tenri-kyo representatives. At length, through the agency of her milkman, Niwano, she was introduced to Reiyu-kai and presumably thereby was healed of her illness.

The team of Niwano and Naganuma was formed specifically for the propagation of Reiyu-kai, and for three years they were diligent in this pursuit; but in 1938, as previously noted, they began a society of their own. This was one of several schisms in Reiyu-kai. Due largely to the erratic, sometimes hysterical behavior of the president, Kotani Kimi, dissension was commonplace in the Reiyu-kai organization. Issues that might have been resolved through good management resulted instead in repeated secessions. It is not completely clear just what precipitated the withdrawal of Niwano and Naganuma. According to a Rissho Kosei-kai official, it was a doctrinal difference. Objecting to what they considered to be a vain reliance upon the magical potency of invocation, Niwano and Naganuma wanted to emphasize instead a quality of personal life that accords with faith.[8] A contrary account is recorded by Joseph M. Kitagawa, who reports that the secession followed an incident in a Reiyu-kai leaders' meeting when Kotani Kimi ridiculed Niwano for his dependence upon divination.[9] It is, of course, entirely conceivable that these two reports supplement rather than contradict each other. In any event, it appears that the new society did not at first differ very substantially from its parent body.

Initially, the new group met in Niwano's home, with Mrs. Naganuma serving as spiritual leader; however, it soon became necessary to provide a more adequate meeting place. In 1941, with a membership of approximately one thousand, they purchased a building in the area where the headquarters now are located.[10] During the war years, the sect continued to grow steadily. Perhaps the horror of air raids impelled some to join, and the fact that Rissho Kosei-kai property escaped damage from these raids seems to have inspired the confidence of many.[11] By the time the war ended in 1945, the membership had increased to about three thousand,[12] but it was with the granting of religious freedom soon thereafter that the rate of growth became phenomenal. For the first decade after the war, Rissho Kosei-kai was the fastest-growing and most publicized New Religion. During the first five years, its membership was doubled annually; and by the end of the decade, the sect could claim approximately one million followers.[13] For the second decade and more, it has continued to expand at a remarkable rate; yet during this period, it has been eclipsed by Soka Gakkai as the fastest-growing and most newsworthy sect.

Later in this chapter we shall return to an examination of some of the factors in the postwar success of Rissho Kosei-kai, and in the next chapter we shall give our full attention to Soka Gakkai. However, inasmuch as both Rissho Kosei-kai and Soka Gakkai (though in many respects essentially dissimilar movements) attribute their strength to the greatness of the *Lotus Sūtra* and identify themselves with the Nichiren Buddhist tradition, this may be the most appropriate point at which to supply necessary background information concerning the *Lotus Sūtra* and Nichiren.

The Lotus Sūtra

The *Lotus Sūtra* has been described by W. E. Soothill as "the most important religious book of the Far East."[14] No other book reflects so faithfully the essential characteristics of the Mahayana (Great Vehicle) branch of Buddhism; no other has been so effective an aid in their dissemination throughout China, Tibet, Mongolia, Korea, and Japan or, in this whole vast area, has been so reverently regarded.

As in the case of numerous other religious classics, questions concerning the authorship, age, and provenance of the *Lotus*

Sūtra remain unanswerable. It is reasonably certain that this work was composed in Sanskrit as the *Saddharma-puṇḍarīka-sūtra.* Presumably it was written in northern India, though it may have been done somewhere in central Asia. It can probably be dated near the beginning of the Christian era. But whatever its earlier history, we know that by the late third century, the *Lotus Sūtra* was in China and was being translated into Chinese. Subsequently, it was a Chinese translation—completed in A.D. 406 and attributed to an immigrant scholar, Kumarajiva—that became the most widely used version of this scripture. From this Chinese text, additional translations into other languages have been made. In Japanese, the *Lotus Sūtra* is called *Myōhō-renge-kyō*, or *Hoke-kyō*, a contraction of the full name.

As literature, the *Lotus Sūtra* is an apocalypse, presented as a great cosmic drama or pageant. It opens with the historical Buddha, Shakyamuni,[15] seated on Vulture Peak in Nepal and prepared to teach an assembled multitude. In this instance, however, he is no longer merely a man who by exceptional diligence had achieved enlightenment (Buddhahood). He is the Eternal Buddha. By a light emanating from his forehead, he illumines every quarter of the universe, and he proclaims his authority over it all.

Doctrinally, this scripture presents a message radically different from the pragmatic humanism and monasticism of the earlier, so-called Hinayana (Small Vehicle) Buddhism. In what is purported to be his final and authoritative discourse, the Buddha rescinds his previous teachings, in which he had urged each individual to seek Nirvana by self-cultivation and merit. Such teachings, he explains, had constituted only an interim doctrine, an expedient means by which he had begun to prepare the totally ignorant to receive his full revelation. In this climactic teaching, the transfigured Shakyamuni promises that by grace through faith and invocation, all mankind—not simply the diligent few—shall be saved. This, of course, is the basic tenet of Mahayana Buddhism.

Closely related to this doctrine are four other features of the *Lotus Sūtra* that, being reflected prominently among the New Religions acknowledging the authority of this scripture, ought to be identified here: (1) the bodhisattva ideal, (2) messianism, (3) salvation by invocation, and (4) conferral of happiness.

THE BODHISATTVA IDEAL

A bodhisattva (Japanese, *bosatsu*) is "one whose essence is enlightenment" or, in other words, one who is in the process of becoming a Buddha. Within the context of the *Lotus Sūtra*, there are two categories of bodhisattvas: in the one are great spiritual beings (deities, in effect), who, though qualified to enter the final bliss of Buddhahood, have postponed that reward in order to remain accessible as saviors to struggling humanity; in the other are all true believers. The bodhisattva ideal, a compassion that impels a person to seek to bring enlightenment and salvation to others, describes the essential ethic of the *Lotus Sūtra*.

MESSIANISM

According to the soteriology of the *Lotus Sūtra*, Shakyamuni was one in a succession of earthly Buddhas, each of whom, in his turn, had also manifested the Eternal Buddha and inaugurated a new Buddha period on earth. In each Buddha period, there are three stages: "that of the true law, that of the semblance of the true law, and that of final decadence and disappearance."[16] At the conclusion of each cycle, a new Buddha appears to restore the true law with power. The next Buddha, whose coming is foretold in the *Lotus Sūtra* and elsewhere, is Maitreya (Japanese, Miroku).

SALVATION BY INVOCATION

Though the promise of the *Lotus Sūtra* is that salvation is by grace through faith and invocation, there are passages, especially in Chapter X,[17] which seem to invite reliance on invocation alone—even invocation of the *Sūtra* itself. Those who "look upon this *Sūtra* with reverence as if it were the Buddha" and pay homage to it in almost any manner are assured of becoming Buddhas in future worlds. No deed is more meritorious than honoring this *Sūtra* or one who proclaims it; no crime is more heinous than defaming the *Sūtra* or one of its advocates.

CONFERRAL OF HAPPINESS

Much of the dramatic quality of the *Lotus Sūtra* is achieved by the use of hyperbole. Such is the wonderful power of this scripture that nothing should seem impossible to a true believer. The most extravagant promises are made to those who will believe and aid in disseminating its doctrines. The literal-minded person may find here a magical guarantee of all the requisites of earthly happiness, particularly prosperity and good health.

The *Lotus Sūtra* was among the early Buddhist imports to Japan. In 606, Prince Shotoku lectured on this scripture to the delight of the Empress Suiko. However, the person most prominently associated with the exposition of this text in antiquity is Saicho, known also as Dengyo Daishi (767–822). Sent to China in 804, he became adept in the eclectic doctrines of the *T'ien-t'ai* sect based on the *Lotus Sūtra*. Upon returning home, he founded a branch of that sect (Japanized as *Tendai-shū*). His headquarters atop Mount Hiei, near Kyoto, continued for centuries as one of the greatest centers of Buddhist learning in Japan. It was there in the thirteenth century that the monk Nichiren studied the *Lotus Sūtra* and concluded that it contained the whole of Buddhism and hence was the key to everything. In this conviction, he began the stormy career which shaped the tradition which, in some of its current manifestations, now engages our attention.

Nichiren

Unlike most other founders of the prominent sects of Japanese Buddhism, Nichiren (1222–1282)[18] did not go abroad for study, nor did he at any time have a noble patron. He was a lonely, long-suffering seeker and fearless protagonist of what he considered to be true Buddhism. Though indubitably earnest in his convictions, he was an unrelenting zealot whose intolerance many people found intolerable. Born to a fisherman's family, he was sent in his early childhood to a monastery near his home. As he grew to young manhood in the monastic life, he became obsessed by the need to solve the problem of the diversity within Buddhism. Which, if any, of the several sects was propounding the true doctrine? In the midst of many conflicting claims, how could one recognize the truth even if he should hear it? In search of an answer, Nichiren went first to Kamakura, the seat of the military dictatorship then ruling the land; but rather quickly concluding that "the capital of a country is a place for disseminating the truth, and not for learning it,"[19] he moved on to the great monastic center on Mount Hiei. There in the *Lotus Sūtra* he supposed that he had found what he sought: a scripture, composed of Shakyamuni's own words, that both comprehended and completed the partiality of all other teachings and promised salvation to all—even to those of meager capacity and simple faith. Though he himself actually was a man of considerable erudition, he capsuled the whole of Buddhism in the simple invocation of the Sacred Title (*Daimoku*) of this scripture, *Namu Myōhō Renge-kyō* ("Adoration to the Lotus of the Wonderful Law"). In 1253, he began a mission based on this holistic conception.

Returning to his home territory, he expounded his teaching, together with denunciations of the various sects, in the presence of the abbot and monks of his former monastery. They were so incensed by his effrontery that they drove him from the province. Thence he went again to Kamakura, where, at a time when many untoward events were affecting the general welfare adversely, he boldly identified these hardships as retributions for false faith. In support of his contentions, he wrote an essay entitled *Risshō-Ankoku-Ron* (*The Establishment of Righteousness and the Security of the Country*), in which, systematically but virulently, he attacked the "errors" of the leading Buddhist sects and warned the government that only ruin could result from its tolerance of heresy. The issuing of this document resulted in Nichiren's being attacked by a mob and, later, in his arrest and banishment to the Izu Peninsula.

While in exile, an unrepentant Nichiren formulated the five

theses that were basic to his mission and prepared himself for its eventual resumption. These may be summarized as follows: (1) the doctrine he preached was that of the *Lotus Sūtra*, the consummate teaching of the Buddha Shakyamuni; (2) because the degeneracy of the "latter days of the Law" (*Mappō*) was upon them, the people had no capacity for complicated doctrine but could be trained only by the simplest form of Buddhist teaching; (3) since the time of *Mappō* had come, only the *Lotus Sūtra* retained the power to save all mankind; (4) according to the prophecy of the *Lotus Sūtra*, Japan was the country in which true Buddhism should prevail and from which it should be propagated worldwide; and (5) other forms of Buddhism had completed their missions and awaited fulfillment in the universal acceptance of the perfect truth. Later, Nichiren was to add a sixth thesis to these five, namely, that he himself was the person whose coming had been foretold as the one who should accomplish this mission.

Thus, after his exile, Nichiren renewed his attack on "false faith." Spurred on by the acquisition of a growing body of followers and by a threatened invasion of Japan by the Mongols, he became increasingly outspoken in his denunciations and warnings. In 1271, thoroughly exasperated by this contentiousness, the government took Nichiren into custody and once again sentenced him to banishment, apparently with the intention that he should be killed on the way. However, the planned execution was foiled miraculously, presumably by a spectacular lightning display that left the executioners in panic. Nichiren proceeded into exile on rugged Sado Island in the Japan Sea. There, during almost three years of extreme hardship, his assurance was strengthened that he was indeed the one predicted in the *Lotus Sūtra*. In an essay entitled *Kaimoku-shō* (*Opening the Eyes*), he recorded his vow: "I will be the Pillar of Japan; I will be the Eyes of Japan; I will be the Great Vessel of Japan."[20] Also while in exile, he devised a schematic representation of Cosmic Being, a diagram consisting of the Sacred Title (*Daimoku*) surrounded by a graded arrangement by titles of all orders of existence. The preparation of this mandala was regarded by Nichiren as the principal work committed to him, for in it he epitomized the whole of Buddhist ontology and soteriology and gave all persons access to saving power.

Permitted to return to Kamakura in 1274, Nichiren still refused to compromise his position; but instead of remaining as a heckler in the capital, he withdrew to an area near Mount Fuji in order to establish a base from which to evangelize the world. There in comparative quiet he spent the last eight years of his life, and when he died in 1282, he bequeathed to the Japanese people their most conspicuous example of resolute belief and faith and their first tradition of arrant exclusivism in religion.

Risshō Kōsei-kai *in the* Lotus Sūtra–*Nichiren Tradition*

Rissho Kosei-kai is, we repeat, one of a rather large company of *Lotus Sūtra* sects that are related in various ways to the Nichiren tradition. Like Kosei-kai, several others of these sects are offshoots of Reiyu-kai, while some, most notably Soka Gakkai, have originated differently. All these sects have at least two features in common: (1) dependence upon the *Lotus Sūtra*, signalized by the recitation of the *Daimoku*, and (2) veneration of Nichiren as the faithful exponent and exemplar of the Buddhist truth revealed in the *Sūtra*. However, the existence of these common traits should not be taken as prima facie evidence of the essential uniformity of these sects, for the discrepancies among them are considerable. This is especially apparent and important in the case of Rissho Kosei-kai and Soka Gakkai, which represent religious orientations that, in their pure forms, are polar opposites. Kosei-kai stresses the recitation of the *Daimoku* as an affirmation of faith in the teaching of the *Lotus Sūtra*. It is very careful to state that no special merit is acquired by frequent repetition of this formula; indeed, opposition to just such a notion reputedly was Niwano and Naganuma's principal reason for seceding from Reiyu-kai. Soka Gakkai, on the other hand, as we shall show more fully in the next chapter, emphasizes the repetition of the *Daimoku* as the means of acquiring saving power.

In addition, while Kosei-kai clearly is identified with the Nichiren tradition, in its case the relationship is prominent without being dominant. Since 1949, this organization has been independent of all the old established Nichiren sects. Moreover, the object of worship in Kosei-kai is declared to be the Eternal Buddha manifested in Shakyamuni, the spokesman of the *Lotus Sūtra*. Nichiren is honored not as the Eternal Buddha but for his recognition and advocacy of the *Sūtra* as the repository of essential truth. Apparently it is the compassion of the *Sūtra*'s message rather than the fiery disposition of Nichiren that Kosei-kai finds most impressive.

Perhaps this purpose and mood are nowhere better exemplified than in Kosei-kai's version of the *Oeshiki*, the traditional rites observed annually by most Nichiren groups on October 12, the eve of the death anniversary of Nichiren (d. October 13, 1282). Kosei-kai observes this occasion with a day-long festival that begins at about 8 A.M. and concludes after 9 P.M. Though the fundamental solemnity of the occasion is preserved in a mid-morning Buddhist mass, the day is chiefly a joyful and colorful celebration, commemorating the life, enlightenment, and teaching of Nichiren rather than mourning his death. The principal activity is a series of processions that wind through the streets surrounding the Tokyo headquarters of the sect. About fifteen thousand people, many of them dressed in traditional costumes, take part in these parades. A group of small children, attired in an ancient style, march to old court music. Young kimono-clad women lend their unique beauty and grace to the occasion. There are also flag bearers and musicians, including a large troupe beating on hand drums (*taiko*), a kind of trademark of Nichirenism. A modern touch is supplied by a three-hundred-member boy-and-girl fife-and-drum corps from the Risshō Gakuen, the Kosei-kai high school. The climax is reached after dark, when about eighty portable pagodas, each surrounded by a cascade of lighted paper lanterns, are borne through the streets by hundreds of male devotees. Since its inauguration in the early 1950's, this festival has been one of the most important annual events of Rissho Kosei-kai. In recent years it has attracted each time approximately two hundred thousand spectators, including many of the general public, to whom the sect always extends a cordial invitation.

In honoring Nichiren the man, therefore, Kosei-kai preserves the tolerant perspective that is generally associated with Buddhism. Here again, however, Soka Gakkai takes an almost opposite position. It is a lay organization in the service of the most uncompromising Nichiren sect, which, stressing the messianism of the *Lotus Sūtra*, sees Nichiren as the pivotal figure in heralding a new age of power exclusively for those who accept his one true religion. Thus, despite seemingly common features, the relation of Rissho Kosei-kai and Soka Gakkai is in important respects essentially a dichotomy and also, not surprisingly, an unrelenting rivalry.

Persistence of Popular Piety

The independence of Rissho Kosei-kai as an association of Buddhist laymen, only loosely affiliated with the Nichiren tradition, has made it possible for this organization, without any great concern for orthodoxy, to adopt or sanction any ideas and practices that are attractive and effective. Especially during the almost two decades of Mrs. Naganuma's leadership (1938–1957), the most salient features of the movement, in addition to *hōza*, were aspects of popular or folk religion. For example, if we inquire concerning the postwar success of Kosei-kai, we find that the attractiveness of three activities in particular contributed to its popularity: (1) veneration of ancestral spirits, (2) divination, and (3) the *hōza* groups. Each of these is a means of identifying and dealing with the "real" causal (karmic) factors in the living situation. The first two were based on traditional commitments and ideas that were too ingrained to be ignored in the midst of crisis; the third, though new to many, was a most timely innovation. We shall explore each of these more fully.

VENERATION OF ANCESTRAL SPIRITS

So-called ancestor worship is one of the oldest, most persistent, and most universal characteristics of Japanese life. To express gratitude and respect to one's ancestors is considered to be a very natural and human act and a sign of sincerity and genuineness. Moreover, such veneration is also both a weighty and an expedient obligation, for the welfare of both the living and the dead, being forever and indissolubly linked, depends upon its being fulfilled. The consolation of the spirits of the dead is contingent upon the faithful devotion of their descendants in the world. The neglect of this responsibility brings indescribable unhappiness to those who have departed, and this in turn can result only in misfortune for the offenders and possibly also their families. Thus, when any suffering or hardship occurs, many Japanese are prepared to assume that its cause may lie in neglect of the ancestors; for even the most diligent person knows that he is subject to occasional forgetfulness or hypocrisy, and one who is less conscientious is likely always to feel some misgiving concerning what he knows to be his negligence. Because of the currency of this outlook, the New Religions that stress the rectification of relations with the ancestors have generally had a good response to this emphasis, especially from women.

It was through the renewed acceptance of her obligations to her ancestors that Mrs. Nagamuna was healed of her illness in Reiyu-kai, the Spirit-Friends Association. Subsequently, in Rissho Kosei-kai, she was the principal spokesman for a family-centered way of life based on the proper veneration of ancestors. As a shamanic type, she also served occasionally as a medium, although spiritualism was never so popular in Kosei-kai as in Reiyu-kai or certain other sects,[21] and apparently it is no longer practiced at all under the official auspices of the sect. Nevertheless, the emphasis on ancestral rites does remain strong. One of the first duties of a new convert is to register his ancestors at the headquarters and receive on their behalf the new posthumous Buddhist names by which thenceforth he will honor them. Also, a large cemetery for the members is carefully maintained at Yamato-cho, just west of Tokyo, and is the site of important mortuary rites, one of which we shall describe subsequently.

DIVINATION

Divination is the occult art of discerning beforehand the course of future events or identifying hidden factors in past events or current circumstances. It is practiced universally in an immense variety of forms, but it is an especially popular and engaging art in the Orient, where it occurs both in very crude forms and in subtle combination with various philosophies and psychological insights. In Rissho Kosei-kai, the type of divination most commonly practiced is onomancy, or name divination. Each person entering this association requests an analysis of his name to determine whether the characters with which it is written are auspicious or inauspicious. This is considered to be a very complex "science," one from which the uninitiated are effectively debarred; though by means of Saki's description of *ōbasami no innen* ("karma of the great pincers"), we can glimpse one small facet of the practice. In this instance, if a character composed of an even number of strokes stands between two characters each of which is formed by an odd number of strokes, that character is said to be "pinched" and is therefore a bad omen.[22] It behooves the person burdened with this ill omen either to write his name with different characters or to change his name entirely.

HŌZA GROUPS

The group-counseling system called *hōza* is one of the features of Reiyu-kai that has been continued in Rissho Kosei-kai. However, in the view of the latter sect, its indebtedness for this practice is not to Reiyu-kai but to the *Lotus Sūtra* and to Shakyamuni, in whose day, so it is believed, this system already was in use. In Reiyu-kai, it is averred, the practice was not highly developed and was not essential from a doctrinal standpoint. In Kosei-kai, however, the development of *hōza* is a necessary concomitant of the doctrine and purpose of this movement, which is committed to solving the problems of individual people. The *hōza* system provides both a suitable medium by which the individual can make his problem known and an effective means for discerning its source or course and prescribing a solution.[23]

In addition to the daily sessions held at the headquarters and described in the introduction to this chapter, *hōza* meetings are also scheduled locally wherever Kosei-kai is active. To encourage spontaneity, these sessions customarily are organized according to sex or age groups; for example, among adults there may be separate sessions for men and women, and for young people of both sexes (up to about thirty years of age) still another session may be scheduled.

Myoko Sensei's Shamanic Legacy

Until the death of Naganuma Myoko in 1957, much of the vigor
of Rissho Kosei-kai derived from the charismatic, revelatory character of her leadership. Honored by the members as a "living
Buddha" (*ikibotoke*, a term comparable in this instance to
ikigami), she tended to encourage among them a vitalistic expectation that owed more to popular piety than to classical Buddhism.
Since her death, though certainly there has been no overt deprecation of her as a person, an effort has been made to supersede
the somewhat shamanistic approach with which she was associated. The period of her leadership is even referred to as a time
of "expediency" or "accommodation" (*hōben*),[24] a transitional
stage, justified and necessary because of prevailing circumstances
but needing now to be updated. Nevertheless, devotion to Myoko
Sensei continues to be an important dimension in the faith and
loyalty of thousands of the believers. One indication of this
fealty is the manner in which her death anniversary is commemo-
rated. Since I was privileged to attend a service held in her
memory on September 10, 1963, I shall document this point by
including a brief description of what transpired on that occasion.

It was the sixth anniversary (seventh according to Japanese
reckoning) of the death of the foundress. In the early morning,
devotees gathered at the headquarters to board chartered buses
and at Seibu-Shinjuku Station to board chartered trains for the
journey to the cemetery (Kōsei Rei-en) at Yamato-cho, to the
west of Tokyo. My associate, Kobayashi Sakae, and I had been
asked to join the pilgrims scheduled to leave by train at about
9 A.M. By 8:25 A.M., several thousand believers already were
assembled in the open area outside the wickets. Each one wore
over his left shoulder and across his body a white band inscribed
with the *Daimoku* and the name of the sect.

The orderliness of the crowd was most impressive. They were
lined up according to the *shibu* (local groups) to which they
belonged. Numbered banners held above the crowd indicated to
each new arrival where he should station himself. Only the
leaders milled about, and they did so only to communicate with

one another and to relay messages to their respective groups. Occasionally, reports or instructions were given to the assembly over a portable loudspeaker. At about 8:50, the entire group was called to attention. Facing the station, all bowed and chanted a ritual that included the *Daimoku* and an expression of gratitude to their *Kaichō Sensei*, President Niwano. Thereafter the first contingent moved in single file through the turnstile. These were followed by other groups at intervals of ten minutes or so (as quickly as the special trains could be brought into position without interfering with the normal rush-hour traffic) until all had been entrained. The whole operation was accomplished with military efficiency minus military severity. All seemed to accept unquestioningly the necessity of following directions, and thus they waited patiently and quietly for their turns to come. I saw no instance of restlessness, exasperation, or ill temper on the part of anyone.

Kobayashi and I were introduced to the head of the *shibu* in whose train we were to ride. He personally escorted us to seats in the first car, and after the train departed from the station, he rejoined us and answered our questions during the entire hour that the journey required.

When we arrived at the cemetery, the service already had begun. On an elevated plot where the tomb of the foundress is located, the principal officials of the sect were seated. President Niwano sat under a large red umbrella, presumably a symbol of his office. On an adjacent plot, identical to the first except that it contained no monuments, musicians and other functionaries were seated. (The second plot eventually will be the burial place for Niwano.) We were ushered to special seats reserved for us on the walkway between the two plots. The throngs of devotees (estimated to have been about twenty thousand for this service) were seated in the roads and paths throughout the vast cemetery.

The service consisted of traditional Japanese music and chanting, including unison chanting by the entire assembly. Following this, President Niwano arose and delivered a short eulogy of Myoko Sensei. When Niwano had resumed his seat, another man stood at the microphone and began to call the roll of the officials. As each person's name was called, he stepped forward and placed an incense stick in the urn before the tomb. This tribute concluded the formal service. With musicians leading the way, President Niwano and the other officials then left the tomb and walked in solemn procession to a nearby building where lunch awaited them.

We lingered for a while in the vicinity of the tomb and watched as hundreds of devout pilgrims began to come forward and stand for a moment before the tomb, there to offer incense and a brief prayer. For the remainder of that day and for four days thereafter, so we were told, others would be coming from many parts of Japan to pay tribute to this one whose spirit is presumed still to be present among those whose affection for her is undying. Perhaps for many of the faithful, the sense of her presence was even further enhanced that day when, after the lunch, the public-address system carried a sermon that she had recorded. Though her voice was surprisingly harsh and gravelly, there was unmistakably a kind of magnetic quality in it. Some of the devotees, upon returning to the headquarters that afternoon, would make a second pilgrimage to the former residence of the foundress, where, for the one day only, some of her clothing and other personal effects were on display. Welcome or not, it would seem, the shamanic aspect of Rissho Kosei-kai will remain for a while, at least as long as there are those who remember Myoko Sensei.

Early in the afternoon, we returned to Tokyo as we had come, by train, although in the company of a different *shibu*. As the train reached the point in its itinerary nearest the headquarters, all were alerted to this fact; whereupon each one clasped rosary beads (*ojuzu*) and chanted the *Daimoku*. Afterward they removed their chest bands and put them away. The pilgrimage was over. They had been desacralized and individualized again, and their departure from the train was undirected.

Lay Buddhism in Action

An approximately literal translation of *Risshō Kōsei-kai* is "Society to Establish Righteousness and Foster Fellowship."

More fully interpreted—avowedly to suggest the intention of those who actually coined the name—it is now said to specify "a society of laymen who seek the perfection of their character and the attainment of Buddhahood by following the religious teaching of the Lord Buddha."[25] However, it seems doubtful, in retrospect, that this is the most adequate way to spell out the movement's original aims. As we have seen, Kosei-kai's early success owed much to its accommodation of a largely undifferentiated popular piety, which included but was not really governed by specifically Buddhistic considerations. Thus, the affiliation with the Nichiren tradition was tenuous; and despite exhortations to live by the principles of the *Lotus Sūtra*, it was not always clear whether that scripture was to be regarded primarily as a source of power or as a source of wisdom. Therefore, as a rapidly expanding movement, Rissho Kosei-kai has had to face up to the necessity of systematizing and clarifying its essential perspectives. In general, as the present interpretation of its name implies, its response has been to move steadily toward a more recognizably Buddhistic definition of its life and character.

Prefigurations of this ongoing trend appeared even in the 1950's —for example, in the definition of the so-called Three Actions (*San-gō*), which were declared to be basic to life in Kosei-kai:

1) *Verbal Action*: Chanting the *Daimoku* (without magical associations), reciting the sacred scriptures (chiefly the *Lotus Sūtra*), and using "right speech" (proper and edifying language) in daily life.

2) *Mental Action*: Repentance of and purification from the sins of the *six* senses: sight, hearing, smell, taste, touch, and consciousness.

3) *Bodily Action*: Practice of the compassionate bodhisattva way of helpfulness to others.[26]

However, this tendency has been especially evident since the death of Naganuma Myoko in 1957, when the leadership of the movement devolved solely upon Niwano Nikkyo. Now, such classical Buddhist teachings as the Four Noble Truths, the Noble Eightfold Path, and the Twelvefold Chain of Causation are being emphasized. Also, in the new Daiseidō (Great Sacred Hall), there are numerous Buddhist motifs and symbols, including pre-eminently a twenty-foot-tall standing figure of Shakyamuni Buddha.

The Buddhism of Rissho Kosei-kai, however, is lay Buddhism—Buddhism without either monks or priests. Its tone and direction principally are set by one man, Niwano, who is untrained for professional Buddhist leadership but whom many people regard now as Japan's "typical man of religion in action."[27] Unassuming and approachable—in contrast to many of the leaders of other New Religions—he uses no grandiose title but is simply called *Kaichō* ("president") or *Kaichō Sensei* ("president-teacher"). A friendly man, smiling almost continually, his manner bespeaks kindness and compassion. Though he aspires to lead his vast membership in the path of the Buddha, he has no reliance upon or indebtedness to Buddhist scholasticism. He professes to have found a faith that works, and he invites others to join him in it, both for their own salvation and for the useful investment of their lives for the sake of humanity. At the present time, it is claimed, more than two million people regularly signify their acquiescence by means of the following affirmation (*kōryō*):

> We, the members of Rissho Kosei Kai, under the leadership of our revered teacher, President Niwano, recognize the essential Way of Salvation in Buddhism and pledge our best efforts, in the spirit of Buddhist laymen, to perfect our character and realize in our lives the Bodhisattva Way. To this end, by improving in knowledge and prac-tice of the faith, in personal discipline and in leading others, we shall endeavor to realize a state of peace for the family, the community, the country, and the world.[28]

Reflections

In the postwar period, says Kitagawa, an "energy hitherto buried and forgotten in the Buddhist tradition in Japan" has been released. "Never in the history of Japanese Buddhism did laymen and laywomen take such an active part in Buddhist affairs as they do today."[29] From the standpoint of Buddhism's own interests, increased lay participation would appear to be one of its strongest hopes for finding anew a relevant and creative relationship to Japanese life. To what extent is Rissho Kosei-kai likely to contribute to this eventuality? It is perhaps too soon to say, for the character of this movement is not yet fully defined. But its resources and opportunities for the future appear to be good. Does it represent *authentic* Buddhism? There are many who will insist, on traditional grounds, that it does not, and perhaps they are the ones who ought to judge. Still, it is not an insignificant fact that the first Buddhist invited to attend the Second Vatican Council as a special guest was Niwano Nikkyo.[30] Who speaks for Buddhism? In this day and time, it is the one who is given a hearing.

Sōka Gakkai:
A Multiphasic Mass Movement

THE STANDS OF KOSHIEN STADIUM near Osaka were filled to capacity with upwards of eighty thousand people. On the field, massed row on row, stood about seven thousand costumed or uniformed performers. The occasion was *Sōka Gakkai's* celebration of the national holiday Bunka Sai (Culture Day), on November 3, 1963. For almost two hours I had watched, somewhat awestruck, as the program of mass performances had unfolded with unvarying precision before an orderly and highly appreciative assembly. There had been calisthenic and gymnastic exhibitions, baton-twirling routines, Hungarian and Japanese folk dances, and fife-and-drum corps maneuvers. Music had been provided by choral groups, bands, and orchestras and by the entire multitude joined in song. Throughout the morning, a card section composed of white-clad boys repeatedly and expertly had flashed the slogan *Dai-san Bunmei* ("The Third Civilization"), by which this society advertises its way as the authentic life for the present dichotomized world. Now all was in readiness for the finale. From his box in the stands came Ikeda Daisaku, the young and vigorous president, to address the gathering. In a very brief speech, he reminded his hearers that no other religion anywhere in the world could have done what Soka Gakkai had accomplished there that day, and he admonished them also to remember that, as Soka Gakkai followers, they were becoming Japan's indispensable citizens. Then, walking briskly, accompanied by a small entourage, he made a circuit of the field. As he passed, the occupants of each section of the stands apparently tried to outdo all the others in the volume and demonstrativeness of their cheers.

As I looked and listened, I felt almost frightened by the possible implications of these manifestations of mass energy and blind obedience. For one who remembers the World War II period, such a spectacle has a haunting effect. His mind flashes back to newsreel clips of Nazi youth rallies and other similar vignettes of the totalitarianism that once nearly destroyed civilization. Is the similarity here more than circumstantial? Is this fascism reborn? This specter frequently arises in the minds of both Japanese and non-Japanese observers of the activities of Soka Gakkai. Not surprisingly, this is an association that the society's leaders deeply resent; for, they ask, "How can a movement whose aim is happiness and peace for all mankind be fascistic?"[1]

As we shall endeavor to show, the fascist label cannot be pinned on Soka Gakkai solely on the basis of the subjective responses of outside observers, nor can it be withheld completely simply because of the protestations of innocence from Soka Gakkai leaders. The most powerful popular movement in the history of Japan, this is an organization whose character and importance are not susceptible of any simplistic analysis. It is a mass movement gathering to itself thousands of lonely and dispirited people. It includes a primitive type of folk religion based upon magic and relic veneration. It is a modern lay association in the service of a seven-hundred-year-old Buddhist sect. It is the sponsor and principal electorate of a new and thriving political party. It is the patron of cultural activities for the masses. It is all this and perhaps more, as we shall see in due course; but first let us consider how Soka Gakkai came to be.

History of the Movement

In his incomparable essay on mass movements, Eric Hoffer wrote: "A movement is pioneered by men of words, materialized by fanatics and consolidated by men of action."[2] Though Soka Gakkai was not among his referents, it fits quite neatly the pattern that he described. Thus far, in this organization's succession of leaders, its three presidents typify respectively these three categories. The first president, Makiguchi Tsunesaburo, was the man of words who founded the society. Toda Josei, the second president, was the fanatic, under whose leadership the organization achieved its most spectacular growth. The man of action is the third president, Ikeda Daisaku, who is succeeding in making more and more observers acknowledge that "Sokagakkai is more than an emotion. It . . . is a monumental reality."[3]

Makiguchi Tsunesaburo (1871–1944) was born in a village in Niigata Prefecture. After completing elementary school there, he moved to Hokkaido and later enrolled in the Sapporo Normal School. Following his graduation, he was retained as a teacher at this same school and began to concentrate on the study of geography, in connection with which he developed his novel theory of value, to which we shall return later. In 1901, he went to Tokyo, where, two years later, he published his first book, *Jinsei Chirigaku (Geography of Life)*. For several additional years, he worked principally as an editor and publisher interested in educational theory, but eventually he returned to active engagement in teaching and school administration. During approximately two decades, he served as the principal of various elementary schools in Tokyo.

In 1921, while Makiguchi was the administrator of the Nishimachi School, Toda Josei, then twenty-one years old, was assigned to his faculty and soon became his personal disciple. After 1928, when both men were converted to *Nichiren Shō-shū* (Nichiren Orthodox Sect), the two worked as close confederates in linking Makiguchi's theories with the intolerant and chiliastic doctrines of what was at that time a very small sect of Buddhism. Makiguchi retired from school work in 1930 and, in that same year, began publishing his magnum opus, *Sōka Kyōikugaku Taikei* (*A System of Value-Creation Education*), the fourth and last volume of which appeared in 1934. Although Soka Gakkai now regards 1930 as its foundation year,[4] the society was not constituted formally until 1937, when about sixty people banded together under the name *Sōka Kyōiku Gakkai* (Value-Creation Education Society) and elected Makiguchi president. Avowedly dedicated to research in education, the society nevertheless from its outset had a religious character and endeavored to extend the faith of the Nichiren Sho-shu. By aggressive personal evangelism and the publication of a monthly paper, *Kachi Sōzō* (*Creation of Value*), first issued in 1941, the society had increased its membership to about three thousand by July of 1942, when harassment from the government began.

As a part of its effort to maximize the unity of the nation in support of the war effort, the government attempted to force all the Nichiren sects to consolidate. Nichiren Sho-shu refused to comply, and Makiguchi and his followers joined with the priests in defying the government order. They also refused to participate in the rites of the national cult of Shinto. Predictably, charges of lese majesty were drawn up, and on July 6, 1943, Makiguchi and Toda, along with twenty-one other members of the society, were arrested. In effect, the organization was disbanded. On November 18, 1944, at the age of seventy-three, Makiguchi died of malnutrition in his cell in Sugamo Prison. Toda and a few others, still choosing to endure imprisonment rather than renounce their principles, remained in custody until 1945.

In retrospect, it appears that Makiguchi's enduring contributions to Soka Gakkai are in fact rather meager. Aside from his role as the organization's founder and first president, he is honored chiefly as a martyr and a "great philosopher." This latter reputation is based on a novel notion that he expounded in an essay called *Kachi-ron* (*The Theory of Value*), a highly prized document for study in Soka Gakkai. The faithful regard this as an epoch-making philosophical treatise, but the unconverted are more likely to see it as the statement of "a naive form of utilitarianism."[5]

This essay is a reexamination of the idea, attributed to Kant, that the objectives of human life are the good, the true, and the beautiful. Makiguchi demurs, saying that, while the good and the beautiful certainly merit this designation, the true does not. The true, being identified with experienced reality or the factual, may be conducive either to happiness or to unhappiness. What really is pivotal is value, a qualitative dimension of life that is the product of the good, the beautiful, and the *profitable*. Thus, "great philosophy" presumably is brought out of the realm of metaphysical concern for truth and is lodged in the day-to-day concern for workability, with human happiness as its goal.

Toda Josei (1900–1958), upon whom devolved the full responsibility for the postwar reorganization of Makiguchi's work, was born in Ishikawa Prefecture but was reared and educated in Hokkaido. Having qualified as an elementary-school teacher, he accepted a position, as we have noted, in the school in Tokyo where Makiguchi was principal and began the intimate association with him that continued until the older man's death. Unwavering in his loyalty to his teacher and in his faith in the *Lotus Sūtra*, Toda is said to have recited the *Daimoku* more than two million times and to have achieved enlightenment during the two years of his incarceration. Upon being released from prison in July, 1945, he began almost immediately to reconstruct the society. Early in 1946, the movement was reconstituted under the name *Sōka Gakkai* (Value-Creation Society). No longer to be identified essentially with the educational field, the reorganized group took as its main purpose "to bring peace and happiness to all mankind."

Not until May 3, 1951, did Toda formally assume the presidency of Soka Gakkai. It was also on this date that the most fanatical drive for converts was begun. In his inaugural address, Toda launched this campaign by saying: "Don't hold a funeral for me, but just throw my remains into Tokyo Bay off Shinagawa if we fail to achieve 750,000 families in the next seven years."[6] The method of evangelism already being employed was what Nichiren had called *shakubuku* ("break and subdue"), essentially a tactic of destroying another's resistance and converting him by the force of one's own arguments. Under Toda's instruction, example, and relentless goading, the techniques of *shakubuku* were sharpened, and throughout the organization, participation in *shakubuku* was accepted by virtually every member as both a duty and a means of blessing. In November, 1951, six months after Toda's inauguration, Soka Gakkai published the *Shakubuku Kyōten* (*Shakubuku Canon*), a manual for the society's evangelistic task, containing summations of Soka Gakkai doctrines, denunciations of rival religions, and techniques for making new converts. Armed with this book and seemingly unlimited enthusiasm, Soka Gakkai devotees began to swarm all over Japan in search of new members. In general, the Japanese people were offended by the intolerance and aggressiveness of these propagandists. Many instances of intimidation, terrorism, coercion, and blackmail were alleged, and some were reported in news media. Nevertheless, the campaign was amazingly effective. Late in 1957, several months earlier than the target date, Soka Gakkai announced that Toda's goal of a membership of seven hundred and fifty thousand families had been achieved. While, to be sure, no one could check the accuracy of the figures, there was no mistaking the fact that Soka Gakkai had become an immensely powerful movement. This was attested not only by the enthusiasm and the vast number of its adherents but also by the tight military type of organization that Toda had effected. He was the society's organizing genius, and much of its success, both during and since his presidency, has been due to the precise control that the top leaders have been able to exercise over the entire movement.

Toda's career ended with the Gakkai definitely on the march. It was growing at an incredible rate. It was well organized and well financed. It had begun to score impressive victories in politics. Appropriately, the last month of Toda's life was devoted to celebration. On March 1, 1958, the Soka Gakkai completed a modern five-storied ferroconcrete building, the Dai-Kōdō (Great Lecture Hall), on the grounds of Taisekiji, the head temple of Nichiren Sho-shu. This achievement provided an occasion for a protracted celebration of all the society's triumphs. For an entire month, devotees came from throughout the nation to join in the grand ceremonies. On April 1, Toda returned to Tokyo, and on the following day he died. On the day of the funeral, an estimated three hundred thousand people crowded into the neighborhood of the mortuary. Even the Prime Minister and the Minister of Education, who had no affiliation with Soka Gakkai, visited the bier and offered incense[7]—a gesture that journalists cynically but probably correctly interpreted as a bow "to some two million votes behind the altar."[8] Toda was buried within the precinct of Taisekiji, and his tomb continues to be a place of pilgrimage.

Toda's legacy was both substantial and complicated. He left Soka Gakkai with a very large membership, a comprehensive and efficient organization, and momentum sufficient to sustain a continued rapid growth. At the same time, because of the rigidly authoritarian character of his leadership, his death left a power void that precipitated a temporary crisis for the movement. Also, largely because of Toda's fanatical intolerance and bluntness and his advocacy of *shakubuku*, the public image of Soka Gakkai was very poor. Toda frequently complained that the press coverage of Gakkai activities was unfair and scurrilous, but it seems clear that his own tactlessness and recklessness were largely responsible for the movement's poor press.

For about two years after Toda's death, no new president was designated. During this time, some signs of factionalism appeared and a few minor schisms occurred;[9] however, the organization survived its trial without any major rift or diminution of effectiveness. On May 3, 1960, Ikeda Daisaku, then only thirty-two years of age, was inaugurated as the third president of Soka Gakkai. Born in Tokyo in 1928, Ikeda was but nineteen years old when he became Toda's disciple. Thereafter, for the remaining eleven years in the life of his master, the young man received careful instruction from him and usually accompanied him on his numerous journeys.

It is not completely clear just how Ikeda was chosen for this top office. In a press conference three years after his installation, two officials of Soka Gakkai were asked, "Was the president of the Gakkai chosen by election?" One replied that it had been evident from the very atmosphere that everyone was agreed that Ikeda should be the president. This, he said, was the ultimate of democracy. The other official stated that the Board of Directors had decided that Ikeda was the man best suited for the job and asked him to accept. This procedure, he said, was in accord with the Buddhist way, which calls for that person who understands Buddhism most adequately to be the teacher.[10] In any event, the selection of Ikeda has proved to be popular with the membership and fortuitous for the organization. Intelligent and self-assured, vigorous and photogenic, he has held a tight rein on the organization and at the same time has kept the common touch. Though, as his many speeches reveal, Ikeda also has the mark of the fanatic upon him (he has said, for example: "The relation between the Sokagakkai and the Rissho Koseikai is that which existed between Buddha and the Devil"[11]), he is much more sensitive to the importance of good public relations than was his predecessor. He seems definitely to be trying to broaden the appeal of Soka Gakkai. Perhaps sensing that "by the very nature of [its] relationship to society . . . the 'attack' type of sect or cult is fairly short-lived,"[12] he has moderated the aggressiveness of *shakubuku* and has redirected some of the energy of his vast following into political and cultural pursuits.

A Lay Movement in the Service of a Buddhist Sect

Technically, Soka Gakkai is neither a religion nor a religious sect. It is a society of Buddhist laymen devoted to the service of Nichiren Sho-shu, a seven-hundred-year-old sect that claims to be Nichiren's only authorized agent and hence the sole proponent of "True Buddhism."

In the view of this sect, Nichiren, not Shakyamuni, stands as the climactic and pivotal figure in Buddhist history. Though Shakyamuni is acknowledged to have been the one who introduced Buddhism to the world, his career, except as it points toward Nichiren, generally is denigrated.[13] For forty-two years after his enlightenment, Shakyamuni is said to have advanced the teachings of Hinayana and Provisional Mahayana Buddhism, but during the last eight years of his life he expounded the *Lotus Sūtra*, the basis of Actual Mahayana Buddhism, and declared its superiority over all his previous teachings. He also is supposed to have issued a prophecy, which he spelled out in the following precise detail. For the first one thousand years after his death, people would be saved by his earlier and simpler teachings. During the second millennium, only the teachings of the *Lotus Sūtra* would be availing for salvation and Buddhism gradually would decline to the level of mere formality. When two thousand years had elapsed, the period known as *Mappō* ("latter days of the Law") would begin. Great wars and continual strife among the various sects would signify that the teachings of Shakyamuni had lost their power. Then would appear a great bodhisattva who, as the materialization of the Eternal Buddha, would propound a more powerful teaching applicable to the new times. This bodhisattva would arise in "a small country to the northeast of India," where, in spite of physical abuse and exile, he would establish True Buddhism and prepare for the salvation of all mankind.

This prophecy is regarded as having been fulfilled in Nichiren, who is now honored as the True Buddha.[14] In a sense, Nichiren's principal task was to complete a process of distillation that would leave quintessential Buddhism easily accessible to all. The fullness of the ancient teaching was embodied in the *Lotus Sūtra*. The *Lotus Sūtra* foretold the coming of Nichiren, none other than the Eternal Buddha. Nichiren reduced the whole of Buddhist truth to the invocation of the Sacred Title (*Daimoku*) and then inscribed its words on a tablet to be the enduring repository of all truth and power. This tablet is the *Gohonzon* (Object of Worship) of Nichiren Sho-shu and is kept in their head temple, Taisekiji, which stands at the foot of Mount Fuji.

Historically, Nichiren Sho-shu is but one of several sects within the Nichiren tradition, each one of which claims to be the guardian of orthodoxy. Because of the tangle of historical data and the intemperate character of the entire controversy, it is perhaps impossible to make a completely objective assessment of the rival claims. Yet, one point at least is clear: more faithfully than any of these other sects, Nichiren Sho-shu reflects Nichiren's own conviction that True Buddhism is clearly identifiable and that devotion to it is the only acceptable way of life. In a land noted for its religious pluralism, this sect is unrelenting in its claim to be the one true religion and is utterly contemptuous of the "heresies" of "false" religions. Soka Gakkai was organized to help press this claim and eliminate the opposition. Its activities in the service of Nichiren Sho-shu are principally of three kinds: (1) evangelism, (2) instruction in doctrine and discipline, and (3) material support.

EVANGELISM

The evangelistic task undertaken by Soka Gakkai may be defined as *shakubuku* for *kōsen-rufu*. *Shakubuku* ("break and subdue") is, as we have noted, the tactic of destroying another's resistance and converting him by the force of one's own arguments. *Kōsen-rufu*, or widespread dissemination, designates the ultimate goal and the anticipated achievement of worldwide acceptance of True Buddhism, when all mankind will live in happiness and peace. The spiel of the evangelist working toward this goal usually proceeds somewhat as follows. The chief end of man is happiness and peace, and the function of true religion is to enable man to achieve this state. There are, however, many different religions issuing contradictory claims and promises. Only one of these religions can be the true religion, and it is absolutely necessary that man identify that one and commit himself to it—but how is he to recognize it? He must examine each religion and subject it to three proofs (*sanshō*): (1) the literary (*monshō*), (2) the theoretical (*rishō*), and (3) the practical (*genshō*). Is it proved in the testimony of valid scripture? Is it consistent with reason and science? Does it actually work by producing happiness in daily life? Having tested all religions against these standards, one must conclude that Nichiren Sho-shu is the only true religion. All others, being heretical, are a source of unhappiness and therefore must be uprooted.

The proposal that the issue of religious supremacy be settled on the basis of a comparative study of various religions is, of course, simply a dodge. The spokesmen for Soka Gakkai are caricaturists, not students, of other religions. Any religion that looms as a rival is presented in stereotype and subjected to ridicule. In contrast, the superiority of Nichiren Sho-shu is "demonstrated" by an appeal to the above-mentioned three criteria. This religion meets the *literary* test, as the *Lotus Sūtra*, the only valid scripture, testifies. It also passes the *theoretical* test, since, as the only religion based on cause and effect, it is invariably consistent with science and reason. Finally, it meets the *practical* test, for, alone among religions, it can demonstrate that its followers are happy and are moving forward. Obviously, in the final analysis, the most effective "proof" is simply the persuasiveness of the leader's proclamation.

By means of *shakubuku*, Soka Gakkai has garnered a vast number of converts for Nichiren Sho-shu; however, in considering this fact, the outsider must be wary of his own tendency to report it in terms of a stereotype. Contrary to what one might expect, the assimilation of people into this sect is by no means uniform. Indeed, there are several distinctive, though sometimes overlapping, levels of religious orientation, ranging from utter naïveté and credulity to a fairly advanced state of sophistication. It may be instructive at this point to characterize these levels briefly.

In the first place, many devotees have found in Nichiren Sho-shu impressive validation and implementation for the rather primitive reliance upon magic and relic worship that is a part of their folk-religious heritage. Among such persons, the *Gohonzon* is treasured especially as a repository of magical power, power accessible to anyone through the recitation of the *Daimoku*, a magical incantation. They are deeply impressed, too, by the sacredness of the Nichiren memorabilia among the treasures of Taisekiji—altar equipment that he used, samples of his handwriting, and, above all, the *Onikuge*, one of his teeth. Reportedly, Nichiren himself pulled this tooth when it became loose and gave it to his favorite disciple. A tiny bit of flesh, so it is said, adhered to the root and has continued to grow until now it covers almost the entire surface of the tooth. Though rarely shown, this "living" tooth is prized as a symbol of the mystery of life.[15]

Secondly, there are those who throughout their lives had been Buddhists but, prior to their contact with Soka Gakkai, had never known why. Though often participating in Buddhist ceremonies, especially mortuary rites, they had known almost nothing of Buddhist doctrine and had never contemplated the relevance of their faith to their daily lives. Through Soka Gakkai, they feel, they now have established their identity as Buddhists. A religion that they had always been encouraged to regard as old and great and rich has at last become concretely meaningful.

At a third level, there are members who are committed specifically to what may be called *Hokke shinkō* ("Lotus faith") and who are deeply interested in the details of the Nichiren Sho-shu doctrines.[16] Soka Gakkai includes a fairly large number of serious lay students of the *Lotus Sūtra*, the writings of Nichiren, and the more recent literature of this tradition.

Finally, at the highest level, there are a few genuine intellectuals who have been attracted to this faith by Soka Gakkai. Uneasiness concerning the religious void in their lives is rather widespread among Japanese intellectuals, but relatively few of them ever find fulfillment in one of the Japanese religions, and most are openly disdainful of all the New Religions. Occasionally, however, one does affiliate with some sect. Joseph J. Spae has reported such an instance involving the conversion of a professor of physics from Roman Catholicism to Soka Gakkai. His generalization from this case seems plausible.

> People like Prof. Yamane seem to have found for the first time in Sōkagakkai the sense of being related to a Power which is truly universal and yet closely connected with themselves and with all aspects of their real lives. They have even found, through Sōkagakkai and not through Christianity, the idea of a Supreme Power, working out a great purpose in history, something that gives them great confidence for the future.[17]

In pursuing its goal of *kōsen-rufu*, worldwide propagation, Soka Gakkai has begun to develop outposts among both Japanese and non-Japanese residents overseas. Particularly in the United States and in several countries of South America where there are substantial colonies of Japanese people, Soka Gakkai has made notable progress. Beachheads also have been established in Australia and in a number of countries in southeast Asia and Europe.

Since the mid-1950's, a large percentage of non-Japanese converts has come from among American servicemen stationed in Japan. In view of the language and cultural barriers that usually hinder such persons from even attempting to penetrate Japanese society, the conversion of several hundred servicemen to a Japanese religion is a remarkable circumstance, one that, to my knowledge, no one has attempted to study carefully.

Most of these men are either married to or dating Japanese women, and their conversions, at least initially, usually are only concessions to their wives or girl friends.[18] In general, it seems, such men are rather poorly educated and culturally rootless. If they received any religious instruction in their younger days, it is likely to have come from a fundamentalistic or legalistic branch of Christianity and to be associated in their minds even yet with parental or social discipline, against which they may be in rebellion. If they have married Japanese women, usually they have done so over the objections of their parents and against the advice of their officers and diplomatic representatives, and probably the women have also had to act in defiance of their families and society.

The effort to achieve harmony in this type of mixed marriage often is very traumatic, especially for the wife, who perhaps tends to make greater sacrifices and also to expect more from the marriage than does the man. As tension and unhappiness increase, she may develop certain psychosomatic ailments. Eventually, desperate for help but psychologically and culturally debarred from finding it in available American medical or religious resources, she may turn to Soka Gakkai. Finding acceptance in an intimate *Japanese* fellowship, she may develop new hope and purpose, which may in turn result in the improvement of her total well-being. Her husband, surprised and genuinely pleased by the change, may then accede to her request that he accompany her to the Soka Gakkai meetings. Attempting to meet such a person at least halfway, Soka Gakkai leaders provide literature and discussions in English. Thereafter, if he becomes a convert, he may remain within the movement simply as a hanger-on, or he may become an active and enthusiastic participant, perhaps engaging in *shakubuku* among his buddies in the service or even among his family back home. In some instances, his zeal may surpass and outlast that of his wife, but generally the most important gain seems to be matrimonial harmony. For a husband and wife of diverse racial and cultural origins and with limited personal resources, there are many difficult adjustments that each must make. In Soka Gakkai they may see an opportunity to live a more fully shared life. Since Soka Gakkai is first of all a Japanese movement, it may enable the wife to reestablish and maintain ties with her own people and culture. Since this movement is also open to non-Japanese, it may seem to the husband to offer him his best opportunity to participate in *Japaneseness*, that which continually renders his wife a stranger to him. At the same time, Soka Gakkai may seem to both husband and wife to be sufficiently new, crisis-oriented, and universalistic to be a proper fellowship for people like themselves, who henceforth will find it almost impossible fully to be identified with either of the cultures whose mores they have violated. For such as these, Soka Gakkai has become a new community, one in which membership is not determined by birth.

INSTRUCTION IN DOCTRINE AND DISCIPLINE

Proud of having been founded by schoolmen and zealously devoted to its role as the warder of True Buddhism, Soka Gakkai assigns high priority to the instruction of its members in doctrine and discipline. Almost every activity that the society sponsors has this function as one of its purposes; however, it is pursued most specifically by three means: discussion groups, lectures, and publications.

Perhaps the most effective instruction takes place at the local level through the *zadankai* (discussion meetings). In these sessions, trained leaders hear the questions raised by the members and attempt to direct the discussions toward an orthodox understanding of the issues. On other occasions, especially large mass gatherings, lectures are delivered by the president and other high officials. Characteristically brief, these are popular and chatty discourses, more on the order of pep talks than of academic presentations, although they do stress doctrinal matters. Most of these speeches are printed or reported in one or more of the society's regular publications, and occasionally collections of them are also published in book form.

Soka Gakkai's publishing activities are extensive. In addition to books and pamphlets, the society issues three vernacular periodicals for propaganda purposes: *Seikyō Shimbun*, a thrice-weekly newspaper; *Seikyō Graphic*, an illustrated weekly; and *Daibyakurenge*, a monthly journal. Since a large percentage of the membership subscribes to these publications and reads them credulously, they are an effective means of indoctrination. Also, for the benefit of non-Japanese members and inquirers, Soka Gakkai publishes in English a weekly newspaper, *The Seikyo News*; a monthly magazine, *Seikyo Times*; and assorted books and pamphlets. On the whole, the Gakkai's publications in both languages are blatantly propagandistic and doctrinaire, and their literary quality is very poor.

As an incentive to study, Soka Gakkai has initiated a series of examinations by which the members may qualify for academic ranks and titles to signify their level of understanding. In ascending order, the various grades are assistant lecturer, lecturer, sub-assistant professor, assistant professor, associate professor, and professor. The seriousness with which the members respond to this system is indicated by the fact that annually several hundred thousand people take the examinations.

Disciplinary instruction in Soka Gakkai pertains chiefly to individual and family worship and pilgrimages to the head temple. When a person becomes a member, he is given a *gohonzon*, a small facsimile of the "original" mandala of Nichiren, to enshrine in his home. Every morning and every evening, he is supposed to pray before this *gohonzon*. Although he has a small service book from which he reads on these occasions, his principal act of worship then and in every circumstance is the recitation of the *Daimoku*, the religious act par excellence.

The chanting of this prayer formula, *Namu Myōhō Renge-kyō* ("Adoration to the Lotus of the Wonderful Law"), is a fairly typical example of a well-known phenomenon in the history of religions, namely, the effort to achieve salvation by invocation. This technique is broadly prominent in Japanese popular Buddhism. Apparently throughout all the Nichiren sects, the *Daimoku* is chanted; in addition, the several Pure Land sects have the *Nembutsu* (*Namu Amida Butsu*, "Adoration to Amida Buddha"). Though interpretations of the use of such formulas vary from sect to sect, the essential character of the practice seems to remain rather constant. Faith is not prerequisite to the recitation. It may be undertaken entirely on an experimental basis. The most important factors initially are quantity and frequency. By the very act of repeated recitation, a process of empowerment and transformation takes place, with the eventual result that the invocation, including all the mystery of which it is the quintessence, becomes a functioning part of one's innermost being, and one is linked effectively with whatever is considered to be the source of saving power.[19] In the Buddhistic frame of reference, the recitation is also a means of altering karma by canceling the untoward effects of previous deeds and by becoming itself the cause of desirable results.[20]

Next to daily worship, the most important aspect of religious discipline is pilgrimage (*tozankai*) to the head temple of Nichiren Sho-shu. This temple, Taisekiji, is a complex of ancient and modern buildings situated "at the most awe-inspiring spot in the world,"[21] at the foot of Mount Fuji.[22] It is magnetically attractive to Soka Gakkai devotees. There the *Gohonzon*, the repository of all saving power, is kept. There, too, are many other Nichiren relics, as well as the tomb of Toda Josei, whose eminence is second only to that of Nichiren within this tradition, and the magnificent new edifices that the members themselves have helped to build. Each member is urged to make a pilgrimage to this place, and most are enthusiastically eager to do so. With so vast a membership, however, the problem has been to maintain orderly traffic patterns in the daily movement of thousands of pilgrims to and from Taisekiji.

Soka Gakkai's ability to handle this problem is a prime example of its organizational efficiency. No one may make the pilgrimage without permission, and all who go must obey the directions of their chaperons and guides. With these two conditions met, it has been possible, using chartered trains and buses, to shepherd an average of about ten thousand pilgrims a day through the temple.[23]

MATERIAL SUPPORT

Outwardly, Soka Gakkai maintains a low-pressure approach to financial matters. When asked to identify the sources of income, spokesmen for the society explain that they receive the bulk of their support from a relatively few wealthy members and the sale of publications. Severely critical of sects that greedily fleece their deluded followers, Soka Gakkai leaders deny that their members have ever been similarly victimized. But no matter the sources and means of collection, it is obvious that this organization has tremendous financial resources and that one of its chief functions is to utilize this potential in providing material support for Nichiren Sho-shu.

The most impressive products of this stewardship are the splendid new buildings that the Gakkai has erected since 1955 in the precinct of Taisekiji. Regarded as the materialization of modern ideas inspired in the human mind through faith in True Buddhism,[24] the erection of these buildings provides concrete goals and symbolizes dramatic achievement. The first to be completed was the Hoanden, a sanctuary within which the *Gohonzon* is enshrined. Among the several other fine facilities that have been built subsequently, the most notable are two large ultramodern buildings, the Daikōdō (Grand Lecture Hall) and the Daikyakuden (Grand Reception Hall).

The Daikōdō was completed early in 1958 and was dedicated in a month-long series of ceremonies in March of that year. It is an impressive six-story building, designed to accommodate five thousand people for lectures. The cost was approximately $1,100,000. Even more impressive and costly is the Daikyakuden. Said to have been planned originally by Toda, it was one of the projects to which Ikeda committed himself in his inaugural address on May 3, 1960. In July of the following year, the projected cost of more than $3,000,000 was oversubscribed about two and a half times in only a four-day financial campaign. The completed building was dedicated on April 1, 1964.

In special ways, the Daikyakuden symbolizes the broadening goals of Soka Gakkai. Into the foundation went stones that had been gathered from forty-seven countries. Among the building materials used are cypress from Taiwan, cedar from Canada, and marble from Italy, Sweden, and France. Decorative pieces include a chandelier from Czechoslovakia and a fountain from Italy, both selected by President Ikeda during a trip abroad. Also, in a surprising gesture, a large number of guests (including the present author) were invited from among the foreign diplomats, scholars, and journalists then residing in Japan to be present for the grand opening of the new structure.

But eventually even these imposing edifices will be surpassed when present plans for a new cathedral are materialized. Already the money is in hand. In the autumn of 1965, the Japanese were astounded to learn that in a four-day campaign, Soka Gakkai had raised almost $100,000,000 for this project. This unprecedented fund-raising feat was made possible by many acts of sacrificial giving, such as surrendering the cash value of insurance policies.

A Proselytizing Mass Movement

If in his book *The True Believer* Eric Hoffer has accurately delineated the characteristics of a mass movement (as I believe he has), then Soka Gakkai is almost a perfect textbook example of this phenomenon. Thus it would appear that although this society is closely affiliated with a sect of Buddhism, its religious character actually is largely accessory to its essential identity as a proselytizing mass movement. If so, its success can be attributed not so much to the appeal of its doctrines or the attractiveness of its object of worship as to the confluence of those factors that seem always to accompany a successful mass movement. Here, following Hoffer, we shall note some of the most important of these factors and comment on their applicability to an analysis of Soka Gakkai.

Unless the social conditions are propitious, a proselytizing movement has no chance of prospering. "The milieu most favorable for the rise and propagation of mass movements is one in which a once compact corporate structure is, for one reason or another, in a state of disintegration."[25] Just such a condition has existed in Japan since the end of World War II. The breakup of totalitarian government and military discipline and the deterioration of traditional institutions, together with increased exposure to the Western ideal of self-advancement, have resulted in widespread individual frustration. Though the new order permits unprecedented freedom, "the palliatives of frustration" are lacking.[26] This condition obtains particularly among the urban poor, many of whom, weighed down by social inequities and by self-distrust and feelings of helplessness, have little sense of personal worth. In short, they are the "poignantly frustrated," those who in every instance, it seems, are the fruits that a mass movement harvests first.[27] Perhaps their principal burden is the consciousness of a worthless or unwanted self from which they long to escape. An effective mass movement may help them to accomplish their desire.

It cures the poignantly frustrated not by conferring on them an absolute truth or by remedying the difficulties and abuses which made their lives miserable, but by freeing them from their ineffectual selves —and it does this by enfolding and absorbing them into a closely knit and exultant corporate whole.[28]

Apparently this is precisely the service that Soka Gakkai has rendered to a large percentage of those who have entered its ranks. Its success is not due to the quality of its ideas but to its ability to reach a person who feels that he is nobody and to impart to him new hope and purpose by showing him a fellowship and a cause within which he can find both acceptance and refuge.

In order to be effective, a mass movement must achieve unity. For this purpose, its best technique "consists basically in the inculcation and cultivation of proclivities and responses indigenous to the frustrated mind."[29] Here again, Soka Gakkai follows the script very closely. If we note Hoffer's own selective list[30] of the propensities of the frustrated mind, we can readily see that Soka Gakkai appeals directly to each of them. (1) *A deprecation of the present.* Mankind now is living in *Mappō*, the "latter days of the Law," a degenerate age. (2) *A facility for make-believe.* All the power of Buddhism resides in the *Gohonzon*, the tablet on which Nichiren is supposed to have inscribed the *Daimoku.* (3) *A proneness to hate.* All other religions are heretical, and their protagonists are deceitful rascals who must be unmasked and defeated. (4) *A readiness to imitate.* By reciting the *Daimoku* and practicing *shakubuku* according to prescription, the members increase their faith and begin to realize concrete benefits in their daily lives. (5) *Credulity*. This is the True Buddhism; therefore, even though one may not understand its profound doctrines, he need never doubt the supremacy of this religion. (6) *A readiness to attempt the impossible*. The goal of Soka Gakkai is *kōsen-rufu*, the evangelization of the entire world.

The unity achieved in this manner can be maintained and strengthened by means of a tightly controlled organization. It is one of the enigmas of a rising mass movement that while its adherents have a strong sense of liberation, they also find congenial and comfortable an atmosphere of strict obedience to rules and commands.[31] Not real freedom but fraternity and uniformity, signifying deliverance from the frustrations of independent, individual existence, are the goals. A mass movement would default on its promises if it failed to provide an authoritarian structure that is conducive to so complete an assimilation of the individual that he will cease to "see himself and others as human beings."[32] This, indeed, has been the result for thousands of Soka Gakkai members. They no longer see themselves as undistinguished members of human society; their primary citizenship is in True Buddhism, through which they are linked to a force and an organization that are changing the world.

The success of a mass movement, of course, depends to a great extent upon the talents of its leader. What qualities are essential to such a one?

Exceptional intelligence, noble character and originality seem neither indispensable nor perhaps desirable. The main requirements seem to be: audacity and a joy in defiance; an iron will; a fanatical conviction that he is in possession of the one and only truth; faith in his destiny and luck; a capacity for passionate hatred; contempt for the present; a cunning estimate of human nature; a delight in symbols (spectacles and ceremonials); unbounded brazenness which finds expression in a disregard of consistency and fairness; a recognition that the innermost craving of a following is for communion and that there can never be too much of it; a capacity for winning and holding the utmost loyalty of a group of able lieutenants.[33]

Within Soka Gakkai, all these traits belonged to Toda Josei, the second president, and all are also present in his successor,

Ikeda Daisaku. However, in both cases, certain characteristics are more prominent than others. In Toda, who was at the helm when Soka Gakkai was on the rise, audacity, fanatical faith, and brazenness—the very qualities most needed at the time—were ascendant. In Ikeda, on the other hand, perhaps delight in symbols, recognition of the importance of communion, and a capacity for surrounding himself with capable and loyal assistants are dominant. These latter traits, it appears, suit well the man whose task, like Ikeda's, is to consolidate a mass movement.

Ikeda is a man of action and is committed to the promotion of united action on the part of his vast following. Under his leadership, the scope of the movement has been greatly expanded. Though it continues to draw the poignantly frustrated from among the poor, it is also reaching deeper and deeper into the middle class to attract large numbers of young people and others who are chiefly interested in the diversified and efficiently run activities of the society. However, this development, too, fits the general pattern for mass movements. "It is rare for a mass movement to be wholly of one character. Usually it displays some facets of other types of movement, and sometimes it is two or three movements in one."[34] Soka Gakkai, as we have observed, is a religious movement, but it is also a political and a cultural movement.

A Sponsor of a Political Party

Ōbutsumyōgō, meaning the "agreement in purpose of government and Buddhism," a principle advocated by Nichiren in the thirteenth century, provides the ideological basis for Soka Gakkai's entrance into politics. Under the presidency of Toda Josei, the society organized a political department, which it called Kōmei Seiji Renmei (often abbreviated as Kōseiren), Fair Politics Federation, and in local elections in 1955 sponsored and elected to office fifty-three candidates. In the national elections of the following year, 1956, three Kōseiren candidates, polling approximately one million votes, were elected to the House of Councillors, the Upper House of the Diet. These victories, coupled with reckless campaign methods, which resulted in the arrest of more than one hundred Soka Gakkai devotees on charges of violating election laws,[35] attracted nationwide attention to this burgeoning mass movement. Subsequent successes have occasioned widespread and increasing alarm among political parties, who do not welcome additional competition, and among many private citizens, who fear the return of fascism.

In 1959, Soka Gakkai ran six more candidates for the House of Councillors and elected them all, thus bringing their total representation in the Upper House to nine. In 1962, when the three original Councillors plus six new candidates waged successful campaigns, Soka Gakkai became the third largest body in the Upper House, with fifteen representatives. Besides the ruling Liberal Democratic Party, only the Socialist Party outnumbered them. Still, the political purpose of Soka Gakkai at that time was somewhat amorphous. Without the backing of a full-fledged political party, the Soka Gakkai members of the Diet organized themselves into the Kōmeikai (Fairness Association) in order to have a base for negotiating with other political units; but generally they tended to favor the policies of the Liberal Democrats. All the while, Soka Gakkai officials disavowed real political intentions. Their members' presence in the Upper House, they said, was principally symbolic, and they had no plan to try to elect candidates to the Lower House, the House of Representatives, where the most effective political power resides. Initially they adopted a muckraker's role, calling attention to corruption and discrimination and lionizing their own elected officials, both at national and local levels, as the only ones really interested in the welfare of the people.

A major turning point was reached on May 3, 1964, when President Ikeda announced that, acceding to its importunate membership, Soka Gakkai would enter candidates in the next Lower House election. However, he indicated that to avoid involving the society directly in politics, a new political party would be formed. Later that year, on November 17, the Kōmeitō (Clean Government Party) was organized. Technically, this party is organically separate from Soka Gakkai, but while membership in the party is not limited to Soka Gakkai adherents, no real effort has been made to disguise the fact that the two actually are interlocking agencies. As one Japanese journalist has observed, "the two bodies are of the same blood and live on the same spiritual pabulum."[36] Not only is Soka Gakkai the Kōmeitō's sponsor, but also its leaders determine the policies and its membership comprises the principal electorate of the party.

At the time of this writing, the anticipated Lower House election had not yet been called. Nevertheless, the new party had had an opportunity to prove itself. In the national elections in 1965, the Kōmeitō increased the number of its seats in the Upper House to twenty. Also, in the local Tokyo elections in the same year, the Kōmeitō made significant gains in the Metropolitan Assembly. Because of public revulsion following the disclosure of extensive scandal among incumbent officeholders, neither the Liberal Democrats nor their major opponents, the Socialists, were able to achieve a majority of seats. Thus, Kōmeitō, though third in numerical strength, was left with the balance of power in that important body.

Thus far, it seems, Soka Gakkai has contributed a generally salutary influence to Japanese politics. Its representatives are sufficiently numerous to be rather effective as gadflies but are still too few to have to assume any real responsibility for policy making. They are helping to arouse the long-entrenched Liberal Democrats from lethargy and to expose the hollowness of the endless demonstrations that the Socialists and Communists offer as substitutes for real political acumen and action. Still, at this juncture, it is perhaps impossible to predict the long-range significance of Soka Gakkai's political ventures or even to be confident concerning their real character.[37] Several important questions remain to be answered.

First, will Soka Gakkai be able to elect enough representatives to the Lower House of the Diet to gain a real voice in the national government? In local and Upper House elections, where its previous successes have been registered, it has with comparative ease planned and directed patterns of voting among its obedient membership that have assured the election of almost all its candidates. In the case of Lower House elections, this will be a more complicated and less predictable procedure; for whereas the majority of the members of the House of Councillors are elected by nationwide balloting, delegates to the House of Representatives are determined by votes within specified electoral districts. Thus, in the latter case, Soka Gakkai bloc voting will be effective only in those districts in which its devotees are concentrated.

Second, does Soka Gakkai stand for a policy that could be implemented politically? The goal of Kōmeitō is to establish "Buddhist democracy" (*buppō minshu shugi*), apparently to be defined as a "parliamentary democracy in which every individual has been awakened to the principles of Buddhism."[38] Such an achievement presupposes the conversion of a majority of the Japanese to Nichiren Sho-shu. Soka Gakkai also sees itself in terms of international outreach as the "Third Civilization," the synthesizer of Eastern spirituality and Western materialism and the obvious alternative to the two major power blocs. This goal, in turn, is tied to *kōsen-rufu*, the worldwide propagation of the faith. On the bread-and-butter issues of Japanese politics, Kōmeitō's policies seem generally to be unoriginal and to reflect the still limited experience and political acumen of its personnel.

Third, will Soka Gakkai's sponsorship of a political party be challenged on constitutional grounds? Presumably it could be, for in Article 20 of the constitution it is expressly stated: "No religious organization shall receive any privileges from the State, nor exercise any political authority." As yet the meaning of this declaration has not been clarified, for it has never been tested in the courts.[39]

Finally, is Soka Gakkai fascistic? If it should gain extensive political power, would it recognize the basic freedoms of the opposition, or would it, invoking the principle that "error has no rights," demand conformity from the opposition? The apparently total lack of parliamentary procedure within both Soka Gakkai and Kōmeitō gives no assurance that their representatives in government will seek to promote democracy, except in the sense that they themselves define this concept.

A Patron of Cultural Opportunities for the Masses

Asserting that, as history indicates, it is one of the functions of Buddhism to inspire cultural developments, Soka Gakkai is committing itself to the promotion of a wide range of cultural movements. Within its organization, it has set up a Cultural Division consisting of departments of public opinion, education, science, art, and economics. In addition, it sponsors a number of associations and institutes for the advancement of such cultural pursuits as music, drama, and scientific and philosophical inquiry. It now seems likely that by 1976, Soka Gakkai will have its own university; and it is entirely possible that the society will eventually decide to form its own nationwide labor organization.

Apparently there are two principal purposes underlying this outreach. One is the widely advertised intention to extend and improve the cultural opportunities of the masses. The other, unspecified but no less obvious, is a bid to diversify the appeal and thereby increase the influence of Soka Gakkai. There is no reason to suppose that this society is incapable of genuinely altruistic interests; at the same time, there is every reason to believe that everything that it does includes a power motive. Certainly the leaders of Soka Gakkai realize that they cannot continue indefinitely to expand their organization solely, or even mainly, on the basis of its religious appeal; but they also know that there are many other ways by which they can "win friends and influence people." Thus they are beginning to experiment with a variety of approaches; for example, they now publish a nonpropagandistic journal, *Ushio* (*The Tide*), intended for a readership among intellectuals, most of whom have been nothing but contemptuous of Soka Gakkai's claims.

Perhaps the dual purpose of this whole cultural outreach can be seen most clearly in reference to the formation of the Minshu Ongaku Kyōkai (abbreviated as Min-on), Democratic Music Association. This is a concert society that was organized in 1963. For the payment of a very small membership fee, the music-loving Japanese of modest financial means can attend a variety of concerts featuring "wholesome" popular music—music considered to be superior to that which usually is available to the masses but not of so high a level as to be beyond the range of their appreciation. (Mitch Miller and his "Sing Along" gang were featured in a Min-on concert on May 19, 1965.) Surely, this is a worthy enterprise, and more than a half-million people have indicated their approval by joining this association. However, it must also be noted that by forming this organization, Soka Gakkai entered a contest already in existence between the rival sponsors of two other popular concert societies. The first to be formed was Ro-on under the sponsorship of Sōhyō, a leftist labor federation. This act was seen as a challenge by certain capitalists, who countered by forming Onkyō, to which they tried to convert Ro-on members. Despite its protestations to the contrary, Soka Gakkai established Min-on partly in order to join this rivalry, for at issue is a question that is being tested on many fronts: Who best serves and represents the masses in present-day Japan?

Reflections

In studying Soka Gakkai, it is very difficult to remain unbiased; for in the course of the inquiry, one's sensibilities almost certainly will be outraged repeatedly by much that one sees, hears, and reads and, above all, by the general brashness and gracelessness of many of the Soka Gakkai people whom one meets. They seemingly have no flair for public relations. Even when they are extending hospitality, their certitude sets them apart and may cause them to appear to be contemptuous of their guests. If for no other reason than this, it is not difficult to comprehend why so many observers, both Japanese and non-Japanese, report that Soka Gakkai is an insidious movement.

There are, of course, still other and more substantial reasons—as we have already observed—why Soka Gakkai is a disturbing presence. Yet, is it not important, so far as possible, to hold these negative responses in abeyance and endeavor also to identify the more positive attributes of this powerful movement? What might they be?

In the first place, there is often a prophetic quality, almost Hebraic in its boldness, in the society's diatribes against institutional religion and entrenched political forces. Though unmistakably libelous in character and self-righteous in tone, these utterances may contain a valid word of judgment. In the infamous *Shakubuku Kyōten*, we read that

. . . from the standpoint of actual practice and practical application, the religious world today has degenerated and forgotten the truths discovered by former great sages. The leaders today have become nothing but clown-like priests or monkey-like religionists, pretending to know the truth and rattling off in a pompous manner. One cannot help but be shocked; one cannot help but be dumbfounded.[40]

In the second place, almost alone among the Japanese religions and religious movements, Soka Gakkai has been able to attract a really large number of young people. Undoubtedly there are many reasons—some perhaps ignoble—why this is so, but one explanation offered by a Soka Gakkai official cannot be taken lightly. Said he:

Today the young people in Japan no longer have a dream. They play baseball and watch television, but this cannot satisfy them completely. They must have some dream. This religion supplies that dream for the future; and, in addition, it gives them happiness now every day.[41]

Finally, one may wonder how much of Nichiren's *total* spirit survives in Soka Gakkai. Has only his bibliolatrous hatred of heresy been retained at the heart of a mythological interpretation of his career? Uchimura Kanzo (1861–1930) insisted that there was something priceless in this Buddhist prophet:

I for one venture my honour, if need be, for this man. Most of his doctrines, I grant, cannot stand the test of the present-day criticism. His polemics were inelegant, and his whole tone was insanoid. He certainly was an unbalanced character, too pointed in only one direction. But divest him of his intellectual errors, of his hereditary temperament, and of much that his time and surroundings marked upon him, and you have a soul sincere to its very core, the honestest of men, the bravest of Japanese.[42]

Then, Uchimura concluded his assessment by saying: "*Nichiren minus his combativity* is our ideal religious man."[43] The expendable subtrahend, it seems, has been fully preserved. How much, if any, of the remainder lives on in Soka Gakkai?[44]

Conclusion

WHETHER THEY ARE CONSIDERED as phenomena or as a phenomenon, as movements or as a movement, the New Religions of Japan are immensely complex, and their essential character and ultimate importance are highly ambiguous. They perpetuate rather unselectively a substantial residue of the old and traditional. They mirror the hurt and frustration of many generations of common people who have suffered deprivations imposed by a too narrowly regimented life. They exemplify the hope that indeed does spring "eternal in the human breast." They also seem to possess, both threateningly and promisingly, the capability for exerting a long-range effect upon the life of Japan. Though the enterprise is highly problematical, it is this capability that we shall examine tentatively now in bringing this study to its conclusion.

Japanese Public Reaction to the New Religions

"The New Religions are terrible! I don't want other people to know about them." Such was the reaction of a Japanese friend of our family when we told her why we had returned to Japan.

It is not an untypical view. Though held with varying degrees of intensity, this is also—and for years has been—essentially the attitude of many middle- and upper-class Japanese. Analyzed more finely, it seems usually to be an outlook in which are mingled feelings of amusement, contempt, and alarm but which nevertheless remains broadly permissive or indulgent and may even reflect an element of personal uneasiness or wistfulness. Let us see some of the ways in which it is manifested.

(1) *The New Religions are amusing.* They are only *goriyaku shūkyō* (religions of personal advantage). Almost anyone, it is said jokingly, no matter his origin or experience, can easily become the spokesman for some deity and quickly amass a group of followers. Virtually any teaching will do, so long as it is ludicrously superficial and illogical. One college professor writes: "I even burst out laughing sometimes when I am reading the doctrines of certain New Religions."[1]

(2) *The New Religions are contemptible.* Some Japanese find them to be not only laughably ridiculous but disquietingly and repulsively so. Sheer disgust is expressed in the following assessment:

I once glanced at a propaganda pamphlet issued by one of these new religions, and found myself more struck by something nasty in the general tone than by any merits or demerits in the actual ideas it propounded. The religions of the past which are worthy of the name somehow give an impression of cleanliness, but about certain of the new religions there clings an odour that is distinctly unsavoury.[2]

(3) *The New Religions are alarming.* The notion seems to be widespread that these sects are a cover-up for extortion and quackery of many sorts. Thus, it is assumed that weak and ignorant people regularly are the prey of the greedy and that the ill and confused frequently are brought to still greater harm. Such is the misgiving, conveyed in awkward but expressive English, in the following statement: "Of course, some patients will be glad being restored their health, but we must know how many innocent people hurry to the grave untimely because of their not consulting the doctors."[3] There are also allegations, supported by very limited statistical data, that the New Religions are contributing to the incidence of mental illness.[4] But currently,

perhaps the greatest alarm is occasioned by the political successes of Soka Gakkai.

(4) *Still, the New Religions are timely, while the old religions are passé.* The spokesmen for these new sects at least know where people hurt. Though their motivations and techniques may be questionable, they seem to have some of the right concerns. Thinking thus, the man cited previously who admitted laughing at the doctrines as being superficial and indiscreet testified later in his article that "after deep consideration you will have a more friendly feeling toward the New Religions than toward the so-called 'existing religions' [*kisei shūkyō*]."⁵ Certainly, he acknowledged, they are simple and naïve, but also they are dynamic. They are conscious of the problems and sufferings of people and are directed toward their alleviation. Furthermore, he asks rhetorically: "Which is it that has a stronger prayer for peace, the 'existing religions' or the New Religions?"

(5) *Only time can tell which, if any, of the New Religions are genuine.* It is generally conceded that man has an innate tendency to seek solace in religion and that if he does not find it in "proper" places, he will search elsewhere.

These are troubled times, and it is perhaps inevitable that if the old religions have lost their authority man should be ready, if only his spiritual weakness is played on, to entrust himself body and soul to something such as these new religions.⁶

Therefore, even though some of the New Religions are unsavory and possibly even antisocial, perhaps it is wise not to try to suppress them, for each one will progress only so far as it deserves to go. "The New Religions must speak to ignorant people at first. As they mature they may become more profound. If they do not, others will arise to take their place."⁷ Furthermore, there is even the possibility that those that do survive may bring some contribution of lasting value. "This age of science may yet produce a new Christ or a new Buddha who will weave a new world of illusion in a truly disinterested attempt to save the masses of mankind."⁸

The raising of this latter possibility helps to open to our view still another dimension in the religious perspectives of Japanese sophisticates. Like their counterparts elsewhere, such persons

on the whole seem rather thoroughly secularized—some com-
mittedly so, some faddishly so. Some who as youths witnessed
the sudden about-face in teachings concerning the divinity of
the Emperor and the sacredness of the Japanese mission still
show the effects of this shock and now find it almost impossible
to believe in anything. However, in many instances, secularization is either sported or borne uneasily. One frequently finds
intimations that this is so. For example, a scientific folklorist
writes: "When we consider that people in bygone days sought to
ward off sickness with . . . a talisman . . . , it arouses feelings
of both pity and amusement, *together with a tinge of envy.*"[9]
A similar feeling may be aroused by exposure to one of the New
Religions. Thus, after observing a young woman kneeling alone
in prayer in the sanctuary of one of the sects, a man of scientific
temperament writes: "I was moved as I watched by mingled
feelings of sympathy and interest. Such simple, unquestioning
piety is mine no longer, *yet I still at times experience a nostalgia
of kinds for that ability to pour out one's heart to some supernatural being,* whether a God, a Buddha, or anything else."[10]
While perhaps it has not happened often that those "who came
to scoff, remain'd to pray,"[11] nevertheless the response in many
cases is at least ambivalent—revulsion from human ignorance and
chicanery, coupled with fascination before the uncanny.

As we might expect, the strongest feelings against the New
Religions usually are expressed not so much by the secularized
laity as by the professional protagonists (such as priests and educators) of the old established religions. They have become increasingly alert to the possible implications of the flourishing of
the new movements, and some among them have published
strong statements alleging that these sects are perversions of
religion and that generally they are being perpetrated by greedy
impostors. However, even among such critics, it seems also to be
generally recognized that in the very success of the New Religions there is unmistakably an element of judgment upon the
incumbent religious leadership and their establishments. Hence,
together with the general populace, they too have found it possible to temper their resentment with a certain degree of mag-
nanimity.

I found this response well exemplified in one of my close

friends, a lay Buddhist scholar and educator in the Jodo Shin-shu, who had authored criticisms of the New Religions. At my request, he set down for me an outline of his reactions to those movements. He began by belaboring them on three counts: (1) their bold and piratical eclecticism, (2) the unprincipled opportunism of their leaders, who prey upon the ignorant and suffering, and (3) their fanatical, misleading, and exaggerated promises of benefits to be received. However, turning next to an examination of the conditions that had fostered the rise of such sects, he proceeded to list thirty-two points detailing the failure of Buddhism to minister to the Japanese people in the period of their greatest social crisis. Thus, while he deplored the existence of the New Religions, he recognized that the ineffectiveness of the old religions had been permissive of their rise. Said he: "The old religions have given room for the activities of the New Religions. . . . It is lamentable that almost all the sects of Buddhism have lost their power and their truth."[12]

Yet, despite the ambivalent, sometimes soul-searching response that the Japanese people have accorded the New Religions, it still may be said that neither as a movement nor as movements have these sects really been taken very seriously. This is the burden of a statement that a Japanese scholar has addressed to his fellow countrymen. Pointing out that largely because of adverse publicity the New Religions sometimes are considered to be abnormal and unhealthful social phenomena, he goes on to say: "Today's New Religions, however, cannot be neglected. They are in the process of growing as a social power, influencing the political, social, and cultural fields in Japan."[13]

In essence, this statement is the thesis which I have attempted to enunciate throughout this book and which, in conclusion, I want to reexamine both descriptively and conjecturally in relation to certain questions concerning the staying power or future significance of the New Religions.

The Issue of "Religious" Adequacy

In terms of the *quality* of their "religious" appeal and the life of faith that they offer, what is likely to be the long-range significance of the New Religions? The phrasing of this question reflects a concern—frequently with pejorative overtones—that many people feel when they become aware of the dramatic success of these sects. There may follow, then, a whole line of questions in somewhat the same vein. Can such sects continue to thrive? If so, will their presence tend to subvert the cause of "creative" or "profound" religion by presenting a prominent but poor image of religion and by perpetuating the delusion of the masses? On the other hand, is it possible that the New Religions (or at least some of them) are actually "diamonds in the rough"? Is it likely, then, that in some fashion—perhaps by helping to thwart the advance or to moderate the severity of secularization— these movements might actually serve the cause of "genuine" religion? Is it even conceivable that "spiritual renewal," so often mentioned by both Japanese and non-Japanese as Japan's great need, could issue from what has been begun in these New Religions?

Almost any questions pertaining to the future of the New Religions are problematic; and they are doubly so if, like the queries just posed, they call for an assessment of these sects on the basis of their "religious" *quality* or *adequacy*. Only a very incautious or arbitrary person would attempt to answer such questions unequivocally. In general, it seems more judicious for the historian of religions, in dealing with these concerns, to eschew rendering opinions that approximate value judgments and to adopt instead some more agnostic stance, such as the following:

Now we have learned better than dogmatically to label this particular action holy and meritorious, and that gesture superstitious and repulsive: the roots of faith lie too deep in human personality for any superficial judgment, or perhaps for any human judgment at all.[14]

Furthermore, for reasons that we shall present later, preoccupation with the *quality* of these sects may actually debar an observer from comprehending their essential character and significance. Nevertheless, it still seems possible and justifiable, without forsaking necessary objectivity, to make a few pointed comments concerning the religious adequacy of the New Religions.

In the first place, we may observe that while Japan has experienced numerous religious revivals of various sorts, it has never undergone a religious reformation in the past, and the New Religions do not represent such in the present or promise it for the future.[15] On the contrary, they are deeply rooted in traditional folk religion, especially in the ancestor cult, shamanism, magic, and miracle. Though they burgeoned particularly just after World War II, when, as many now think, Japan was ripe for a religious reformation, the New Religions offered mainly only a sanctuary and a palliative, largely reversionary in character, which imparted a measure of hope to many among the frustrated masses but offered nothing to the nation as a whole.

Therefore, it can be said, in the second place, that while these sects consistently have addressed themselves to the assuagement of real needs, their approach frequently has been superficial. Characteristically, they have not explored the sources of man's problems in the depths of human nature or in the intricacies of social structure and personal interaction.[16]

Consequently, in the third place, being generally incapable of analyzing and solving personal and social problems in depth, the New Religions have often resorted to religious escapism. By so doing, Saki charges, they hinder the development of freedom and democratic participation. If they are to serve a more positive function, he says, three transitions must be effected: "from blind obedience to democratic spontaneity, from unrealistic idealism to realistic concreteness, from mere word to positive action."[17]

From the comments thus far, it appears that there is little of enduring religious value to be expected from the New Religions; but we must be clear in emphasizing that there is also a range of more positive characteristics to be noted. First, through their typically strong organizations, the New Religions follow up individual expressions of need or interest by providing a sustained pattern of activities, companionship, consultation, and specific goals and programs. Such an approach is an innovation for many Japanese, who, though long accustomed to seeking personal benefits through religion, customarily have pursued their religious interests sporadically and unsystematically. For example, seeking some specific boon or just general good fortune, a Japanese may go to a shrine, throw a small coin into the alms box, offer a brief prayer, then go on his way and, for an indefinite time thereafter, have nothing more to do with such activity. Through systematization, the New Religions attempt to move religious interest and participation from the periphery to the center of life. To the considerable extent that they have succeeded in this effort, they have transformed religious involvement into something that is much more purposeful than it characteristically had been.

Second, the purposefulness engendered by these sects, though often crassly utilitarian, may be opening the way to more considered thought and discussion of the potential relevance of religious faith and commitment to the conditions of modern life. As they evolve, certain of these new movements are playing down their earlier promises of immediate benefits and are beginning to take cognizance of "the conflicts and the institutions that make life harsh and meaningless for many"[18] and to urge that what goes on politically and socially is properly the concern of religious man qua religious man.

Third, though the emphasis upon healing and worldly success is waning somewhat, the strength and appeal of the New Religions seem not to be abating. Does this mean that the motivations of the devotees are becoming more "spiritual" and less mundane? According to Oishi Shuten, the clearheaded executive secretary of the Union of New Religious Organizations (Shinshūren), this is precisely what it does mean.[19]

Fourth, it is unmistakable that the New Religions of Japan are evolving according to the same general pattern that has long been observable in similar movements elsewhere. That is, they are steadily becoming more highly institutionalized and sophisticated. In some instances, it is obvious that the lingering association with shamanism, faith healing, and magical elements has become an embarrassment to current leaders, who aspire now to be identified instead with perspectives and programs that more members of the middle and upper classes of society will recognize as viable.

If we return now to the question with which we began this section, how may we formulate an answer? In terms of the *quality* of their "religious" appeal and the life of faith that they offer, what is likely to be the long-range significance of the New Religions? We must say, I think, that the issue is highly ambiguous. Both by design and by natural evolution, some of the sects are becoming more sophisticated, hence presumably more respectable. At the same time, it is evident that the attainment of greater sophistication is usually accompanied by a decline in the rate of growth and a general loss of vitality.[20] Perhaps this trend will continue. Perhaps it will also result in the stabilizing of some of these movements as solid middle-class sects. However, it still remains pertinent to ask whether it is at all likely that, since folk beliefs are their basic resource, the New Religions can bring forth teachings that can command an extensive hearing among the real pacesetters and decision makers in the complex society of modern Japan. Again, the chief significance of these movements lies not so much in their intrinsic quality as in their social function. Let us ask, then, what this fact presages.

The "Bridging" Character of the New Religions

"It is easy to be contemptuous of popular culture; it is important also to recognize its broadening social role."[21] This observation is wholly and directly pertinent to the study of the new religious movements in Japan. As we have stressed repeatedly, they are products of Japanese popular culture and, as such, retain prominently much of the naïveté and credulity of folk faith, in consequence of which they often are denigrated by those who are repelled by their seeming grossness. At the same time, they are what sociologist J. Milton Yinger calls "bridging" sects, which are fashioned, in sometimes bizarre ways, "out of materials at hand" but "have at least the potentiality of helping to carry their members over into a new life."[22] From the standpoint of their long-range significance, the performance of such a "bridging" role seems clearly to be the most distinctive and important function of the New Religions.

This is also essentially what I attempted to anticipate in the introductory chapter when I observed that while the New Religions arose primarily to shelter the masses from the impact of a larger and threatening world, some of these sects are turning out to be also a means of contact with and admission to that larger world—a world that increasingly is seen to be less threatening or daunting than promising and alluring. Throughout this study, I have endeavored to present the data and characterize the individual sects in such ways as to suggest the emergence of this "bridging" function. Though it is still not possible to predict with confidence the eventual results of this process, certain of its current aspects can be indicated. The New Religions serve as: (1) pressure chambers for the socially disadvantaged, (2) media of expression for the common man, and (3) agencies of a quest for a "vocational symbol."

PRESSURE CHAMBERS FOR THE SOCIALLY DISADVANTAGED

A human being may be disabled by an abrupt and extreme change in environmental pressure even though such pressure never exceeds his range of tolerance. Therefore, in certain enterprises, such as deep-sea exploration, it is sometimes necessary to use a pressure chamber in which a person can adjust to gradual alterations in pressure until he is able to step forth into a different environment and survive and function there.

In one of their roles, the New Religions are analogous to the pressure chamber. Rapid social change also results in greatly modified "pressures," especially affecting those who are socially disadvantaged. Under such circumstances, recurrent throughout an extended period in Japan, the New Religions have arisen, offering among their several boons an opportunity for gradual adjustment to new social pressures. The availability of such a resource has been especially important since the war, as millions of people have faced the dilemma of *two* Japans. Where shall one live? Where *can* one live? In the old and traditional or in the new and modern? Perhaps most Japanese have ambivalent feelings concerning each option and are not incapacitated by the tension between the two. Thus, while they actually may be domiciled in one or the other, they will resist having to specify the locus of their primary citizenship. However, there are many others for whom neither a both-and choice nor an either-or choice is really possible. Because of social disadvantage, they are not equipped to live in the new and modern Japan; at the same time, the old and traditional Japan no longer is wholly accessible as an exclusive option.

To thousands of such persons, the New Religions have seemed to offer a solution to a frightful quandary. There, regardless of qualifications, one can retain the security and comfort of the old and traditional and simultaneously experience the excitement of the new and modern. To be sure, many who respond to this opportunity become permanent refugees from reality who never really establish their citizenship anywhere. In such instances, of course, the analogy of the pressure chamber breaks down, for a pressure chamber is not intended to be a permanent dwelling. For many others, however, this is indeed their means of access to an eventually fuller participation in the larger society.

MEDIA OF EXPRESSION FOR THE COMMON MAN

In every modern society, there is an urgent need that there be adequate media through which the common people can speak on their own behalf. The more respectable languages of art, literature, science, and philosophy tend to be preempted by the upper social and intellectual strata. Usually, however, if they are free to do so, the common people will find languages of their own. In Japan, the New Religions serve in part as media for such expression.

One of the chief roles of the earliest of these sects was social protest. Indeed, as I attempted to show in Chapter III, the sublimation of violent social protest to patterned religious activity in the late Tokugawa period perhaps was the step that marked the beginning of the New Religions as a distinguishable category of sects. Consciously or unconsciously, overtly or covertly, these movements have continued to be media through which the masses can express their protest; but the resulting satisfactions have generally been more psychological and illusory than actual. Now, however, given their own greater maturity and the increased freedom of the postwar years, these sects can be really effective agencies through which the masses can speak. Con-

versely, due to their strongly traditional character, they are also
media through which the masses can be addressed. Perhaps both
these aspects, with their dangers and possibilities, can be seen
most clearly in the relationships between the New Religions and
politics.

Except for Soka Gakkai, none of the New Religions has sought
to set up the organizational machinery for a sustained and purposeful involvement in politics. Generally they support conservative views. Occasionally some sect will openly endorse a candidate
from among its own members. However, despite their rather low-
key involvement, it is obvious that the political potential of these
movements is far from inconsequential.

From what I have been able to observe, it appears that the
political world and the New Religions are engaged in a mutual
but cautious and ambivalent courtship. For their part, the sects
have inherited a desire for recognition by the government. The
masses still instinctively tend to look upon governmental authority
with awe and to feel that somehow recognition by the government is the ultimate recognition. It may seem strange that this
should be so, for many of the sects formerly were inclined to be
antigovernment, and both these and others have suffered harassment and persecution at the hands of the government. Furthermore, according to their present testimony, they ardently cherish
their constitutionally guaranteed freedom to organize and to
propagate.[23] Nevertheless, in their current eagerness to improve
their image and to cast off the label of "false religions," many
sects are seeking to be noticed by government. Hence, on a
really big and important occasion, a sect usually will invite one
or more governmental officials to attend its gathering and perhaps
even to address the assembled devotees. I have been present on
many such occasions when a Cabinet member, a member of the
Diet, a prefectural governor, a mayor, or just a local councilman
has been presented. The deferential treatment accorded such
guests suggests that their presence is quite flattering to the
sponsors.

From the standpoint of the political world, its courtship of the
New Religions seems to be motivated by crassly political considerations. In general, Japanese politicians have little interest

in religion as such, and privately many of them probably despise these newer movements. However, in the great tradition of their counterparts throughout the world, they do not find it too difficult to be gracious when several million votes are involved.

Here again, as at so many other points, the importance of this circumstance is ambiguous. On the one hand, there is the completely obvious danger that almost any of these sects could become—if indeed it is not so already—a captive electorate. Spokesmen for the left sometimes allege that political officeholders and leaders of New Religions often collude in order to perpetuate the tractability of the masses. Though such a charge cannot easily be proved, neither can it easily be refuted.

On the other hand, it is also true that for the first time in the history of Japan, the masses have been given political power. Though theoretically this power rests on a one-man, one-vote theory of democratic process, its real effectuation may depend rather upon political action en bloc. It may not be possible to predict what the long-range result will be, but this much at least is clear: the common people in Japan now have a political voice, and the New Religions are strategically situated media through which it can be expressed.

QUEST FOR A "VOCATIONAL SYMBOL"

It now appears that the loss of their sense of national identity and purpose remains almost the sole instance of major wartime devastation that the Japanese have found to be irreparable. But it is a vast hiatus, the closing of which is unquestionably Japan's greatest current need.

In reflecting on this circumstance, after an extended visit to Japan, theologian Paul Tillich observed: "Present-day Japan is looking for a vocational symbol."[24] His statement is an apt summation, especially in its subtle connotation of the essentially religious character of this vital concern. Have the New Religions anything to do with this?

Where Tillich speaks of a "vocational symbol," others may wish to speak of "nationalism" or "patriotism"; but while all these expressions do impinge upon one another, they are not necessarily synonyms. There are important distinctions that must be sorted out in the light of the Japanese experience.

In his study of mass movements, Eric Hoffer notes "that in modern times nationalism is the most copious and durable source of mass enthusiasm, and that nationalist fervor must be tapped if the drastic changes projected and initiated by revolutionary enthusiasm are to be consummated."[25] The perceptiveness of this observation cannot be gainsaid. It is universally so applicable in the contemporary world that it seems almost truistic. It also describes the Japanese situation—but in the past, not in the present, and this is the important point to be noted.

From 1868 to 1945, nationalism was just such a resource in the Japanese efforts to modernize their nation and expand their territory and hegemony. However, since the war, nationalist fervor as such has been both weak and generally distasteful. Having gone this way already, Japan has a maturity of perspective that many other nations, now in the throes of assorted revolutions, have yet to achieve. Hence, though deeply troubled by their lack of national identity, the Japanese thus far have tended to be wary of all efforts to rekindle nationalist fervor. To return to this, they seem generally to agree, would be a tragic regression. They hope instead to achieve a new sense of identity at a more advanced and more authentic level; or, as Tillich said, they are "looking for a vocational symbol."

In this situation, the New Religions have been, in certain respects, substitutes for nationalism without necessarily becoming nationalistic themselves. Their leaders often have functioned effectively as Emperor substitutes, and the close-knit fellowship and corporate goals that they foster have helped to undergird a sense of identity and purpose. At the same time, they have encouraged dreams of peace and happiness that clearly transcend nationalistic self-interest. But can the New Religions continue indefinitely to function in this manner?

As the memories and lessons of former years grow dim, there is now in Japanese society an inclination—as yet limited but growing—to glorify the war years and to call for a return to patriotism. Also, in some of the more successful New Religions, there are, as we have noted, signs of growing nationalistic interests. Will this trend continue? Will there come a time when the New Religions will have to tap the resources of nationalistic fervor if they are to survive and flourish, or have they developed an inner reserve from which they can contribute to a reorientation that is authentically Japanese yet supranationalistic?

Such quetsions, with their inevitable ambiguities, seem to call for further examination of the international outreach in which many of the sects, some quite conspicuously, are now engaged. What is the range of motivations operative here? What is the effective purpose? It is obvious that this activity is a significant part of the "bridging" function of the sects, for in such outreach they are often the means by which their devotees are introduced to the larger world and thereby develop a sense of participation in the emerging world culture. It seems also to be the case that many devotees, being assured that they have been "saved" by their new faith, have a genuinely altruistic interest in sharing the "good news" with others. At the same time, as our experience in the West has taught us, evangelistic zeal often reflects deeply rooted needs in the evangelists themselves and almost invariably has imperialistic overtones. How is it among the Japanese? There surely must be among them a widespread and quite understandable psychological need to conquer their conquerors, to missionize their missionizers, and to secure worldwide recognition for Japan. While in most of the New Religions these factors are not obtrusive, in some of them they do tend to be. For example, James Allen Dator notes that one factor contributing to the success of Soka Gakkai is *"a Japanese explanation of the world,"*[26] one that holds ultimately that "since the Japanese are an advanced people with the true religion, they must assume the responsibility of saving the world."[27] He then goes on to report that "some of the Sōka Gakkai's Asian critics find in its missionary enthusiasm much which reminds them of the Greater East Asian Co-Prosperity Sphere,"[28] Japan's grand imperialistic design of the 1930's and 1940's.

I have no intention of suggesting that the New Religions may lead or contribute to the rebirth of militaristic imperialism in Japan. This is highly improbable. My purpose, rather, is to point out that in the quest for a "vocational symbol," the role of these religions is potentially very important but is as yet unclear. As "bridging" sects, they could attempt to relink the present to the past, that is, to build a bridge *back* to nationalism. On the other hand, they could endeavor to link the present to the future and help build a bridge to a new and more responsible life that at least transcends omnipresent nationalistic interests.

It all seems to add up to this: the New Religions of Japan, fashioned largely of materials at hand, have provided and still provide a refuge, a basis for hope, and a bridge to a new life for many millions of people in various states of disprivilege and frustration. It does not yet appear what they will become, but at least for the foreseeable future it seems certain that they will continue, and it seems likely that they will contribute importantly, both for good and ill, to the emergent life of Japan. Let them not be judged with haste, but let them be observed with care.

Notes

CHAPTER I: Introduction

1. Nishida Kitaro, *Intelligibility and the Philosophy of Nothingness*, trans. Robert Schinzinger (Tokyo: Maruzen Company, Ltd., 1958), p. 166.
2. Kobayashi Sakae, Assistant Professor of History of Religions, Kwansei Gakuin University, Nishinomiya, Japan.
3. Inui Takashi, Oguchi Iichi, Saki Akio, and Matsushima Eiichi, *Kyōso* (Tokyo: Aoki Shoten, 1955), p. 242.
4. The Japanese people received their first assurance of complete religious freedom in the terms of Article I of the Basic Directive on "Removal of Restrictions on Political, Civil, and Religious Liberties," issued on October 4, 1945, by the Supreme Commander for the Allied Powers. Subsequently, this guarantee was also written into Article 20 of the 1947 Constitution. In the abrogated Meiji Constitution of 1889, Article 28 was also a carefully qualified guarantee of religious freedom, but real freedom of religion was never actually a part either of the thought or of the experience of the Japanese people prior to the end of World War II.
5. Especially noteworthy are the reports in *Look*, Vol. 27, No. 18 (September 10, 1963), pp. 15–26; *Life*, Vol. 57, No. 11 (September 11, 1964), pp. 72–74; *Time*, Vol. 84, No. 24 (December 11, 1964), pp. 38–45; and *The New York Times Magazine* (July 18, 1965), pp. 8–9, 36, 38–39.
6. Takagi Hiroo, Assistant Professor of Sociology of Religion, Toyo University. Personal interview, February 14, 1964.
7. Shinshūren is the common abbreviation of Shin Nippon Shūkyō Dantai Rengō Kai, which was constituted on October 15, 1951.
8. J. Milton Yinger, *Sociology Looks at Religion* (New York: The Macmillan Company, 1961), p. 25.
9. Quoted by Gino K. Piovesana in *Recent Japanese Philosophical Thought, 1862–1962* (Tokyo: Enderle Bookstore, 1963), p. 105.
10. Yinger, *op. cit.*, p. 40.
11. The literature on this subject includes the following: Alexander F. Chamberlain, "New Religions," *Journal of Religious Psychology*, Vol. 6 (1913), pp. 1–49; James Mooney, *The Ghost-Dance Religion*, 14th Annual Report of the Bureau of Ethnology for 1892–1893 (Washington, D.C.: Government Printing Office, 1896); Peter Worsley, *The Trumpet Shall Sound* (London: MacGibbon & Kee, Ltd., 1957); Vittorio Lanternari, *The Religions of the Oppressed*, trans. Lisa Sergio (New York: New American Library, 1965).
12. Margaret Mead, *New Lives for Old* (New York: William Morrow & Company, 1956), pp. 214–215.

CHAPTER II: *Japan's Religious Heritage*

1. The purpose of this chapter is more to epitomize than to describe the religions of Japan. Among the many books treating this subject more fully, the following may be especially useful to the general reader: Anesaki Masaharu, *History of Japanese Religion* (London: Kegan Paul, Ltd., 1930; Tokyo: Charles E. Tuttle Company, 1963); Raymond Hammer, *Japan's Religious Ferment* (Fair Lawn, N.J.: Oxford University Press, 1962); and Joseph M. Kitagawa, *Religion in Japanese History* (New York: Columbia University Press, 1966).

2. An alternate reading of the Chinese characters, which usually are read as *Shintō*, is *Kami no Michi*, the "way of the *kami*." If a definition of the term *kami* is supplied, this is the preferable way to translate the name. For a definition of *kami*, see the section entitled "The Concept of *Kami*" further along in this chapter.

3. Taoism generally has functioned in Japan in such a suffused state that no effort is made in this study to describe it as an entity or to trace its impact. Nevertheless, it is important to keep in mind that it is a real but often unidentifiable factor in many situations and to note that in the persistence of *yin-yang* magic its role is quite conspicuous.

4. *Shūkyō Nenkan* (Tokyo: Mombusho, 1963), pp. 542–543.

5. Kawasaki Eisho, "Kōri danchi shūkyō chōsa," *Shūhō*, No. 23 (June, 1963), pp. 5–13.

6. Limiting this discussion to only two basic perspectives is admittedly an oversimplificaton, but neither the space nor the occasion permits a fuller treatment. Readers interested in pursuing the analysis in detail are encouraged to consult Nakamura Hajime, *The Ways of Thinking of Eastern Peoples: India, China, Tibet, Japan*, rev. ed. (Honolulu: East-West Center Press, 1964).

7. Plato's *Apology*, section 38.

8. Imamura Taihei, "The Japanese Spirit as It Appears in Movies," in Kato Hidetoshi (ed. and trans.), *Japanese Popular Culture* (Tokyo: Charles E. Tuttle Company, 1959), p. 140.

9. *Ibid.*, p. 141.

10. Nishida, *Intelligibility and the Philosophy of Nothingness*, p. 168.

11. Anesaki, *op. cit.*, p. 21. See also D. C. Holtom, "The Meaning of Kami," *Monumenta Nipponica*, Vol. 4 (1941), pp. 391–392.

12. *An Outline of Shinto Teachings* (Tokyo: Jinja Honcho, 1958), p. 8.

13. Cf. Ono Sokyo, *The Kami Way* (Tokyo: International Institute for the Study of Religions, 1959), p. 7.

14. This type of solicitude was a factor in the establishment of Yasukuni Shrine in Tokyo in 1869 for the enshrinement of the spirits of the war dead. For a discussion of the rise and development of the *goryō-shin* concept, see Hori Ichiro, "On the Concept of *Hijiri* [Holy-Man]," *Numen*, Vol. 5, Fasc. 2 (April, 1958), pp. 157–160.

15. Anesaki, *loc. cit.*

16. Ono, *op. cit.*, p. 8.

17. Kato Genchi, *What Is Shinto?* (Tokyo: Maruzen Company, Ltd., 1935), pp. 53–54.

18. Ono, *loc. cit.*

19. *An Outline of Shinto Teachings*, p. 23.

20. *Ibid.*, p. 7.

21. Kuroda Kazuo, "Devotion or Diversion?", *The Japan Times*, October 7, 1959. For a more extended discussion of Shinto, especially in the postwar period, the general reader may wish to see Floyd H. Ross, *Shinto: The Way of Japan* (Boston: Beacon Press, 1965).

22. For an informative brief essay that characterizes Buddhism in Japan and focuses upon the contemporary situation, see Joseph M. Kitagawa, "The Buddhist Transformation in Japan," *History of Religions*, Vol. 4, No. 2 (Winter, 1965), pp. 319–336.

23. Warren W. Smith, Jr., *Confucianism in Modern Japan* (Tokyo: Hokuseido Press, 1959), p. 6. For a translation of this document, see Tsunoda Ryusaku *et al.* (eds.), *Sources of the Japanese Tradition* (New York: Columbia University Press, 1958), pp. 49–53.

24. See Robert King Hall (ed.) *Kokutai no Hongi: Cardinal Principles of the National Entity of Japan*, trans. John Owen Gauntlett (Cambridge, Mass.: Harvard University Press, 1949). This "bible" of Japanese militarism was first published in 1937.

25. For a detailed exposition of the early Christian epoch in Japanese history, see C. R. Boxer, *The Christian Century in Japan, 1549–1650* (Berkeley, Calif.: University of California Press, 1951).

26. In the English language there is at present no adequate synoptic study of Japanese folk religion. However, the acknowledged authority in this field, Hori Ichiro, delivered the 1965 Haskell Lectures at the University of Chicago on the subject, "Folk Religion in Japan: Continuity and Change." The publication of these lectures will help to fill this need. Additional useful studies already in print include the following: Hori, "On the Concept of *Hijiri* [Holy-Man]," *Numen*, Vol. 5, Fasc. 2 and 3 (April and September, 1958), pp. 128–160 and 199–232; Hori, "Japanese Folk-Beliefs," *American Anthropologist*, Vol. 61, No. 3 (June, 1959), pp. 405–424; and Richard M. Dorson (ed.), *Studies in Japanese Folklore*, trans. Ishiwara Yasuo (Bloomington, Ind.: Indiana University Press, 1963).

27. Fanny Hagin Mayer, "Religious Elements in Japanese Folk Tales," in Joseph Roggendorf (ed.), *Studies in Japanese Culture* (Tokyo: Sophia University, 1963), p. 16.

28. Quoted by Oliver Statler, *Japanese Inn* (New York: Random House, 1961), p. 168.

29. Okada Rokuo (ed.), *Japanese Proverbs and Proverbial Phrases*, Tourist Library Series, No. 20 (Tokyo: Japan Travel Bureau, 1955), pp. 113–115.

30. *The Japan Times*, November 17, 1964.

31. Anesaki, *op. cit.*, p. 6.

CHAPTER III: *Social Crisis and the Rise of New Religions*

1. Cf. Edwin O. Reischauer, *Japan Past and Present*, 3d ed. rev. (New York: Alfred A. Knopf, 1964), p. 80.

2. *Ibid.*, pp. 80–81.

3. The most notable were Kamo Mabuchi (1697–1769), Motoori Norinaga

(1730–1801), and Hirata Atsutane (1776–1843). For well-edited excerpts from their writings, see Tsunoda *et al.* (eds.), *Sources of the Japanese Tradition*, pp. 506–551.

4. A translation of this Imperial Rescript is appended to D. C. Holtom, *Modern Japan and Shinto Nationalism*, rev. ed. (Chicago: University of Chicago Press, 1947), pp. 219–220.

5. Quoted in Arthur Tiedemann, *Modern Japan: A Brief History* (Princeton, N.J.: Anvil Books, D. Van Nostrand Company, 1955), p. 186.

6. *Idem.*

7. Cf. Okakura Kakuzo, *The Awakening of Japan*, spec. ed. (New York: Japan Society, Inc., 1921), pp. 45–46.

8. Herbert Zachert, "Social Changes During the Tokugawa Period," *The Transactions of the Asiatic Society of Japan*, Second Series, Vol. 17 (December, 1938), p. 237.

9. For a collection of such stories, see Ihara Saikaku, *The Japanese Family Storehouse*, trans. G. W. Sargent (London: Cambridge University Press, 1959).

10. For literary reflections of the merchant-dominated urban culture of this period, see *Major Plays of Chikamatsu*, trans. Donald Keene (New York: Columbia University Press, 1961).

11. Hugh Borton, "Peasant Uprisings in Japan of the Tokugawa Period," *The Transactions of the Asiatic Society of Japan*, Second Series, Vol. 16 (May, 1938), p. 39.

12. Reischauer, *op. cit.*, p. 94.

13. Shibusawa Keizo (ed.), *Japanese Life and Culture in the Meiji Era*, trans. Charles S. Terry, Centenary Culture Council Series, Vol. 5 (Tokyo: Obunsha, 1958), p. 325.

14. *Ibid.*, p. 293.

15. Reischauer, *op. cit.*, p. 133.

16. Shibusawa, *op. cit.*, p. 294.

17. Reischauer, *op. cit.*, pp. 128–129.

18. Shibusawa, *op. cit.*, p. 305.

19. Cf. *ibid.*, pp. 307–308.

20. Reischauer, *op. cit.*, p. 160.

21. Except as otherwise noted, statistics used in this section have been adapted from *Statistical Handbook of Japan* (1964), pp. 17–22, and from Shibusawa, *op. cit.*, pp. 332–336.

22. According to the report of the Agriculture and Forestry Ministry of the Japanese government, the number of persons leaving rural areas was 600,000 in 1961, 524,000 in 1962, and 710,000 in 1963. Youths under twenty years of age and middle-aged "breadwinners" make up the majority. Reported in *The Japan Times*, July 26, 1964.

23. Kishimoto Hideo and Wakimoto Tsuneya, "Introduction," in Kishimoto Hideo (ed.), *Japanese Religion in the Meiji Era*, trans. John F. Howes, Centenary Culture Council Series, Vol. 2 (Tokyo: Obunsha, 1956), pp. 5–6.

24. The term *saisei itchi* sometimes is translated quite misleadingly as "the unity of church and state." The Western experience that such a rendering recalls should be set aside, so far as possible, during any effort to comprehend this Japanese phenomenon.

25. This was one of the discoveries of the Iwakura Mission, an embassy led by Iwakura Tomomi, which visited Europe and the United States in 1871–1873 in order to observe government administration and discuss treaty revision. See Kishimoto (ed.), *Japanese Religion in the Meiji Era*, pp. 83–84.
26. Yanagida Kunio (ed.), *Japanese Manners and Customs in the Meiji Era*, trans. Charles S. Terry, Centenary Culture Council Series, Vol. 4 (Tokyo: Obunsha, 1957), p. 8.
27. Jean Stoetzel, *Without the Chrysanthemum and the Sword* (Paris: UNESCO, 1955), p. 20.
28. Inouye Syuzi, "Japan in Search of a Soul," *Japan Quarterly*, Vol. 4, No. 1 (January–March, 1957), p. 100.
29. I am indebted to several Japanese scholars for suggestions concerning periodization; however, there is no agreement among these gentlemen as to how it should be done. For example, Takagi Hiroo (personal interview, February 14, 1964) designated three periods: (1) early Meiji, (2) late Meiji through Taisho to World War II, and (3) the end of the war to the present; Murakami Shigeyoshi ("Shinkoku nippon seisui-shi—gendai shinkō shūkyō no saihatsu-mi," *Taiyō*, No. 15 [September, 1964], 150) also specifies three periods but defines them somewhat differently: (1) the World War I era, (2) 1930–1935, and (3) the post-World War II period; Saki Akio (*op. cit.*, p. 37) stresses the importance of two periods, those immediately after the Russo-Japanese War (1904–1905) and World War I (1914–1918), respectively, in addition to the post-World War II period. Therefore, I must assume personal responsibility for the improvisations on expert opinion that have produced the present fivefold scheme.
30. Oguchi Iichi and Takagi Hiroo, "Religion and Social Development," in Kishimoto (ed.), *Japanese Religion in the Meiji Era*, p. 348.
31. Anesaki, *History of Japanese Religion*, p. 299.
32. For a more complete survey of *Shingaku* and the life and teaching of its founder, Ishida Baigan, see Robert N. Bellah, *Tokugawa Religion* (New York: The Free Press, 1957), pp. 133–177.
33. For additional discussion of Ninomiya Sontoku and excerpts from his teachings, see Tsunoda *et al.* (eds.), *Sources of the Japanese Tradition*, pp. 578–588, and Ishiguro Tadaatsu (ed.), *Ninomiya Sontoku: His Life and "Evening Talks"* (Tokyo: Kenkyusha, 1955).
34. Quoted in Tsunoda *et al.* (eds.), *ibid.*, p. 586.
35. Uchimura Kanzo, "Ninomiya Sontoku—A Peasant Saint," in Ishiguro (ed.), *op. cit.*, p. 10.
36. Bellah, *op. cit.*, p. 128.
37. Oguchi and Takagi, *op. cit.*, p. 317.
38. *Idem.*
39. *Ibid.*, p. 320. According to these authorities, "the literal meaning of this name was that any action was all right." "Let's go!" might be another way to render its spirit. Actually the words probably were much more important for their presumed magical potency than for their intrinsic meaning.
40. Anesaki, *op. cit.*, p. 316.
41. *Ibid.*, pp. 314–315.
42. Oguchi and Takagi, *op. cit.*, p. 334.

43. It provides an interesting sidelight to note that it was in 1880 that the first "lonely-hearts column" to appear in a Japanese magazine was printed in the thirty-fifth issue of *Jogaku Zasshi* (*Women's Learning Magazine*). See Baba Kyoko, "Choice from the Weeklies," *The Japan Times*, April 16, 1964.

44. Anesaki, *op. cit.*, p. 31.

45. Saki, *op. cit.*, p. 37. Also see *Shūkyō Nenkan* (1963), p. 206.

46. Inui *et al.*, *Kyōso*, pp. 141–142.

47. Cf. Offner and Van Straelen, *Modern Japanese Religions*, pp. 91–93.

48. For a discussion of the *Lotus Sūtra*, see Chapter VIII.

49. Murakami, *op. cit.*, p. 151.

50. Deguchi Isao, "Omoto," *Contemporary Religions in Japan*, Vol. 4, No. 3 (September, 1963), 231–232.

51. The Imperial Rescript on Education, issued in 1890, was a statement of Confucian and Shinto ethics considered to be essential to the support of the state. In time it became one of the chief symbols and devices of jingoism. For a translation of the text, see Tiedemann, *op. cit.*, pp. 113–114.

52. Inui *et al.*, *op. cit.*, pp. 158–159.

53. Murakami, *loc. cit.*

54. *Sengo Shūkyō Kaisōroku* (Tokyo: Shinshuren, 1963), p. 55.

55. Murakami, *loc. cit.*

56. *Idem.*

57. *Sengo Shūkyō Kaisōroku*, p. 55.

58. *Ibid.*, pp. 170–171.

59. Murakami, *loc. cit.*

60. *Sengo Shūkyō Kaisōroku*, p. 52.

61. Oishi Shuten, "The New Religious Sects of Japan," *Contemporary Religions in Japan*, Vol. 5, No. 1 (March, 1964), 58.

62. Cf. Yinger, *Sociology Looks at Religion*, pp. 41–42.

63. Space does not permit a description of these small sects. The doctrines of Toitsu Kyokai are expounded in Young Oon Kim, *The Divine Principles* (San Francisco: The Holy Spirit Association for the Unification of World Christianity, 1960). Descriptions of the other two movements may be found in the following articles by William P. Woodard in *The Japan Times*: "Original Gospel Movement Shows Religious Fervor" (May 1, 1964) and "Spirit of Jesus Church Shows Rapid Expansion" (June 12, 1964).

64. Harry Thomsen, *The New Religions of Japan* (Tokyo: Charles E. Tuttle Company, 1963).

65. *Shūkyō Nenkan* (1963), p. 206; Saki, *op. cit.*, p. 37.

66. Yinger, *op. cit.*, p. 55.

CHAPTER IV: *Recurrent Characteristics of the New Religions*

1. Within a Buddhistic orientation, the honorific might be *ikibotoke* or *katsubutsu* ("living Buddha"). In some cases, also, the leaders eschew all such exalted designations in favor of the straightforward title *kaichō*

("president"). This is the choice of Niwano Nikkyo of Rissho Kosei-kai, for example. Nevertheless, the attitudes and expectations of many of the devotees may be little affected by such seemly modesty.

2. *Tenrikyō Kyōten* (Tenri, 1949), p. 3, translated in Offner and Van Straelen, *Modern Japanese Religions*, p. 45.

3. An approximately literal translation of this term would be "Honorable Lord Kami." In this instance, it is essentially synonymous with *ikigami*. The story of Kitamura Sayo is told in English in *The Prophet of Tabuse* (Tabuse, Yamaguchi Prefecture: Tensho Kotai Jingu-kyo, 1954).

4. Interview with Kitamura Sayo, March 29, 1964.

5. Hori Ichiro, "Penetration of Shamanic Elements into the History of Japanese Folk Religion," in Eike Haberland, Meinhard Schuster, and Helmut Straube (eds.), *Festschrift für Ad. E. Jensen* (München: K. Renner, 1964–1965), pp. 251–257.

6. The experiences of other founders are reported in the discussions of specific religious movements in Chapters V–IX.

7. Murakami, "Shinkoku nippon seisui-shi," *op. cit.*, p. 151; Saki, *Shinkō Shūkyō*, pp. 77–78.

8. Cf. Murakami, *loc. cit.*

9. *Idem.*

10. Saki, *op. cit.*, p. 51.

11. Hall (ed.), *Kokutai no Hongi*, p. 83.

12. Saki Akio (*op. cit.*, p. 123) specifically names the following as persons displaying symptoms of abnormality: Deguchi Nao of Omoto-kyo, Kitamura Sayo of Tensho Kotai Jingu-kyo, Jikoson of Jiu-kyo, Kotani Kimi of Reiyu-kai, and Naganuma Myoko of Rissho Kosei-kai. He also lists those whom he believes to be quite normal, even though they are supposed to have had mystical experiences: Miki Tokuchika of PL Kyodan, Taniguchi Masaharu of Seicho no Ie, Okada Mokichi of Sekai Kyusei-kyo, Makiguchi Tsunesaburo and Toda Josei of Soka Gakkai, and Niwano Nikkyo of Rissho Kosei-kai.

13. *Sengo Shūkyō Kaisōroku*, pp. 166–168.

14. Tsunoda *et al.* (eds.), *Sources of the Japanese Tradition*, p. 93.

15. Quoted in Saki, *op. cit.*, p. 111.

16. Quoted in Offner and Van Straelen, *op. cit.*, p. 139.

17. Interview with three officials of Soka Gakkai: Kuroyanagi Akira (member of the Board of Directors and editor in chief of *The Seikyo News*, an English-language propaganda newspaper), Shinohara Makoto (member of the Board of Directors), and Ikeda Katsuya (member of the editorial staff of *Seikyō Shimbun*, the Soka Gakkai newspaper), September 12, 1963.

18. Saki, *loc. cit.*

19. For a more detailed study of healing among the New Religions, see Offner and Van Straelen, *op. cit.*, especially Chapters 8–10.

20. *The Japan Times*, May 18, 1965.

21. Hall (ed.), *Kokutai no Hongi*, p. 81.

22. Saki, *op. cit.*, pp. 196–203.

23. Eric Hoffer, *The True Believer* (New York: Harper & Row, 1951), p. 44.

24. Personal interview, April 24, 1964.

25. Lanternari, *The Religions of the Oppressed*, p. 249.

26. Personal interview, February 6, 1964.

27. Hanayama Training Center, Wakayama City, March 7–8, 1964.

28. Sugimoto Etsu, A Daughter of the Samurai (New York: Doubleday & Company, 1925), pp. 11–14.

29. Ibid., p. 12. Reprinted by permission of the publisher.

30. Osaragi Jiro, Homecoming, trans. Brewster Horwitz (New York: Alfred A. Knopf, Inc., 1954), p. 242. The temple on Mount Hiei is the Enryakuji, headquarters of the Tendai sect. It was founded in 788 by Saicho (Dengyo Daishi), one of the most distinguished of the Japanese Buddhist leaders.

31. The Japan Times, November 17, 1958.

32. Cf. the discussion of Japanese obligations and their reciprocals (on, gimu, and giri) in Ruth Benedict, The Chrysanthemum and the Sword (Boston: Houghton Mifflin Company, 1946), pp. 114–132 et passim.

33. Cf. Lanternari, op. cit., pp. 248–249.

34. Cf. Revelation 21:2–4.

35. These events marked the official opening of the following edifices: (1) the Daikyakuden (Grand Reception Hall) of Soka Gakkai at the head temple Taisekiji near the foot of Mount Fuji, April 1, 1964; (2) the Daiseidō (Great Sacred Hall) of Rissho Kosei-kai in Suginami-ku, Tokyo, May 15, 1964; and (3) the Dōjō (Training Hall) of Tensho Kotai Jingukyo in Tabuse, Yamaguchi Prefecture, May 31, 1964.

36. Statistical Handbook of Japan (1964), p. 125. This publication also reports (p. 127) that more than eighty-six percent of the total population lives within television-service areas.

37. See Kobayashi Sakae, "Religious Syncretism in Japan," Kwansei Gakuin University Annual Studies, Vol. 7 (March, 1959), pp. 203–236.

38. Quoted in Tsunoda et al. (eds.), op. cit., p. 585.

CHAPTER V: Konkō-kyō: A Functional Monotheism

1. In some instances, an individual's purpose is not to seek deliverance from a problem but simply to express his joy at having been delivered already.

2. In references to the deity worshiped in Konko-kyo, the term "Kami" will be used in this discussion rather than "kami" or "God." This is to suggest that while the concept of deity is derived largely from Shinto, it importantly transcends the usual notions of kami and tends toward monotheism; however, it remains sufficiently different from basic Judeo-Christian concepts to suggest that the use of "God" might be somewhat misleading.

3. More detailed descriptions of Konjin and the folk customs that he called forth are quoted in Delwyn B. Schneider, Konkokyo: A Japanese Religion (Tokyo: International Institute for the Study of Religions, 1962), pp. 67–68.

4. As it is now used in Konko-kyo, the name Tenchi Kane no Kami signifies the "Parent-God of the Universe." Etymologically, the name is something of a puzzle, one that reflects the enigmatic but pregnant character of Kawate's experience. The name includes that of Konjin (which may be read Kane no Kami), but it also reaches toward a universality that the

name Konjin traditionally did not represent. Schneider (*op. cit.*, pp. 114–118) wrestles with this problem of etymology inconclusively but somewhat helpfully.

5. *Konkō-kyō Kyōten*, "Gorikai," Verse 7, translated in Schneider, *op. cit.*, p. 88.
6. *Ibid.*, verse 18, p. 89.
7. *Ibid.*, verse 3, p. 87.
8. It is impossible to translate this name in such a way as to indicate its implicit allusions to various aspects of Japanese popular piety. For additional commentary, see the discussions of *kami* and *ikigami* elsewhere in this book.
9. Murakami, "Shinkoku nippon seisui-shi," *op. cit.*, p. 150.
10. Murakami, *loc. cit.* Probably also this is another example of playing on words. The Chinese character that is read *Kane* in the name of the deity (Tenchi Kane no Kami) and *Kon* in the name of the sect and is the principal feature in the Konko-kyo crest may mean "metal," "gold," or "money." While none of these specific meanings is important in the manner in which the character is used by Konko-kyo, it is not difficult to see why Japanese businessmen, already fond of playing with the ambiguities of their language, would seize this opportunity to make a pun.
11. Interview with priests of the Konko-kyo Church of Izuo, Osaka, April 20, 1957.
12. Hori Ichiro and Toda Yoshio, "Shinto," in Kishimoto (ed.), *Japanese Religion in the Meiji Era*, p. 95.
13. *Ibid.*, p. 96.
14. For the names and brief characterizations of the thirteen sects of *Kyōha Shintō*, listed in the order in which they were officially recognized by the government, see *ibid.*, pp. 96–97.
15. In 1963–1964, approximately one hundred students, divided almost equally between men and women, were enrolled in the Institute. More than sixty of these, including all but seven of the women, were in the third-level course. The first-level course had fifteen men and only one woman; the second-level course included fourteen men and six women.
16. Interview with Takahashi Masao, the *Kyōkan* (second-ranking official) of Konko-kyo, October 29, 1963. At that time, there were 3,896 ordained ministers, of whom 1,749 were women.
17. Interviews with Takahashi Masao, October 28 and 29, 1963. (Mr. Takahashi died on May 25, 1965, at the age of seventy-eight.)
18. Takahashi Hakushi, "Kyōsō Shinkan no sochi ni tsuite," *Konkō-kyō Gaku*, No. 6 (1950), p. 16. Translated in Raymond Hammer, "The Idea of God in Japan's New Religions" (unpublished PhD dissertation submitted to the Faculty of Theology of the University of London, 1961), p. 94.
19. Tamura Yoshiro, "What Is Religion?: A Report of a Round-Table Conference," *Contemporary Religions in Japan*, Vol. 5, No. 4 (December, 1964), p. 299.
20. Seto Mikio, "Konkō-kyō to Kirisuto-kyō no hikaku-kenkyu," *Konkō-kyō Gaku*, No. 5 (1962), pp. 64–83.
21. Statistical data included in this discussion were supplied by the chief minister, Miyake Toshio, in a personal interview on March 19, 1964, and

in a letter dated August 26, 1965, commenting on the first draft of this chapter.

CHAPTER VI: PL Kyōdan: *An Epicurean Movement*

1. Inui *et al., Kyōso,* p. 140. Except as otherwise noted, the historical sketch that follows is adapted mainly from pages 138–170 of this work.
2. Sanskrit: *Mahavairocanasa-tathāgata.* The Chinese characters used in writing *Dainichi* mean "Great Sun."
3. In common parlance, *furikae* (that is, *ofurikae* minus the honorific prefix) is used mainly in reference to the "transfer" of financial accounts. This is an example of a businessman's term being adopted for use in a businessman's religion.
4. For two examples, see Richard M. Dorson, *Folk Legends of Japan* (Tokyo: Charles E. Tuttle Company, 1962), pp. 37–41. This folkloric basis for *ofurikae* is suggested more specifically by the reversionary character of its later use in Hito no Michi: thousands of metal images of the sect leader were made and distributed with the promise that *ofurikae* would be granted to any person who prayed to one of them (Inui *et al., op. cit.,* p. 157).
5. "Himorogi no yurai" ("History of *himorogi*"), inscribed on a sign near the tomb of Miki Tokuharu at Tondabayashi. A *himorogi* is an offering to a deity; in this instance, it is a *sakaki* tree (*cleyera ochnacea*), especially sacred to Shintoists. This tree, or an offshoot from it, has been transplanted in front of Miki's own tomb.
6. The full name of the original movement was *Shintō* ("way of the *kami*") *Tokumitsu-kyō.* The sect that Miki organized in 1924 was called *Jindō* ("way of man") *Tokumitsu-kyō* in order to distinguish it from the other sect—which still continued—and to identify it with its founder, whose real successor Miki claimed to be. In effect, the change of name in 1931 involved dropping only the words *Tokumitsu-kyō,* for *Jindō* and *Hito no Michi* are alternate ways of reading the same characters.
7. *Sengo Shūkyō Kaisōroku,* p. 59.
8. Inui *et al., op. cit.,* p. 140.
9. Interview with two PL teachers, Tondabayashi, May 11, 1957.
10. *Perfect Liberty—How to Lead a Happy Life* (Tondabayashi: PL Kyodan, 1951), pp. 2–3.
11. Miki Tokuchika, "The True Way of Life" (unpublished typescript given to the present author on the occasion of a visit to PL headquarters on May 11, 1957).
12. *Idem.* At the time of my visits in 1963–1964, there were only six *Oyasama;* but according to a personal letter dated October 16, 1965, nine additional persons (including Yano Jiro, my correspondent) recently had been appointed to this position.
13. Yuasa Tatsuki, "PL (Perfect Liberty)," *Contemporary Religions in Japan,* Vol. 1, No. 3 (September, 1960), p. 25.
14. Inui *et al., op. cit.,* p. 140.
15. Saki, *Shinkō Shūkyō,* pp. 148–149.

16. Yuasa, *op. cit.*, p. 26.
17. The various rites and prayers, together with instructions for their use, are listed in a forty-two-page manual, *PL Saiten Hō* (Tondabayashi: PL Kyodan, 1962).
18. Interview with a PL member (a college student), June 5, 1964.
19. The Kyōso-sai is one of the four major annual festivals of PL Kyodan. The other three are the Gantan-sai (the New Year's Day celebration), the Kyōshu-tanjō-sai (celebration of the *Oshieoya's* birthday) on April 8, and the PL-sai or Rikkyō Kinenbi (commemoration of the founding of PL Kyodan) on September 29.
20. The music is composed specially for this occasion and is amplified through a sixty-foot tower equipped with sixty 30-inch speakers.
21. "PL" (Tondabayashi: PL Kyodan, 1964), p. 17.
22. When written with the character used in this instance, the word *tama* means "spirit." The same word rendered by another character means "jewel." Much of PL terminology is characterized by such mingling of verbal associations.
23. The most elaborate development of hand symbols has occurred in the esoteric (*mantrayana*) sects of Buddhism. Among the New Religions, the use of hand symbols also is prominent in Tenri-kyo. PL Kyodan acknowledges no indebtedness to other sects for its symbols. According to Yano Jiro, a *Yūso* or *Oyasama*, "The PL hand symbol as we know it today originated at about 1 A.M., September 29, 1946, when our *Oshieoya* received a divine inspiration" (letter to the author, October 16, 1965).
24. Personal interview, December 21, 1963.
25. "Gendai no shinkō shūkyō," *Taiyō*, No. 15 (September, 1964), p. 122.
26. Inui *et al.*, *op. cit.*, p. 167.
27. Yuasa, *op. cit.*, p. 27.
28. Interview with PL officials, December 21, 1963.
29. "Gendai no shinkō shūkyō," *ibid.*, pp. 122–124.
30. The Union of New Religious Organizations of Japan (Shin Nippon Shūkyō Dantai Rengō Kai, abbreviated as Shinshūren) and the Union of Japanese Religions (Nihon Shūkyō Renmei).
31. Osaragi, *Homecoming*, pp. 211–212.

CHAPTER VII: Seichō no Ie: *Divine Science and Nationalism*

1. Taniguchi Masaharu, *Truth of Life* (Tokyo: Seicho no Ie Foundation, 1961), p. 28.
2. *Ibid.*, p. 1.
3. The principal source of my discussion of Taniguchi's career is an interpretive study included in Inui *et al.*, *Kyōso*, pp. 97–135, which in turn is based primarily on Taniguchi's autobiography.
4. *Ibid.*, pp. 106–107.
5. Fenwick L. Holmes, *The Law of Mind in Action* (New York: Robert M. McBride Company, 1921). The author was a leader of the New Thought movement in the United States. It would be difficult to overestimate the influence of this book upon Taniguchi. The book takes ideas that Tani-

guchi already held, states them clearly and vividly, elaborates them within a universal scientific context, and sets forth detailed steps by which one may become a "master of life" and then a "great philosopher" and a "master teacher of life." Except in the area of nationalistic particularism, there appears to be little in Taniguchi's basic teachings that is not found or foreshadowed in this book.

6. Inui *et al., op. cit.,* pp. 123–126.
7. Richard Storry has published a helpful study of these societies in *The Double Patriots* (Boston: Houghton Mifflin Company, 1957). "By 1936," he says, "there were nearly 750 [patriotic] associations in Japan" (p. 26).
8. Inui *et al., op. cit.,* p. 130.
9. William K. Bunce (ed.), *Religions in Japan* (Rutland, Vt.: Charles E. Tuttle Company, 1955), pp. 33–34.
10. Storry, *op. cit.,* p. 18.
11. Taniguchi Masaharu, *Ware-ra nihonjin toshite* (Tokyo: Nihon Kyobunsha, 1958), pp. 150–158.
12. *Ibid.,* p. 152. I am grateful to Hori Ichiro for pointing out that these two lines are just a fragment of a poem in the *Manyōshū* and are virtually meaningless apart from that context. The *Manyōshū* is the earliest (eighth century) compilation of Japanese poetry and has as one of its principal themes the affection and loyalty of the people for the Emperor. The lines quoted by Taniguchi are the first two lines of a song included in a much longer poem. The entire quatrain is translated as follows:

> At sea be my body water-soaked,
> On land be it with grass overgrown,
> Let me die by the side of my Sovereign!
> Never will I look back.

(*The Manyōshū: One Thousand Poems Selected and Translated from the Japanese* [Tokyo: Iwanami Shoten, 1940], pp. 150–152. Reprinted by permission of the publisher.) Though originally the poems of the *Manyōshū* were not martial songs, some of them were adapted for that use in the World War II period.

13. *Ibid.,* p. 154.
14. Interview with staff personnel at the Seicho no Ie headquarters in Tokyo, September 9, 1963.
15. Taniguchi, *Ware-ra nihonjin toshite,* pp. 170–171.
16. *Ibid.,* p. 177.
17. *Sengo Shūkyō Kaisōroku,* pp. 162–163.
18. Taniguchi Masaharu already has designated Taniguchi Seicho as his heir apparent and has decreed that the transmission of leadership in this movement shall continue to be by hereditary succession. Formerly a psychology major, Seicho was adopted into the Taniguchi family soon after the war. Apparently he has been carefully prepared for his eventual leadership role.
19. Taniguchi reports in one of his books: "The Humanity Enlightenment Movement of the Seicho-No-Ie is now spreading like wild-fire in the United States, and is contributing to national diplomacy by coming in contact with the American people" (*Recovery from All Diseases* [Tokyo: Seicho no Ie Foundation, 1963], p. 125). This, of course, is a gross exag-

geration. Very few people in the United States have even heard of Seicho no Ie. Nevertheless, it is quite possible that its essential message would appeal to many people in this country, as we may assume from the persistence here of various other "peace of mind" and "divine science" cults, from some of which indeed Taniguchi initially appropriated some of his central teachings. An interesting sidelight is that the 1965 National AAU gymnastic champion Makoto Sakamoto, a Tokyo-born naturalized American, credits his winning performance to the faith given him by Seicho no Ie.

20. "Anyone who reads [the magazine] *Seicho-no-Ie* will easily understand how wonderful his own religion is, whether it be Shintoism, Christianity or any sect of Buddhism" (Taniguchi Masaharu, *Divine Education and Spiritual Training of Mankind* [Tokyo: Seicho no Ie Foundation, 1956], p. 5).

21. At the current rate of exchange, $1 (U.S.) is equal to 360 yen; therefore, 100 yen would be approximately equivalent to 27.8 cents, and 1,000 yen would be about $2.78.

22. Hatoyama Ichiro, a veteran politician and close friend of Taniguchi, was purged during the Occupation; but he returned to power as the Prime Minister in 1954–1956. He and his wife were strong supporters of Seicho no Ie.

23. Cf. Taniguchi, *Recovery from All Diseases*, p. 45.

24. "The state of unhappiness and inharmony in the final analysis comes about from lack of gratitude" (*ibid.*, p. 53).

25. Seicho no Ie finds "truth" not only in religions but in numerous additional sources as well. Some of those specifically identified here and there in the literature are Japanese classics, the philosophies of East and West, psychology, psychoanalysis, spiritualism, the electron theory, and modern science.

26. Taniguchi, *Divine Education and Spiritual Training of Mankind*, p. 114.

27. It is inevitable that any person who goes to the literature of various religions trusting in his intuition and seeking validation there for his own dogmas will ignore or distort some of the fundamental insights and perspectives of those religions. Taniguchi certainly has done so in his interpretations of Buddhism and Christianity. This is perhaps most obvious in his treatment of the concepts of karma and sin. Since it is necessary to his own doctrine that there be no punitive or judgmental or predestinarian factor, he denies the reality of both karma and sin. However, in seeming to solve one of his problems, he unwittingly opens the way to a still more serious one. Taniguchi sees man as being originally pure, even divine, but it is obvious from his voluminous analyses of human problems that he also recognizes that man is mentally vulnerable—that is, he is susceptible to delusion. In the doctrine of Seicho no Ie, however, there is no way to account for this vulnerability and no acknowledgment of the necessity to do so. Apparently, Taniguchi is unaware that in Buddhism and Christianity the concepts of karma and sin are different ways of accounting for the basic predicament of man—the mark of the race upon him. In Buddhism, man is said to be vulnerable to ignorance and thus becomes exposed to suffering. His vulnerability is explained by the doctrine of karma and dependent origination. In Christianity, man is said to be vul-

nerable to self-centeredness and rebelliousness and thus comes under judgment. His vulnerability is explained conceptually and mythologically as sin resulting from the fall of man. Whether either of these explanations is adequate is not the issue here. The point to be made is that both these religions attempt to face squarely the problem of man's vulnerability. Taniguchi does not do so, even though the problem is implicit in his system of thought. Though denying the reality of sin, he recognizes the possibility of delusion (the distortion of original purity), which in itself is a concept of the fall of man. While he denies the reality of karma, his acknowledgment of mental aberrancies as the cause of suffering belongs essentially to the thoughtway of karmic sequence.

28. Taniguchi, *Divine Education and Spiritual Training of Mankind*, p. 92.
29. *Idem.*
30. Cf. *Seichō no Ie seiji katsudō no kihonteki tachiba to tōmen no kihon hōshin* (Tokyo: Seicho no Ie Foundation, 1963), p. 7.
31. *Ibid.*, pp. 13–14.
32. Taniguchi, *Ware-ra nihonjin toshite*, pp. 47–54.
33. Cf. Kirasawa Kazushige, "Politics in Review," *The Japan Times*, April 11, 1964.
34. One of the principal targets of the conservatives is Article 9, which renounces war and bans the maintenance of all war-making potential. The conservatives feel that Japan should be free to rearm for the defense of the country—which it is doing anyway on a limited basis. Others, however, look upon the maintenance of the no-war clause as necessary insurance against a return to militarism. In general, the issue seems to be argued along emotional rather than substantive lines.
35. Cf. *Seichō no Ie seiji . . .*, p. 10; Taniguchi Masaharu, *Nippon o kizukumono* (Tokyo: Nihon Kyobunsha, 1960), pp. 130 ff.
36. *Seichō no Ie seiji . . .*, p. 9.
37. *The Japan Times*, October 5, 1957.
38. In 1959, Prince Mikasa compiled a book entitled *Nippon no akebono* (*The Dawn of Japan*), to which many historical scholars contributed in an effort to discredit the view of the nation's origin that Kigensetsu seems to symbolize.
39. For a very helpful summation of the issues and the intransigence accompanying them, see William P. Woodard, "Attempts to Revive Kigensetsu Discussed," *The Japan Times*, April 23 and 30, 1965.
40. Taniguchi, *Ware-ra nihonjin toshite*, p. 47 *et passim.*
41. *The Japan Times*, December 10 and 14, 1963.
42. "Kokki keiyō suishin kondankai," *Asahi Journal*, Vol. 6, No. 18 (May 3, 1964), p. 37.
43. Taniguchi, *Ware-ra nihonjin toshite*, p. 228.

CHAPTER VIII: Risshō Kōsei-kai: *Buddhism of and for Laymen*

1. Fairly typical of the reports of what is seen on these visits is the following statement: "Each person joins a group of ten to twenty people, who sit close together in a circle, talking over their personal experiences and the

problems that concern them most. Their faces light up with lively interest as they eagerly listen and respond to each other" (Paul E. Johnson, "New Religions and Mental Health," *Journal of Religion and Health*, Vol. 3, No. 4 [July, 1964], p. 333).

2. *Hōza* has no precise English equivalent. It is a compound of two Chinese characters. The first one, *hō*, meaning "law," is the Sino-Japanese rendering of *dharma*, the key Buddhist term, roughly translatable as "truth" or "teaching." The second, *za*, means "sitting" or "gathering" and is also the initial character in *zazen*, the cross-legged meditation of Zen.

3. This name now seems rather fulsome, but it must be remembered that the 1930's was "a period of ultranationalism and people generally used such names to show their patriotic spirit regardless of the nature and purpose of their organization. In the postwar period the 'Dai Nippon' was dropped from the name" (William P. Woodard, "Rissho Kosei Kai Takes Rise from Small Start," *The Japan Times*, May 22, 1964). Quite commonly, in general usage, the name is still further shortened to Kosei-kai.

4. *Sengo Shūkyō Kaisōroku*, p. 169.

5. Except as otherwise noted, these biographical sketches are based on Inui *et al.*, *Kyōso*, pp. 220–239.

6. Offner and Van Straelen, *Modern Japanese Religions*, p. 96.

7. Inui *et al.*, *op. cit.*, p. 220.

8. Kamomiya Jokai, "Rissho Kosei Kai," *Contemporary Religions in Japan*, Vol. 2, No. 1 (March, 1961), p. 30.

9. Joseph M. Kitagawa, *Religion in Japanese History*. (New York: Columbia University Press, 1966), p. 325.

10. Woodard, *loc. cit.*

11. Inui *et al.*, *op. cit.*, p. 229.

12. Woodard, *loc. cit.*

13. Based on figures reported by the Shinshūren in *Sengo Shūkyō Kaisōroku*, p. 169.

14. W. E. Soothill, *The Lotus of the Wonderful Law* (Oxford: Clarendon Press, 1930), p. v.

15. The founder of Buddhism, Siddhartha Gautama (c. 563–c. 483 B.C.), the "sage" (*mūni*) of the Shakya clan in northern India, present-day Nepal.

16. Soothill, *op. cit.*, p. 46.

17. *Ibid.*, pp. 149–156.

18. The standard English-language biography of Nichiren is by Anesaki Masaharu, *Nichiren, the Buddhist Prophet* (Cambridge, Mass.: Harvard University Press, 1916), from which this sketch has been digested. There is in addition the following excellent interpretive essay, which unfortunately is not often accessible: Uchimura Kanzo, "Saint Nichiren: A Buddhist Priest," in *Japan and the Japanese, or Representative Men of Japan* (1908), Vol. 15, *Uchimura Kanzō Zenshū* (Tokyo: Iwanami Shoten, 1933), pp. 288–314.

19. Quoted in Uchimura, *op. cit.*, p. 299.

20. Quoted in Anesaki, *History of Japanese Religion*, p. 198.

21. Inui *et al.*, *op. cit.*, pp. 231–232. Perhaps the sect in which spiritualism is most prominent is *Ananai-kyō*, which is not described otherwise in this

book. For a brief survey of this sect, see Thomsen, *The New Religions of Japan*, pp. 143–152.

22. Saki, *Shinkō Shūkyō*, p. 162.

23. Interview with Kamomiya Jokai, an official of Rissho Kosei-kai, September 11, 1963.

24. Kamomiya, *op. cit.*, p. 33.

25. "Rissho Kosei Kai: A New Buddhist Laymen's Movement in Japan" (a pamphlet prepared by Rissho Kosei-kai in cooperation with the International Institute for the Study of Religions, Tokyo, 1963), p. 4.

26. Adapted from Kamomiya, *op. cit.*, p. 32, and "Rissho Kosei Kai," p. 10.

27. *The Japan Times*, September 9, 1965.

28. "Rissho Kosei Kai," inside front cover.

29. Joseph M. Kitagawa, "The Buddhist Transformation in Japan," *History of Religions*, Vol. 4, No. 2 (Winter, 1965), p. 335.

30. *The Japan Times*, September 9, 1965.

CHAPTER IX: Sōka Gakkai: *A Multiphasic Mass Movement*

1. Cf. *The Buddhist Democracy*, This Is the Sokagakkai Series, No. 7 (Tokyo: The Seikyo Press, n.d.), p. 1.

2. Eric Hoffer, *The True Believer* (New York: Harper & Row, 1951), p. 146.

3. Gerald A. Delilkhan, "Sokagakkai's Startling Success," *The Asia Magazine*, Vol. 4, No. 42 (October 18, 1964), pp. 4–5.

4. *The Sokagakkai* (Tokyo: The Seikyo Press, 1960), p. 27.

5. Ivan Morris, "Soka Gakkai Brings 'Absolute Happiness,'" *The New York Times Magazine* (July 18, 1965), p. 9.

6. *The Sokagakkai*, p. 30.

7. *The Japan Times*, April 21, 1958.

8. Kuroda Kazuo, "Religion of Purgation," *The Japan Times*, May 23, 1959.

9. *The Japan Times*, August 23, 1960.

10. "Sōkagakkai ni taisuru sobokuna nijugo no shitsumon," *Bungeishunju* (July, 1963), pp. 116–117.

11. Ikeda Daisaku, *Lectures on Buddhism*, Vol. 1 (Tokyo: The Seikyo Press, 1962), p. 22.

12. Yinger, *Sociology Looks at Religion*, p. 49.

13. For example, in a publication issued by Soka Gakkai, the following statement appears after the listing of the sacred treasures (mostly Nichiren memorabilia) of Nichiren Sho-shu: "There are also some of Shakyamuni's true ashes, but these are not especially treasured" (*The Sokagakkai*, p. 53).

14. In what is generally regarded as the main-line Nichiren tradition, Nichiren himself is looked upon as the last or the *seal* of the bodhisattvas. Nichiren Sho-shu and Soka Gakkai insist that while he took the form of a bodhisattva as a concession to mankind, he is in reality the Eternal Buddha.

15. *The Sokagakkai*, pp. 53–54.

16. I am indebted to Oguchi Iichi of Tokyo University for calling my attention to the distinctiveness of this segment of the membership. Personal interview, February 14, 1964.

17. Joseph J. Spae, *Christian Corridors to Japan* (Tokyo: Oriens Institute for Religious Research, 1965), p. 198.
18. Interview with Kuroyanagi Akira, editor in chief of the Soka Gakkai English-language paper, *The Seikyo News*, September 12, 1963.
19. The essential character of salvation by invocation is portrayed with remarkable clarity in J. D. Salinger's novel *Franny and Zooey* (Boston: Little, Brown and Company, 1961). See the comments regarding the "Jesus prayer" on pages 37 and 112.
20. *The Sokagakkai*, pp. 113–118.
21. *Seikyō Graphic*, April 11, 1963, p. 18.
22. See Noah Brannen, "A Visit to Taisekiji," *Contemporary Religions in Japan*, Vol. 2, No. 2 (June, 1961), pp. 13–29.
23. For a more detailed description of some of the procedural problems that Soka Gakkai has had to solve, see Murata Kiyoaki, "The Soka Gakkai Today," *The Japan Times*, February 13, 1964.
24. Cf. *Seikyō Graphic*, February 13, 1964, p. 8.
25. Hoffer, *The True Believer*, p. 40.
26. "It would seem . . . that the most fertile ground for the propagation of a mass movement is a society with considerable freedom but lacking the palliatives of frustration" (*ibid.*, p. 30).
27. The readiness of such people to be enlisted is what Seymour Martin Lipset has called "working-class authoritarianism." See his *Political Man* (New York: Doubleday & Company, 1960), pp. 87–126. "The social situation of the lower strata . . . predisposes them to view politics as black and white, good and evil. Consequently, other things being equal, they should be more likely than other strata to prefer extremist movements which suggest easy and quick solutions to social problems and have a rigid outlook" (p. 90). It appears also "that extremist religion is a product of the same social forces that sustain authoritarian political attitudes" (p. 97). Reprinted by permission of the publisher and the author.
28. Hoffer, *op. cit.*, p. 39.
29. *Ibid.*, p. 59.
30. *Ibid.*, p. 58.
31. "Both evidence and theory suggest . . . that the lower strata are relatively more authoritarian, that . . . they will be more attracted to an extremist movement than to a moderate and democratic one, and that, once recruited, they will not be alienated by its lack of democracy" (Lipset, *op. cit.*, p. 92).
32. Hoffer, *op. cit.*, p. 61.
33. *Ibid.*, p. 112.
34. *Ibid.*, p. 17.
35. It was reported that Soka Gakkai electioneers, engaged in illegal door-to-door canvassing, used threats of damnation in an effort to coerce voters into supporting their candidates. When arrested for these and other offenses, they showed no remorse, insisting that they regarded faith as more important than law and imprisonment as only a necessary sacrifice (*The Mainichi Daily News*, June 16, 1957).
36. Murata Kiyoaki, "The New Political Party," *The Japan Times*, November 19, 1964.
37. Edwin O. Reischauer reports: "Many Japanese political analysts . . .

feel that [Soka Gakkai] is likely to lose its original religious cohesiveness if it attempts to go more deeply into politics and that therefore its political influence will probably level off" (*Japan Past and Present,* p. 290).

38. Murata Kiyoaki, "Buddhist Democracy," *The Japan Times,* August 13, 1964.

39. Cf. William P. Woodard, "1964 Religious Affairs in Japan Sketched Out," *The Japan Times,* January 8, 1965.

40. *Shakubuku Kyōten,* excerpt from Chapter 4. Translated by Noah Brannen in an unpublished manuscript in the files of the International Institute for the Study of Religions, Tokyo.

41. Personal interview with Kuroyanagi Akira, September 12, 1963.

42. Uchimura, *op. cit.,* p. 311.

43. *Ibid.,* p. 314. Italics in original.

44. After this chapter was completed, an article was published that I should like to commend to all readers as a useful supplement to my discussion of Soka Gakkai. See James Allen Dator, "The Sōka Gakkai: A Sociopolitical Interpretation," *Contemporary Religions in Japan,* Vol. 6, No. 3 (September, 1965), pp. 205–242.

CHAPTER X: *Conclusion*

1. Naramoto Tatsuya, "Kamigami no tanjō," *Asahi Shimbun,* October 16, 1955.

2. Masamune Hakucho, "Thoughts on the New Religions," *Japan Quarterly,* Vol. 4 (1957), p. 66. Reprinted by permission of the author's widow.

3. Inagaki Saizo, principal of Seitoku Gakuin, Kobe, in a personal note to the author (Spring, 1957). Mr. Inagaki has since retired.

4. See Saki, *Shinkō Shūkyō,* p. 121.

5. Naramoto, *loc. cit.*

6. Masamune, *op. cit.,* pp. 67–68.

7. Interview with Nakamura Naokatsu, retired Professor of History, Kyoto University, June 14, 1957.

8. Masamune, *op. cit.,* p. 69.

9. Shishido Misako, "Folk Toy Talismans of Shrines, Temples," *The Mainichi Daily News,* May 27, 1964. Italics supplied.

10. Masamune, *op. cit.,* p. 65. Italics supplied.

11. Oliver Goldsmith, "The Deserted Village."

12. Inagaki Saizo, *vide supra* note 3.

13. Murakami, "Shinkoku nippon seisui-shi," *op. cit.,* p. 149.

14. Vincent Cronin, *The Golden Honeycomb* (New York: E. P. Dutton & Company, 1954), p. 238.

15. Cf. Saki, *op. cit.,* p. 86.

16. In discussing this same limitation in the "new religions" of the West, J. Milton Yinger (*Sociology Looks at Religion,* p. 35) quotes the following observation from William James: "To ascribe religious value to mere happy-go-lucky contentment with one's brief chance at natural good is but the very consecration of forgetfulness and superficiality. Our troubles lie indeed too deep for *that* cure" (*The Varieties of Religious Experience* [New York: Longmans, Green & Company, 1902], p. 128).

17. Saki, *op. cit.*, p. 203.

18. Yinger, *op. cit.*, p. 26. In the discussion from which this quotation is taken, Yinger contends that a religion that disregards such conflicts and institutions is not likely to continue as a persuasive force.

19. William P. Woodard cites Oishi as having estimated in 1961 that sixty to seventy percent of the adherents were participating for "spiritual reasons, that is, to 'solve the problems of human existence'" ("Religion in Japan in 1961," *Contemporary Religions in Japan*, Vol. 3, No. 1 [March, 1962], p. 41). I can agree that he has discerned a definite trend, but I doubt that the distinction between "spiritual" and "mundane" concerns in religion is sufficiently clear-cut to be statistically measurable.

20. Interview with Takagi Hiroo, February 14, 1964.

21. Ithiel de Sola Pool, "Foreword," in Kato Hidetoshi (ed. and trans.), *Japanese Popular Culture* (Tokyo: Charles E. Tuttle Company, 1959), p. 12.

22. Yinger, *op. cit.*, p. 43.

23. One of the principal purposes of the Union of New Religious Organizations (Shinshūren) is to help safeguard the freedom of its members by remaining alert for any threat of the return of government control or intervention.

24. Paul Tillich, *Christianity and the Encounter of the World Religions* (New York: Columbia University Press, 1963), p. 17.

25. Hoffer, *The True Believer*, p. 14.

26. Dator, "The Sōka Gakkai: A Socio-political Interpretation," *op. cit.*, p. 220. Italics in original.

27. *Ibid.*, p. 221.

28. *Idem.*

Index

Index